Toward a Strategy of Peace

Toward a Strategy of Peace

Edited by

WALTER C. CLEMENS, JR.

Center for International Studies
Massachusetts Institute of Technology

RAND McNALLY & COMPANY

RAND M?NALLY POLITICAL SCIENCE SERIES
Bayley, *Public Liberties in the New States*
Becker, *Political Behavioralism and Modern Jurisprudence*
Bobrow, ed., *Components of Defense Policy*
Eldersveld, *Political Parties: A Behavioral Analysis*
Froman, *Congressmen and Their Constituencies*
Goldwin, ed., THE RAND M?NALLY PUBLIC AFFAIRS
SERIES
America Armed: Essays on United States Military Policy
A Nation of States: Essays on the American Federal System
100 Years of Emancipation
Political Parties, U.S.A.
Why Foreign Aid?
Golembiewski, *Behavior and Organization*
Haight and Johnston, eds., *The President: Roles and Powers*
Hanna, ed., *Independent Black Africa*
Milbrath, *Political Participation*
Milbrath, *The Washington Lobbyists*
Peabody and Polsby, eds., *New Perspectives on the House of Representatives*
Press, ed., *The Polity: Selected Articles by Norton E. Long*
Schmidhauser, ed., *Constitutional Law in the Political Process*
Schubert, ed., *Judicial Behavior*
Singer, ed., *Human Behavior and International Politics*
Strauss, *The City and Man*
Strauss and Cropsey, eds., *History of Political Philosophy*
Ulmer, ed., *Introductory Readings in Political Behavior*
Williams and Press, eds., *Democracy in Urban America*

Copyright © 1965 by Rand M?Nally & Company
All rights reserved
Printed in the U.S.A. by Rand M?Nally & Company
Library of Congress Catalog Card Number: 65-25355

. . . For Our Children's Children . . .

Acknowledgements

The editor wishes to thank his colleagues at the Massachusetts Institute of Technology and Harvard University for valuable suggestions in the preparation of this book.

Special thanks are due to Hallock Hoffman, Director of the Study of the Political Process, Center for the Study of Democratic Institutions, Santa Barbara, California, for his role in organizing the World Affairs Institute for which many of the papers in this symposium were originally prepared, and to the University of California, Santa Barbara, for offering its facilities to the Institute.

Acknowledgement is made to the following publications for permission for reprint rights: to the *Bulletin of the Atomic Scientists* for "Advancing the American National Interest Without War," by Arthur I. Waskow; to *World Politics* for "Arms Control and World Government," by Lincoln P. Bloomfield; to the National Catholic Welfare Conference for the translation of *Pacem in Terris*.

Acknowledgement is made to the following authors for permission to use their contributions: Lincoln P. Bloomfield, Samuel Gould, Paul Hoffman, Seymour Melman, Walter Millis, Fred W. Neal, Anatol Rapoport, Adlai E. Stevenson, and Arthur I. Waskow.

The Authors

•

JOHN F. KENNEDY

President of the United States, January 1961-November 22, 1963. His address at American University, "Toward a Strategy of Peace," has been widely regarded as a major contribution to the movement that led to the limited arms control agreements documented and analyzed in this book.

ADLAI E. STEVENSON

Late United States Ambassador to the United Nations 1961-July 14, 1965; Governor of Illinois 1948-1952; author of numerous books and articles.

WALTER MILLIS

On the staff of the Fund for the Republic. His books include *Road to War, This is Pearl, Arms and Men.* He is the co-author of *The Abolition of War,* and he edited the *Forrestal Diaries.* He was formerly an editorial and staff writer for the *New York Herald Tribune.*

FRED W. NEAL

Professor of International Relations and Government, Claremont Graduate School. He was formerly a Consultant on Russian Affairs, United States State Department. He is the author of *Titoism in Action, Yugoslavia and the New Communism, U.S. Foreign Policy and the Soviet Union,* and *War and Peace and Germany.*

ARTHUR I. WASKOW

A Resident Fellow of the Institute for Policy Studies in Washington, D.C. He is the author of *The Limits of Defense, The Worried Man's Guide to World Peace,* and *The 1919 Race Riots: A Study in The Connections Between Conflict and Violence.* He has also written a number of articles in such periodicals as the *Atlantic Monthly, Commentary, Yale Review, Scientific American, Saturday Review,* and *Bulletin of the Atomic Scien-*

The Authors

tists. Mr. Waskow took his doctorate in American history at the University of Wisconsin, and spent two years as legislative assistant to a United States Congressman.

MIKHAIL A. SUSLOV

A Secretary and Presidium Member of the Central Committee of the Communist Party of the Soviet Union. Noted as an expert on ideology and propaganda.

ANATOL RAPOPORT

Professor of Mathematical Biology and Senior Research Mathematician in the Mental Health Research Institute of the University of Michigan. He is presently conducting empirical and theoretical research on conflict and cooperation in situations characterized by mixed or ambivalent motives, using games specially designed for such studies. He has authored four books, *Science and the Goals of Man, Operational Philosophy, Fights, Games, and Debates, Strategy and Conscience.*

LINCOLN P. BLOOMFIELD

Professor of Political Science at the Massachusetts Institute of Technology and Director of the Arms Control Project. He is a consultant to the State Department, the United States Arms Control and Disarmament Agency, and the Institute for Defense Analyses. Dr. Bloomfield is the author of *Evolution or Revolution? The U.N. and the Problem of Peaceful Territorial Change* and *The United Nations and U.S. Foreign Policy,* editor and co-author of *Outer Space—Prospects for Man and Society,* and numerous articles.

NIKOLAI A. PITERSKY

Rear Admiral in retirement, Candidate of Naval Science, oldest member of the research group on disarmament of the Institute of World Economics and International Relations. He has published a number of books and articles mainly devoted to theories of naval warfare. During World War II he was in the United States for over two years as head of a group of Soviet officers who organized the convoy

The Authors

of cargo ships going from the U.S.A. to the U.S.S.R. He participated in negotiations for Lend-Lease settlements and in the London Suez Canal Conferences as a consultant. He is a member of the Commission on Disarmament of the Institute of Soviet-American Relations.

SAMUEL B. GOULD

President, State University of New York. He was formerly President, Educational Broadcasting Corporation; Chancellor, University of California at Santa Barbara; and President, Antioch College.

PAUL G. HOFFMAN

Managing Director, United Nations Special Fund since 1959; United States Delegate to the United Nations, 1956-1959; President of the Ford Foundation, January 1951-March 1953; first Administrator of the Marshall Plan, April 1948-October 1950; first Chairman, Committee of Economic Development, 1943-1948; President of the Studebaker Corporation, 1935-1948.

SEYMOUR MELMAN

Professor of Industrial Engineering at Columbia University. He has served as a consultant to industrial managements, and government, and the United Nations. He was a member of the Advisory Committee of Experts on Industrial Development Activities of the United Nations System. His books include: *Dynamic Factors in Industrial Productivity, Decision-Making and Productivity,* and *The Peace Race.*

JOHN XXIII

Pope 1958 to 1963.

WALTER C. CLEMENS, JR.

Assistant Professor of Political Science and Research Associate at the Center for International Studies, Massachusetts Institute of Technology; an Associate of the Harvard University Russian Research Center. His books include: *World Perspectives on International Politics; Soviet*

The Authors

Disarmament Policy, 1917-1963; he has contributed to *Soviet Foreign Relations and World Communism,* edited by Thomas H. Hammond; he has written for the *Slavic Review, American Political Science Review, Orbis, Journal of Conflict Resolution, International Affairs* (London), *The Journal of International Affairs,* and the *New York Herald Tribune.* Dr. Clemens has studied at the Universities of Moscow and of Vienna and took his doctorate at Columbia University.

ROBERT F. KENNEDY

•

FOREWORD

In the pages that follow, Professor Clemens has assembled a group of stimulating essays, organized around the central themes of President Kennedy's address at American University in June of 1963. The selections examine the possibilities of peace, the common interests of the United States and the Soviet Union, the pursuit of peace, and the relationship of peace and human rights. They cover a broad range of thinking—from the United States, from Russia, from Communist China. This anthology should be of great help to students of international relations, both college and armchair, in their efforts to gain some perspective on the essential question of our time—our direction and the purpose as a nation in regard to the achievement of lasting peace and well-being for all the peoples of the world.

The essays collected here will, hopefully, help the student in understanding for himself what is entailed in a strategy for peace in our age, and in understanding the significance of the efforts made by President Kennedy and President Johnson toward international peace and the lessening of tensions among nations these past four years.

Perhaps I can add a personal note to supplement the ideas expressed in this volume. What President Kennedy felt was the greatest failure during the first two and one-half years of his Presidency was the fact that we had reached no concrete agreement with the Soviet Union in the direction of the lessening of international tensions. After the Cuban nuclear confrontation, however, he felt the world was changed and that perhaps there would be less opposition to a renewed effort for agreement.

Foreword

This view was not shared in many quarters of the government, although it was shared by Averell Harriman, among others. Based on this view and on the encouragement he received from Averell Harriman, President Kennedy made the speech at American University which is the focal point of Professor Clemens' anthology.

From the American University speech and the efforts that followed came the nuclear test ban treaty. To President Kennedy this was the first step which had been missing during the first two and one-half years. He felt, however, that it was only a first step, and he took every opportunity to indicate the importance of our keeping up the momentum that had been generated and of our continuing to move ahead.

Today we seem to be bogged down in that effort. I hope we can recapture our momentum, for every month that passes without some agreement on the proliferation of nuclear weapons brings a number of nations closer to possession of nuclear capability and makes achievement of such an agreement that much more difficult. In my judgment the question of nuclear proliferation — and of the mounting threat posed by the spread of nuclear weapons — is the most vital issue now facing our nation and the world.

I hope the readers of this volume will bear in mind not only the critical relationship between the scattering of nuclear weapons and the prospects of peace, but also the extent to which the issue of nuclear spread interacts with the other political and economic problems discussed in these pages. There are many crises confronting us today, but if and when nuclear weapons become commonly available, each new crisis may become the last crisis for all mankind. Upon the success of our efforts to prevent nuclear proliferation depends the only future our children will have. We must keep moving on as many fronts as possible to halt the spread of nuclear weapons, for the passage of time will only aggravate the dangers.

At the same time that we are concerned with government-to-government activities such as those I have discussed, we must not forget the human element involved in a strategy of peace. Despite occasional manifestations of anti-American feeling, one on the whole encounters respect for the American people among the people of Eastern Europe and the nonaligned nations.

The Peace Corps and the increasing flow of students and other visitors in both directions have created a climate for better understanding. Such contacts among young people are particularly important, because these are the leaders of tomorrow—a most immediate tomorrow in many of the emerging nations. The reservoir of admiration for the United States that is already visible among the people of these countries needs to be cultivated and developed. Too often assumption of the responsibilities of leadership causes a change in perspective. If we continue to work at broadening exchange-of-persons programs, the result can be a better mutual knowledge of institutions, culture, and traditions, which should go far toward bringing about better understanding when the young people involved attain positions of leadership.

This is the human element in a strategy for peace. It is the element we dare not neglect. If the leaders of tomorrow can understand not only that the world is today a seamless web, but also how the strands are woven, then we will have come at least part way toward the mutual understanding that is one of the foundation stones of a permanent peace.

Contents

●

Contents

WALTER C. CLEMENS, JR.

•

INTRODUCTION

1. WHY A "STRATEGY OF PEACE"?

Because of the "new face of war," peace has become "the necessary rational end of rational men." This thesis which President Kennedy set forth in his Commencement Address at American University on June 10, 1963, provides the starting point of this book. The President called on "every thoughtful citizen" to look inward and re-examine his own attitude toward four central problems—"toward the possibilities of peace, toward the Soviet Union, toward the course of the cold war, and toward freedom and peace here at home." Because the purpose of this book is to stimulate consideration of these problems, the essays collected here are presented in the framework of the four main themes of the President's address: first, the possibilities of peace; second, the common interests of the United States and the Soviet Union; third, the pursuit of peace; and fourth, the relationship between peace and human rights. Under these four headings the essays collected here suggest both the opportunities and obstacles in moving toward a world without war, a world safe for diversity, a world without want.

In no instance do we wish to skirt the difficulties, but neither do we wish to ignore whatever avenues may be open to future progress. Therefore it has been judged particularly important to include here the views of Chinese and Soviet spokesmen, as well as of Western scholars and statesmen, and of a man respected in Moscow as well as the West—Pope John XXIII. From this rich admixture of ideology and power politics, caution and hope, parochial and humanistic concerns the reader may sharpen and perhaps redefine his own attitude toward the desirability and limitations of a strategy of peace.

1

Walter C. Clemens, Jr.

No single blueprint for peace pervades these essays, and some authors agree on ends but not on means, while others dispute each other on both counts. But the conflict and confrontation of views — within the West and between Western and non-Western worlds — is essential if we are to grope *toward* the formulation of a strategy for peace. As the President said, by "defining our goal more clearly, by making it seem more manageable and less remote, we can help all peoples to see it, to draw hope from it, and to move irresistibly toward it."

The essays presented here endeavor to leapfrog the crises of tomorrow morning's news to look at the medium-range and long-term prospects of peace, hopefully not in a utopian but a practical way. All the authors deal in some fashion with the concept of a "world without war," but some consider how war can be prevented short of the elimination of national armaments while others speculate on the nature of a warless world assuming that general disarmament were achieved. Thus, at one level the essay by Ambassador Stevenson focuses on the next steps that would strengthen the United Nations to sustain "cease-fire" and promote peaceful change. Similarly, the essay by Neal evaluates the political prerequisites to large-scale disarmament. On another level the essays by Millis, Waskow, Bloomfield, and Pitersky grapple with what Millis has termed a "demilitarized" world — one in which national armaments have been reduced to police levels and in which some United Nations machinery ensures peace between states. The idea of a "world without arms is a world without war" became an article of Soviet faith under Khrushchev and is defended here against Peking by Mikhail Suslov (who later led in denouncing Khrushchev). Intermediate between these two levels, the essays by Rapoport, Gould, Hoffman, Melman, and Clemens consider the essential conditions for building the road from cease-fire and détente to an at least partially demilitarized world.

Finally, on a plane difficult to compare with the others we have the disparate ideals propounded by Peking and Pope John XXIII, the former asserting that the way to peace is via struggle and revolution, the latter declaring that the key to peace and the standard by which all governments should rule is respect for the dignity and equality of individuals and nations.

Introduction

While most "peace research" has been functional, prescribing what to do or how to do it, this book is predicated on the assumption that a fresh look at goals may suggest new ways of approaching them. Therefore the end of the road as well as the possible ways to get there are considered. The emphasis on what seems possible in the here and now, an orientation endemic to American pragmatism, has probably weakened our ability and even our interest in planning for the future, but deeper analysis of our ends could force us to rethink our tactics as well as our strategy. The objective of a world without war may not be so infeasible as is generally assumed. That, at least, is the argument of one paper in this symposium, the essay by Walter Millis.

Naturally we are concerned with the question of who would "win" in a world free from the Damocles sword of global war. If United States interests can be safeguarded only by maintaining heavy military forces, we may prefer to live with the arms race. But, if—as Waskow, Melman, and others in this symposium argue—our economic and political interests would be enhanced in a demilitarized world, the incentive to control armaments would extend beyond the mere survival instinct. We must also consider the advantages and disadvantages that Communist and other countries see in a world without war, for this will affect the kind of arms controls we advocate and the general nature of our strategy of peace.

Talking about something does not necessarily make it come true, but efforts to plan our future should at the least increase our chances of shaping it. The international political system is a product of both voluntarism and determism. It is an artifice that men make; and it is an organism that grows in unforeseen ways as a result of the forces impacting upon it. To say that men have no control over this growth is the counsel of despair, perhaps an admission of the inevitability of war. "Our problems are man-made," John F. Kennedy told his American University audience, "therefore they can be solved by man." We should not expect an absolute peace contingent upon a sudden revolution in human nature, he cautioned, but we can nevertheless strive for an attainable peace based upon "a gradual evolution in human institutions—on a series of concrete and effective agreements which are in the interest of all concerned."

3

Walter C. Clemens, Jr.

In the spirit of Kennedy's admonition that we should examine the requirements of a practical peace, we shall now trace briefly the similarities and differences of approach in the essays presented here under the four headings of the President's address.

2. THE POSSIBILITIES OF PEACE

It may be true that peace in the thermonuclear age is "necessary," but the real question is whether it can be achieved and sustained. Because we must assume that nations' interests will continue to conflict, the President suggested at American University that peace should be viewed as a "process, a way of solving problems." The view that we must expect conflict to persist but endeavor to resolve it by peaceful means is central to the first two essays here. That of Adlai E. Stevenson analyzes the basic changes that seem to be taking place in the world since the Cuban confrontation. *Perhaps* the policy of containment has served its purpose and *perhaps* the world's leaders "are edging toward a consensus on the proposition that nobody can afford an uncontrolled skirmish any more — that the only safe antidote to escalation is cease-fire." But we must act, if peace is to be ensured. "Violence — which there will be — without war — which there must not be — is unthinkable without an effective and reliable system of peacekeeping." Stevenson notes recent progress and problems in the strengthening of United Nations peacekeeping machinery but calls for an attack on the fundamental causes of violence. "What the world needs is a *dynamic* system of order — a system capable of bringing about not just a precarious halt to hostilities, but a curative resolution of the roots of hostility."

Historian Walter Millis agrees that conflict is inevitable, both within and between states. The central question of his essay is how this conflict can be "structured" so it does not result in war between states. Already, he believes, the nation-state has gone far toward reducing not only domestic but international anarchy. When wars do come, however, they tend to be "total" in every respect, a condition no longer compatible with human survival. The problem then is to exploit tendencies already at work in the international system to curb the role of violence and to enhance the rule of law.

Two major alternatives are posed by Millis — either to abol-

4

Introduction

ish the nation-state and establish a world federal government, or to demilitarize the nation-state and safeguard interstate peace by a supranational police force. The second alternative is seen as the more feasible. It would entail reduction of national armed forces to police levels and creation of a supranational, veto-free police force to keep order between states and to prevent violation of the disarmament treaty, while refraining from intervention in strictly domestic affairs.

How would such a demilitarized world deal with the tensions that would strain its seams—revisionist demands of the have-not nations, border disputes, civil war, power-hungry individuals seeking to use foreign adventures to build domestic power? Contrary to those who assume that nations will always fight, if only with clubs, Millis contends that the elimination of major national armaments would transform world politics, making it much easier to structure international conflict and casting many tensions, now exacerbated by their implications for the unsteady military balance, in a different light.

Before large-scale disarmament of the kind contemplated by Millis can come about, of course, certain political preconditions must be fulfilled, for armaments may be a source of tension, but they also reflect distrust and enmity between nations. The essay by Fred Warner Neal analyzes two of the key political obstacles to détente and—in consequence—to disarmament: the unresolved problems associated with Germany and China. Until compromise agreements are found for these issues, little progress is possible toward far-reaching measures of arms control and disarmament. Further, unless the major powers can demonstrate their willingness to coexist without threatening one another's security, disarmament will remain a pipe dream.

Underscoring Neal's thesis that some political accommodation with Communist China must precede progress toward disarmament, the section entitled "The Fantasy of a Warless World" pinpoints the hostile suspicion with which Peking views the West, particularly the United States. The Chinese quote from Lenin's pre-1917 writings to attack the Soviet view evolved since Stalin's death on the possibility and desirability of peaceful coexistence between Socialist and capitalist states. No lasting peace or disarmament is possible, Peking contends, until the root cause of war—the capitalist system—is extirpated and sup-

5

planted by socialism. Moscow's attempts to come to terms with the United States are futile and treasonable to the socialist cause. Peace will come not by negotiation but by struggle and, ultimately, by revolution.

The Chinese attack upon Soviet foreign policy and ideology is part of the jockeying for power between Peking and Moscow within the international Communist movement and should not be taken as an altogether frank and precise statement of Chinese views and preferences with respect to improved relations with the West. As the Suslov speech in the next section notes, Peking has frequently utilized a double standard, welcoming improvement of Chinese relations with Western Europe while condemning Soviet efforts toward détente with the United States. Were the opportunities for Chinese-United States rapprochement so evident as they are between Peking and Paris, the Chinese line toward Washington might be less acid. However, it appears that a major concern of the Communist Chinese stems from anxiety that Moscow and Washington may unite to freeze the political and military balance to their joint advantage. Thus, while Khrushchev welcomed the Kennedy address at American University, Peking termed it "Kennedy's Big Conspiracy."[1]

3. Common Interests of United States and Soviet Union

As we re-examine our attitude to the Soviet Union, President Kennedy suggested that we should "not be blind to our differences" but that we also pay "direct attention to our common interests and to the means by which those differences can be resolved." He indicated that the United States and Soviet Union have a mutually deep interest in avoiding a central war in which they would be the major targets. But while both sides may have an objective interest in a just and genuine peace and an end to the arms race, they may not perceive this interest or may regard it as of less priority than other goals. Kennedy therefore suggested that "if we cannot now end our differences, at least we can make the world safe for diversity."

The first two essays in this section—by Arthur Waskow and Mikhail Suslov—point to the "common interests" that bind and

[1]See below, p. 198.

the "differences" that divide the two superpowers, providing strong limitations as well as inducements to United States-Soviet cooperation in questions of security and other joint concerns. Both essays indicate an awareness of the importance of avoiding nuclear war, but they also reveal a confidence that their respective countries should and could pursue their foreign policies by vigorous means short of war in a demilitarized world. Waskow, unlike Suslov, holds no government post, so his views are not so authoritative. Nevertheless his judgment may be realistic that the people of the United States will not settle for a passive external policy, but will seek one or both of two major aims: (1) enlarging the domain of liberty or (2) enhancing American power. Which policies Americans choose is up to them, Waskow affirms. But both goals may be advanced in a warless world.

Waskow contends that the United States can and should plan to advance its interests in a warless world by a variety of nonviolent means, ranging from intense propaganda to an expanded Peace Corps. The pluralism and dynamism of the American system will enable it to compete favorably in the realm of ideas and of power. The Rand Corporations of the future will engage the country's best minds in planning this strategy.

It may be argued that Waskow's plan amounts to an intensification of some aspects of the cold war and that continued tension of this kind would preclude meaningful disarmament. Waskow himself foresees that the warless world may be so conflict-ridden that a nation which seems to be "losing" may try to rearm. At this point, he predicts, the warless world will either collapse or be jolted into a tighter-knit federation of states.

Waskow, like Millis, considers world federation out of reach for this generation. The problem of the present, Waskow avers, is to eliminate war; it is for another generation to build from a merely disarmed world an orderly and lawful one. Whatever one thinks about the thesis that the disarmed world will abound in political warfare, Waskow's proposals present a vigorous challenge to those who fear that American interests would passively wither if not upheld by a mailed fist.

If we reversed Waskow's main argument and substituted Moscow for Washington as the probable "winner" in a disarmed world, we would approximate the defense by Suslov of "peaceful coexistence" as interpreted in the Kremlin. "We know that peace is the true ally of socialism," Suslov argues. "The situation created by peaceful coexistence also favorably influences the development of the national liberation movement and the revolutionary struggle of the working class in the capitalist countries."

If the Waskow essay could easily be used against right-wing American opposition to détente, the Suslov essay was explicitly designed to rebut "dogmatists" in Peking. "For Marxist-Leninists," Suslov avers, "there neither is nor can there be a dilemma of whether to wage a struggle for peace or a revolutionary struggle." He defines the Soviet slogan "a world without arms, a world without wars" as a "mighty means of uniting and mobilizing the popular masses"—including those who are non-Communist.

Suslov's apologia of Moscow's peace policy in revolutionary terms was made in a secret meeting in February 1964 at a time when Moscow was refraining from public disputation with Peking. By April 1964, however, when the Khrushchev government was marshaling its forces for a compaign to hold an international Communist meeting to ostracize Peking, the Suslov speech was published as a major salvo to rally support for the Soviet stand. In sharp contrast with the Suslov statement, the other Soviet essay in this book, the Pitersky article in Part IV, "The Soviet View of a Warless World," is pitched to moderate the liberal elements in the West. The moral is clear: both the Suslov and Pitersky statements must be evaluated in light of the audience they aim to persuade. It must be further realized that the Kremlin's operative beliefs may not even lie between these two propaganda extremes, since many factors uppermost in the minds of the Soviet leaders may never be articulated publicly.

Assuming that the ideological and political pronouncements are a suggestive but imperfect guide to Communist thinking, the Clemens article "Peking, Moscow, and the West in a Warless World" attempts to analyze the strategic, political, and economic factors that seem likely to determine the nature of Chinese and Soviet interest in arms control and limited collaboration with the capitalist adversary. From analysis of the material problems confronting the two governments the article finds that, on balance, Moscow has much stronger incentives than Peking to

Introduction

join the West in efforts to control the arms race and reduce the threat of violence in international politics.

The Clemens essay raises the question, however, whether a demilitarized world could ever come about if the superpowers remain so actively hostile to one another as Waskow and Suslov advocate. Such aggressive policies would probably preclude the political settlements and mutual trust necessary for either side to take the blind leap of faith ultimately required to stake its security on arms control rather than a quest for military superiority. A sense of common purpose deriving from mutually advantageous cooperation in mastering the challenges of human ecology must supplement fear of atomic war if the superpowers are to perceive and act upon the shared interests resulting from the opportunities and dangers of modern technology. Competition and cooperation, both sides may come to realize, can be a source of mutual enrichment.

A similar view is expressed in Anatol Rapoport's essay on "The Needs of American and Soviet Science." In both the United States and the Soviet Union, he suggests, there is a need for greater freedom and responsibility in natural as well as in social science. American science suffers less from centralized controls than from a weak sense of the social implications of science and technology, while in Russia the situation is reversed. But in both countries the existence of covert and explicit restraints and the absence of social awareness in science are in large part a function of the harnessing of research to the requirements of the cold war. Movement toward a world without war would free science in both the East and the West of its commitment to destructive purposes. "Science so emancipated can then begin truly to embrace the emancipation of man," Rapoport concludes. Freedom and responsibility, we would find, are complementary, not opposed.

4. The Pursuit of Peace

The paradox that a crisis — at least when it is well-managed — may sometimes lead to a relaxation of tensions was dramatically illustrated by the setting and content of Kennedy's American University address.[2] Speaking in the aftermath of Cuba and after

[2]Text below, pp. 22-29.

rejecting advice that he exploit and press the Soviet retreat, the President declared that "nuclear powers must avert those confrontations which bring an adversary to a choice of either a humiliating retreat or a nuclear war." In part perhaps because the United States had demonstrated the right mix of firmness and flexibility, the time had become ripe for progress in arms control.[3] The Cuban crisis had intensified the awareness on both sides of the need for improved communications, and Kennedy spoke of the proposed direct line between Washington and Moscow—an agreement that was signed in Geneva ten days later.[4] He announced also that high-level negotiations were soon to begin that led on July 25 to the initialing of the nuclear test ban treaty, formalized on August 5, 1963.[5] Both sides may have been aware of the potential role of unilateral initiatives to reduce tension: thus Kennedy announced at American University that the United States would not resume atmospheric nuclear testing so long as other powers also refrained, and several days after his speech the Soviet Union stopped jamming the Voice of America. It was also a sign of the times that *Pravda* and *Izvestia* on June 13, 1963, printed the entire American University speech. Comment was deferred for several days until Khrushchev replied to questions by the editors of the two papers.[6]

The momentum of the "Moscow Treaty" on nuclear testing continued when the United States and Soviet governments agreed to a United Nations resolution of October 17, 1963, prohibiting the placing of nuclear weapons in space.[7] And— after Kennedy's death—the joint pledges in April 1964 by Washington, London, and Moscow to reduce production of fissionable materials again showed the flexibility afforded by

---

[3]The American University address nevertheless posed the delicate question of how to strike the proper balance between firmness and flexibility, for Kennedy reiterated Washington's commitment to defend Western Europe and West Berlin, and to make no deal with Moscow at the expense of other nations. These aspects of the speech drew from Khrushchev the comment that the President was refusing to settle the basic problems of the cold war. See *Pravda,* June 15, 1963, and *Izvestia,* June 16, 1963.

[4]Text below, pp. 207-211.

[5]Text below, pp. 211-213.

[6]*Pravda,* June 15, 1963, and *Izvestia,* June 16, 1963.

[7]Text below, p. 214.

Introduction

unilateral initiatives or tacit agreements in slowing the arms race.[8]

While limited measures such as the test ban were the immediate and most feasible objectives of United States arms control policy, the President declared at American University that the long-range United States interest was "general and complete disarmament, designed to take place by stages, permitting parallel political developments to build the new institutions of peace which would take the place of arms." This goal had been affirmed by the United States on September 21, 1961, in a joint United States-Soviet agreement on the principles that should guide disarmament negotiations[9] and on September 25, 1961, in a speech by President Kennedy to the General Assembly. While Washington in this agreement made explicit its commitment to general and complete disarmament (GCD), Moscow conceded that control should be proportionate to the disarmament achieved and that progress from one stage to another should be contingent on the successful verification that the disarmament pledged had been carried out and that the control organ was ready to verify the next stage of the process.[10]

The spring of 1962 saw the United States and Soviet Union introduce detailed GCD programs at the Eighteen-Nation Disarmament Conference. These two documents provide the points of departure for the analyses here by Lincoln P. Bloomfield and N. Pitersky who, both unofficially, speculate on how the framework of the draft United States and Soviet treaties might be filled in to provide a picture of the operating principles of a disarmed world.

Bloomfield's essay "Arms Control and World Government" differs fundamentally in some respects from the views of Millis, Waskow, and Pitersky. Whereas Millis and Pitersky believe a demilitarized world to be feasible in the not-too-distant future,

[8]Texts below, pp. 214-218. After Khrushchev's ouster, the new Soviet Government continued part of his policy by pledging to reduce its defense budget, allegedly on the understanding that Washington would reciprocate. *The New York Times,* December 10, 1964.

[9]Text below, pp. 202-204.

[10]However the Soviet Government refused what it termed United States proposals for "control over armaments," that is, inspection of the forces not to be reduced or limited. See below, pp. 205-207.

Walter C. Clemens, Jr.

Bloomfield argues that if we await the evolutionary development of the political preconditions, at least 25 to 50 years are required. History might, however, be short-circuited if a crisis of some kind appears so menacing that it produces a revolution in world political arrangements.

One reason for Bloomfield's more protracted time scale is that he is perhaps more impressed than Millis or Pitersky with the problems of creating the international arrangements required to oversee disarmament to police levels and ensure order by a supranational security force. While Millis contrasts a "federal global state" to a "demilitarized" nation-state system, Bloomfield maintains "there is a Rubicon that divides the Gaul of basically untrammeled national sovereignty from the Tuscany of meaningful supranational authority." By whatever process and by whatever name, the agency that is to control world affairs must be termed a "limited world government." The obstacles to such an arrangement are summed up in a paradox: if Communist dynamism continues, neither the East nor the West can submit to such a government; if this dynamism is abated, the West might lose whatever incentive it has for world government.

A second reason for the discrepancies between Bloomfield and the other three authors is that his argument, like the United States draft treaty, postulates the necessity of establishing a supranational security force so powerful that "no state can challenge it." The Bloomfield essay spells out what is almost implicit in the United States draft treaty: that the United Nations police force should be armed with nuclear weapons. Millis, Waskow, and Pitersky, by contrast, seem to place less importance on the need for armaments capable of deterring aggression should a state clandestinely violate the disarmament agreement. The Pitersky essay, in turn, proposes a still weaker force than that envisaged by Millis and Waskow. While these two authors call for a permanent, veto-free but lightly armed United Nations police force, the Soviet GCD program elaborated by Pitersky proposes only that states place contingents of their national forces at the disposal of the Security Council. One interesting result of these contrasting emphases is that Bloomfield proposes a United Nations force of 500,000 men while Pitersky posits that individual states will designate contingents for United Nations purposes from their own forces, which for some states could number up to 300,000 men The Soviet plan may thus hope to rely on quantity if not on quality to repulse aggression.

A third area of difference between Bloomfield and the other three authors is that he puts much greater emphasis on the importance of developing an international judicial procedure to settle disputes and hear grievances. Pitersky, while eschewing the detailed court system discussed by Bloomfield, does nevertheless state that all disputes could in a disarmed world "be settled by peaceful, diplomatic and constitutional means." The Soviet author also suggests the possibility of "reviewing" treaties to take account of the interests of small and economically underdeveloped countries and of amending the United Nations charter to help the United Nations to function more effectively to uphold peace and security. In contrast to Bloomfield's thesis that some sovereignty must be surrendered to a limited world government, however, Pitersky ostensibly expects that—even though an International Disarmament Organization would observe each country—national sovereignty would remain untrammeled.

All four authors—Millis, Waskow, Bloomfield, and Pitersky —assume that conflict would continue in a disarmed world. Pitersky makes the classical Leninist assumption that there will be strife between capitalism and the classes and nations which it exploits, but he makes explicit what Lenin only hinted at as a remote possibility toward the end of his life—that disarmament could be achieved despite the continued existence of the capitalist system. Like Millis, the Soviet commentator assumes that the removal of the strategic factor from the calculus of foreign policy would significantly reduce and even transform present sources of tension. And Pitersky shares the concern of several Western authors in the book that United States-Soviet ties be strengthened by joint projects of mutual economic advantage. However he soft-pedals Suslov's thesis that in a disarmed world the Socialist camp would defeat capitalism in economic competition.

The Pitersky article does not take account of two important modifications in Moscow's negotiating position made since September 1962: first, the proposal that the United States and the Soviet Union retain a "nuclear umbrella" until the end of the second or third stage of the GCD process; and second, the suggestion that United Nations members which are not permanent members of the Security Council place national contingents at the service of the Security Council. The extent to which either or both of these proposals might be compatible with United States interests is discussed in the Clemens essay "Implications for United States Policy."

The Clemens article also considers the military, political, and economic policies the United States might pursue on the assumption that Washington wished to convince Moscow and eventually Peking that their interests could be best promoted in a stable political and military environment without resort to force. In the President's words at American University, we must "persevere in the search for peace in the hope that constructive changes within the Communist bloc might bring within reach solutions which now seem beyond us. We must conduct our affairs in such a way that it becomes in the Communists' interest to agree on a genuine peace." The task is to work toward conditions that give all countries including the Communist states a stake both in stability and in orderly change.

The five agreements reproduced in the section "First Documents of a Warless World" register the limited extent to which Moscow and Washington have reached agreement in principle or on partial measures in the pursuit of peace and control of armaments.

5. PEACE AND HUMAN RIGHTS

Last but by no means least, President Kennedy called on Americans to examine their attitude toward peace and freedom in the United States itself, for the "quality and spirit of our own society must justify and support our efforts abroad. . . . In too many of our cities today the peace is not secure because freedom is insecure."

The relationship between domestic factors in Russia and America on the one hand and international politics on the other was acutely defined in 1947 by an architect of the "containment" policy, George F. Kennan. The Stalinist dictatorship, he wrote, was of direct concern to the United States, because it depended in part upon a semimyth of implacable foreign hostility and a perpetuation of "struggle" against the external foe. And the most important way the United States could promote its security was "to measure up to its own best traditions and prove itself worthy of preservation as a great nation." To be sure, Kennan argued, United States military strength would have to contain Soviet expansion, but the influence America exerted upon the internal development of the Communist movement would depend on "the degree to which the United States can create among the peoples of the world generally the impression of a country which knows what it wants, which is coping successfully with the problems of the internal life, and with the responsibilities of a World Power, and which has a spiritual vitality capable of holding its own among the major ideological currents of the time."[11]

The domestic prerequisites for the maintenance of the containment policy are probably still more decisive as we endeavor to move from containment toward cease-fire and peaceful change. It was relatively easy to harness the nation's will and strength to stand firm against a readily perceived external threat. But it takes more imagination and greater resolve in the presence of less visible dangers to embark upon and sustain a strategy of peace. For the purpose of short-term defense against Communist aggression it might suffice to prop up a foreign country with sufficient military power to suppress internal dissension and to keep the Chinese tiger or Russian bear at the gates. But the requirements of creating and maintaining a demilitarized world, in which the Communist movement is still held in check, are infinitely more complex.

This argument points to the conclusion that an enduring peace depends, in the final analysis, on the dynamic fulfillment of man's spiritual and material needs in a way that makes real the ideals proclaimed in the United Nations Universal Declaration of Human Rights. A strategy of peace will therefore have to embody an enlightened, long-range policy toward education, economic development, and moral philosophy that contributes to the fundamental conditions for a world without war.

[11]"X" [George F. Kennan], "The Sources of Soviet Conduct," Foreign Affairs, July 1947, in *The Soviet Union: 1922-1962*, Philip E. Mosely (ed.), New York: Praeger, 1963, pp. 174, 184-85.

Walter C. Clemens, Jr.

What does American education contribute to such a strategy? We are torn, Samuel Gould suggests, between preparing our youth for a world as it is and a world as it should be. American education "finds itself on a tightrope with the increasingly present danger of falling in the wrong direction." A great part of education is devoted to satisfying the demands of students for material wealth and social status, strengthening egotistical impulses that shut off an interest (not to speak of an ability) to take a responsible role in the world at large. Efforts at frenetic escapism will not lead to a warless world. Gould joins Rapoport in lamenting the emphasis on applied military research and the failure to anticipate or plan for the tremendous social implications of technological invention. "The lag in human adjustment grows greater day by day, and our educational systems are almost timid about pointing this out, to say nothing of taking action." Finally, the activist *Zeitgeist* of American life pervades education, almost precluding opportunities for sober contemplation.

Education for a world without war, Gould suggests, must take in a far more encompassing horizon than now exists in United States universities. Foreign cultures must be much better understood. The meaning of the different social sciences must be distilled and interpreted in a more integrated manner than is possible given the rigid departmental separation of most United States campuses. A deeper knowledge of man himself as an individual with mysterious drives, fears, and joys is also necessary to education for peace. Finally, education for a world without war must come to grips with the ethical problems of life, criticizing where necessary present patterns and suggesting where possible other avenues.

The inner faces between economic development, education, and peace are discussed in Seymour Melman's "Converting America's Economy to a Warless World." Melman indicates the involvement of the federal government both in industry and in higher education as a result of the defense effort. On the assumption that United States security can be maintained even while reducing the defense budget to lower levels, Melman contends that the partial conversion of military to civilian economy could have an exhilarating effect on the economy as a whole. It could set free the human and material resources

Introduction

required to generate new markets and new jobs in a massive effort aimed at sparking and sustaining economic growth and eliminating the many areas of severe poverty still blemishing the national life. A concerted program to improve the education and the economic well-being of all classes would help to create equal opportunities for all races. Both public and private investment and planning will be required to accomplish these tasks.

Melman's analysis of the strengths and weaknesses of the United States economy and Paul Hoffman's report on the needs of the emerging nations lead both men to advocate a world-wide attack on poverty. The items which the United States could most profitably "export"—industrial goods and the technology for resource surveys and capital construction—are precisely the items that the emerging nations need most. Unlike the Soviet Union, the United States has a major block of industrial and agricultural capacities which now lie partly idle, but which could be gainfully employed in development programs in Asia, Africa, and Latin America.

Looking at world development from the viewpoint of United States interests, Melman argues that a global assault on poverty could assist the United States to shift resources from defense while maintaining an expanding, full-employment economy. A healthy mix of public and private investment by the United States in the developing nations could do much to create the conditions for economic pluralism and even for political democracy. In consequence the Soviet Union would be pressed increasingly to choose between defense expenditures at home and economic and political influence abroad. In the United States the war on poverty—domestic and abroad—would "transform the conditions under which the American people must consider solutions for international and domestic problems."

The Melman and Hoffman essays point to vivid parallels between poverty, ignorance, unequal opportunity, frustration, and violence as they interact in the United States and in the less-developed countries. If the result in America is violence in the streets, the result in countries like the Congo is civil war that threatens world peace as well as internal stability. If America is failing fully to develop its human resources, the lack of educational facilities in the emerging nations is much more appalling. Here again, as President Kennedy noted in his June 10, 1963, address, great opportunities exist for American youth willing to serve in the Peace Corps and other programs designed to lay the foundations for mass education in the emerging nations. Again there is a complementary relationship between what Americans can do and what the less-developed countries most need.

One more parallel should be stressed between the economic and educational situation in America and in the world's poorer nations. The problems in both cases are severe, but the opportunities are immense, particularly if a portion of the resources given to defense could be transferred to development. Hoffman's estimate is that 20 of the world's 100 poverty-ridden communities could achieve decent living conditions within the next decade — thereby demonstrating to the other disadvantaged countries that they too can hope for such progress.

Hoffman's calculation that we might achieve within this century a world without want dovetails in some respects with Bloomfield's suggestion that comprehensive arms control might be possible in 25 to 50 years as a result of political evolution. Progress toward either objective would tend to accelerate progress toward the other. Virtually all the contributors to this volume agree that instability in the new nations constitutes a major obstacle to the achievement and maintenance of a warless world.

The relationship between world peace and human rights was incisively stated by Pope John XXIII in his encyclical that won the praise of believers and nonbelievers around the world — *Pacem in Terris.* The universal common good and the dignity of the individual are the standards by which the Pope justified his support for many of the elements in a strategy of peace suggested by the various essays in this book. All nations like all men should be seen as equal in dignity. The more fortunate should aid the less fortunate. The rule of reason and a willingness to cooperate should supplant the use of force. Disarmament is recommended not only by fear of thermonuclear war but by the economic advantages disarmament could bring to all peoples.

However the Pope goes on to a conclusion more radical in some respects than any made by the essays in this volume except perhaps the Chinese demand for a universal struggle against capitalist imperialism. *Pacem in Terris* argues that the moral order and the solution of common human problems require the

Introduction

establishment of a "universal public authority" sufficiently powerful to deal with the tasks confronting all nations. The nation-state system is simply not capable of dealing with these tasks because its constituent parts are juridically equal. "Therefore . . . both the structure and form of governments as well as the power which public authority wields in all the nations of the world, must be considered inadequate to promote the universal common good."

How can this universal public authority be established? It must rest not on force but on mutual accord. How can it be effective without endangering the rights of individual peoples and persons? A high but perhaps unattainable standard is proposed: all governments—those in the individual countries and that of the universal public authority—must deal with each other and with their respective citizens with the fundamental objective of promoting the rights of the human person.

The extent to which Pope John was calling for a union, a federation, or a confederation of states is not clear. He wrote that the "world-wide public authority is not intended to limit the sphere of action of the authority of the individual state, much less to take its place. On the contrary, its purpose is to create, on a world basis, an environment in which the public authorities of each state, its citizens and intermediate associations, can carry out their tasks, fulfill their duties and exercise their rights with greater security." While this statement suggests strong limits upon the functions of the central authority, the encyclical concluded with the wish that the United Nations Organization might become ever more equal to its tasks and provide "every human being an effective safeguard for the rights which derive directly from his dignity as a person, and which are therefore universal, inviolable and inalienable rights."

Was the Pope proposing a utopia? Perhaps not, but merely a rededication to an ideal—respect for the dignity of each man—and an affirmation of hope in the feasibility of a better life that could inspire persistence in the pursuit of a strategy of peace.

With this introduction as the setting, let us consider the full text of President Kennedy's address "Toward a Strategy of Peace" and the essays collected here to indicate the salient opportunities and obstacles on the road to a world without war—with or without disarmament.

I

•

TOWARD A STRATEGY OF PEACE

John F. Kennedy

•

TOWARD A STRATEGY OF PEACE: COMMENCEMENT ADDRESS BY PRESIDENT KENNEDY AT AMERICAN UNIVERSITY, WASHINGTON, D.C., JUNE 10, 1963[1]

"There are few earthly things more beautiful than a University," wrote John Masefield, in his tribute to the English universities — and his words are equally true here. He did not refer to spires and towers, to campus greens and ivied walls. He admired the splendid beauty of the university, he said, because it was "a place where those who hate ignorance may strive to know, where those who perceive truth may strive to make others see."

I have, therefore, chosen this time and this place to discuss a topic on which ignorance too often abounds and the truth is too rarely perceived — yet it is the most important topic on earth: world peace.

What kind of peace do I mean? What kind of peace do we seek? Not a *Pax Americana* enforced on the world by American weapons of war. Not the peace of the grave or the security of the slave. I am talking about genuine peace, the kind of peace that makes life on earth worth living, the kind that enables men and nations to grow and to hope and to build a better life for their children — not merely peace for Americans but peace for all men and women, not merely peace in our time but peace for all time.

[1]White House Press Release; text from *Department of State Bulletin,* July 1, 1963, pp. 2-6.

Toward a Strategy of Peace

I speak of peace because of the new face of war. Total war makes no sense in an age when great powers can maintain large and relatively invulnerable nuclear forces and refuse to surrender without resort to those forces. It makes no sense in an age when a single nuclear weapon contains almost 10 times the explosive force delivered by all of the Allied air forces in the Second World War. It makes no sense in an age when the deadly poisons produced by a nuclear exchange would be carried by the wind and water and soil and seed to the far corners of the globe and to generations yet unborn.

Today the expenditure of billions of dollars every year on weapons acquired for the purpose of making sure we never need to use them is essential to keeping the peace. But surely the acquisition of such idle stockpiles — which can only destroy and never create — is not the only, much less the most efficient, means of assuring peace.

I speak of peace, therefore, as the necessary rational end of rational men. I realize that the pursuit of peace is not as dramatic as the pursuit of war, and frequently the words of the pursuer fall on deaf ears. But we have no more urgent task.

Some say that it is useless to speak of world peace or world law or world disarmament — and that it will be useless until the leaders of the Soviet Union adopt a more enlightened attitude. I hope they do. I believe we can help them do it. But I also believe that we must reexamine our own attitude, as individuals and as a nation, for our attitude is as essential as theirs. And every graduate of this school, every thoughtful citizen who despairs of war and wishes to bring peace, should begin by looking inward — by examining his own attitude toward the possibilities of peace, toward the Soviet Union, toward the course of the cold war, and toward freedom and peace here at home.

THE POSSIBILITIES OF PEACE

First: Let us examine our attitude toward peace itself. Too many of us think it is impossible. Too many think it unreal. But that is a dangerous, defeatist belief. It leads to the conclusion that war is inevitable, that mankind is doomed, that we are gripped by forces we cannot control.

We need not accept that view. Our problems are manmade; therefore they can be solved by man. And man can be as big as he wants. No problem of human destiny is beyond human beings. Man's reason and spirit have often solved the seemingly unsolvable, and we believe they can do it again.

I am not referring to the absolute, infinite concept of universal peace and good will of which some fantasies and fanatics dream. I do not deny the values of hopes and dreams, but we merely invite discouragement and incredulity by making that our only and immediate goal.

Let us focus instead on a more practical, more attainable peace, based not on a sudden revolution in human nature but on a gradual evolution in human institutions—on a series of concrete actions and effective agreements which are in the interest of all concerned. There is no single, simple key to this peace, no grand or magic formula to be adopted by one or two powers. Genuine peace must be the product of many nations, the sum of many acts. It must be dynamic, not static, changing to meet the challenge of each new generation. For peace is a process, a way of solving problems.

With such a peace there will still be quarrels and conflicting interests, as there are within families and nations. World peace, like community peace, does not require that each man love his neighbor; it requires only that they live together in mutual tolerance, submitting their disputes to a just and peaceful settlement. And history teaches us that enmities between nations, as between individuals, do not last forever. However fixed our likes and dislikes may seem, the tide of time and events will often bring surprising changes in the relations between nations and neighbors.

So let us persevere. Peace need not be impracticable, and war need not be inevitable. By defining our goal more clearly, by making it seem more manageable and less remote, we can help all peoples to see it, to draw hope from it, and to move irresistibly toward it.

COMMON INTERESTS OF UNITED STATES AND SOVIET UNION

Second: Let us reexamine our attitude toward the Soviet Union. It is discouraging to think that their leaders may actually believe what their propagandists write. It is discouraging to read a recent authoritative Soviet text on military strategy and find, on page after page, wholly baseless and incredible claims—such as the allegation that "American imperialist circles are preparing to unleash different types of wars . . . that there is a very real threat of a preventive war being unleashed by American imperialists against the Soviet Union . . . [and that] the political aims of the American imperialists are to enslave economically and politically the European and other capitalist countries . . . [and] to achieve world domination . . . by means of aggressive wars."

Truly as it was written long ago: "The wicked flee when no man pursueth." Yet it is sad to read these Soviet statements—to realize the extent of the gulf between us. But it is also a warning—a warning to the American people not to fall into the same trap as the Soviets, not to see only a distorted and desperate view of the other side, not to see conflict as inevitable, accommodation as impossible, and communication as nothing more than an exchange of threats.

No government or social system is so evil that its people must be considered as lacking in virtue. As Americans we find communism profoundly repugnant as a negation of personal freedom and dignity. But we can still hail the Russian people for their many achievements—in science and space, in economic and industrial growth, in culture and in acts of courage.

Among the many traits the peoples of our two countries have in common, none is stronger than our mutual abhorrence of war. Almost unique among the major world powers, we have never been at war with each other. And no nation in the history of battle ever suffered more than the Soviet Union suffered in the course of the Second World War. At least 20 million lost their lives. Countless millions of homes and farms were burned or sacked. A third of the nation's territory, including nearly two-thirds of its industrial base, was turned into a wasteland—a loss equivalent to the devastation of this country east of Chicago.

Today, should total war ever break out again—no matter how—our two countries would become the primary targets. It is an ironical but accurate fact that the two strongest powers are the two in the most danger of devastation. All we have built, all we have worked for, would be destroyed in the first 24 hours. And even in the cold war, which brings burdens and dangers to so many countries—including this nation's closest allies—our two countries bear the heaviest burdens. For we are both devoting massive sums of money to weapons that could be better devoted to combating ignorance, poverty, and disease. We are both caught up in a vicious and dangerous cycle in which suspicion on one side breeds suspicion on the other and new weapons beget counter-weapons.

In short, both the United States and its allies, and the Soviet Union and its allies, have a mutually deep interest in a just and genuine peace and in halting the arms race. Agreements to this end are in the interests of the Soviet Union as well as ours, and even the most hostile nations can be relied upon to accept and keep those treaty obligations, and only those treaty obligations, which are in their own interest.

So let us not be blind to our differences, but let us also direct attention to our common interests and to the means by which those differences can be resolved. And if we cannot end now our differences, at least we can help make the world safe for diversity. For in the final analysis our most basic common link is that we all inhabit this planet. We all breathe the same air. We all cherish our children's future. And we are all mortal.

The Pursuit of Peace

Third: Let us reexamine our attitude toward the cold war, remembering that we are not engaged in a debate, seeking to pile up debating points. We are not here distributing blame or pointing the finger of judgment. We must deal with the world as it is and not as it might have been had the history of the last 18 years been different.

We must, therefore, persevere in the search for peace in the hope that constructive changes within the Communist bloc might bring within reach solutions which now seem beyond us. We must conduct our affairs in such a way that it becomes in the Communists' interest to agree on a genuine peace. Above all, while defending our own vital interests, nuclear powers must avert those confrontations which bring an adversary to a choice of either a humiliating retreat or a nuclear war. To adopt that kind of course in the nuclear age would be evidence only of the bankruptcy of our policy—or of a collective death wish for the world.

To secure these ends, America's weapons are nonprovocative, carefully controlled, designed to deter, and capable of selective use. Our military forces are committed to peace and disciplined in self-restraint. Our diplomats are instructed to avoid unnecessary irritants and purely rhetorical hostility.

For we can seek a relaxation of tensions without relaxing our guard. And, for our part, we do not need to use threats to prove that we are resolute. We do not need to jam foreign broadcasts out of fear our faith will be eroded. We are unwilling to impose our system on any unwilling people, but we are willing and able to engage in peaceful competition with any people on earth.

Meanwhile we seek to strengthen the United Nations, to help solve its financial problems, to make it a more effective instrument of peace, to develop it into a genuine world security system — a system capable of resolving disputes on the basis of law, of insuring the security of the large and the small, and of creating conditions under which arms can finally be abolished.

At the same time we seek to keep peace inside the non-Communist world, where many nations, all of them our friends, are divided over issues which weaken Western unity, which invite Communist intervention, or which threaten to erupt into war. Our efforts in West New Guinea, in the Congo, in the Middle East, and in the Indian subcontinent have been persistent and patient despite criticism from both sides. We have also tried to set an example for others — by seeking to adjust small but significant differences with our own closest neighbors in Mexico and in Canada.

Speaking of other nations, I wish to make one point clear. We are bound to many nations by alliances. Those alliances exist because our concern and theirs substantially overlap. Our commitment to defend Western Europe and West Berlin, for example, stands undiminished because of the identity of our vital interests. The United States will make no deal with the Soviet Union at the expense of other nations and other peoples, not merely because they are our partners but also because their interests and ours converge.

Our interests converge, however, not only in defending the frontiers of freedom but in pursuing the paths of peace. It is our hope — and the purpose of Allied policies — to convince the Soviet Union that she, too, should let each nation choose its own future, so long as that choice does not interfere with the choices of others. The Communist drive to impose their political and economic system on others is the primary cause of world tension today. For there can be no doubt that, if all nations could refrain from interfering in the self-determination of others, the peace would be much more assured.

This will require a new effort to achieve world law, a new context for world discussions. It will require increased understanding between the Soviets and ourselves. And increased understanding will require increased contact and communication. One step in this direction is the proposed arrangement for a direct line between Moscow and Washington, to avoid on each side the dangerous delays, misunderstandings, and misreadings of the other's actions which might occur at a time of crisis.

We have also been talking in Geneva about other first-step measures of arms control, designed to limit the intensity of the arms race and to reduce the risks of accidental war. Our primary long-range interest in Geneva, however, is general and complete disarmament, designed to take place by stages, permitting parallel political developments to build the new institutions of peace which would take the place of arms. The pursuit of disarmament has been an effort of this Government since the 1920's. It has been urgently sought by the past three administrations. And however dim the prospects may be today, we intend to continue this effort—to continue it in order that all countries, including our own, can better grasp what the problems and possibilities of disarmament are.

The one major area of these negotiations where the end is in sight, yet where a fresh start is badly needed, is in a treaty to outlaw nuclear tests. The conclusion of such a treaty—so near and yet so far—would check the spiraling arms race in one of its most dangerous areas. It would place the nuclear powers in a position to deal more effectively with one of the greatest hazards which man faces in 1963, the further spread of nuclear arms. It would increase our security; it would decrease the prospects of war. Surely this goal is sufficiently important to require our steady pursuit, yielding neither to the temptation to give up the whole effort nor the temptation to give up our insistence on vital and responsible safeguards.

I am taking this opportunity, therefore, to announce two important decisions in this regard.

Toward a Strategy of Peace

First: Chairman Khrushchev, Prime Minister Macmillan, and I have agreed that high-level discussion will shortly begin in Moscow looking toward early agreement on a comprehensive test ban treaty. Our hopes must be tempered with the caution of history, but with our hopes go the hopes of all mankind.

Second: To make clear our good faith and solemn convictions on the matter, I now declare that the United States does not propose to conduct nuclear tests in the atmosphere so long as other states do not do so. We will not be the first to resume. Such a declaration is no substitute for a formal binding treaty, but I hope it will help us achieve one. Nor would such a treaty be a substitute for disarmament, but I hope it will help us achieve it.

PEACE AND HUMAN RIGHTS

Finally, my fellow Americans, let us examine our attitude toward peace and freedom here at home. The quality and spirit of our own society must justify and support our efforts abroad. We must show it in the dedication of our own lives, as many of you who are graduating today will have a unique opportunity to do, by serving without pay in the Peace Corps abroad or in the proposed National Service Corps here at home.

But wherever we are, we must all, in our daily lives, live up to the age-old faith that peace and freedom walk together. In too many of our cities today the peace is not secure because freedom is incomplete.

It is the responsibility of the executive branch at all levels of government — local, State, and national — to provide and protect that freedom for all of our citizens by all means within their authority. It is the responsibility of the legislative branch at all levels, wherever that authority is not now adequate, to make it adequate. And it is the responsibility of all citizens in all sections of this country to respect the rights of all others and to respect the law of the land.

All this is not unrelated to world peace. "When a man's ways please the Lord," the Scriptures tell us, "he maketh even his enemies to be at peace with him." And is not peace, in the last analysis, basically a matter of human rights — the right to live out our lives without fear of devastation, the right to breathe air as nature provided it, the right of future generations to a healthy existence?

29

John F. Kennedy

While we proceed to safeguard our national interests, let us also safeguard human interests. And the elimination of war and arms is clearly in the interest of both. No treaty, however much it may be to the advantage of all, however tightly it may be worded, can provide absolute security against the risks of deception and evasion. But it can, if it is sufficiently effective in its enforcement and if it is sufficiently in the interests of its signers, offer far more security and far fewer risks than an unabated, uncontrolled, unpredictable arms race.

The United States, as the world knows, will never start a war. We do not want a war. We do not now expect a war. This generation of Americans has already had enough—more than enough—of war and hate and oppression. We shall be prepared if others wish it. We shall be alert to try to stop it. But we shall also do our part to build a world of peace where the weak are safe and the strong are just. We are not helpless before that task or hopeless of its success. Confident and unafraid, we labor on— not toward a strategy of annihilation but toward a strategy of peace.

II

•

THE POSSIBILITIES
OF PEACE

ADLAI E. STEVENSON

•

FROM CONTAINMENT TO CEASE-FIRE AND PEACEFUL CHANGE[1]

The United Nations and therefore the world has been fortunate to have three strong Secretaries-General—Trygve Lie of Norway, Dag Hammarskjöld of Sweden and U Thant of Burma. While serving on the American delegation in London in the first days of the United Nations and latterly in New York, I had something to do with the selection of Trygve Lie and U Thant. And it was my good fortune to know Dag Hammarskjöld well, and my sad lot to attend his funeral in the lovely old cathedral at Upsala. Like the others who came from all over the world, I walked behind him to the cemetery through the streets of the ancient town, lined with thousands of silent, reverent people. Upsala was the world that day when he was laid to rest in the northern autumn twilight, for he was a hero of the community of man.

Norman Cousins tells a story that says a lot about Dag Hammarskjöld as a peacemaker.

He had scheduled an interview with a magazine writer one evening. The writer suggested that they have dinner at a restaurant, which the Secretary-General accepted. He further suggested that they take his car, which the Secretary-General also accepted.

Upon leaving the building, the writer recalled to his embarrassment that he had driven into town in a battered old jeep. The Secretary-General was delighted. "Sometimes I think I was born in one," he said.

[1]Dag Hammarskjöld Memorial Lecture by Ambassador Adlai E. Stevenson, United States Representative to the United Nations, at Princeton University, March 23, 1964.

From Containment to Cease-Fire

But the writer's embarrassment had only begun. Four blocks away, a taxicab darted in front of the jeep and there was a harmless collision.

I don't have to suggest the reaction of the cab driver or the quality of his prose. But the writer was not without a temper himself, or the prose to match the cab driver. It looked as though the disagreement was about to escalate into active hostilities. At this point, Hammarskjöld climbed out of the jeep and stepped around to the cab driver.

"You know," he said, "I don't think anyone quite realizes how tough it is to drive a cab in New York City. I don't know how you fellows do it—ten, twelve, fourteen hours a day, day after day, with all the things you've got to contend with, people weaving in and out of traffic and that sort of thing. Believe me, I really have to take my hat off to you fellows."

The cab driver defused immediately. "Mister," he said, "you really said a mouthful." And that was the end of the incident.

But it wasn't the end of the story. A few blocks later the unfortunate writer ran out of gas. And who should drive by? The same cab driver pulled up and said, "What's the matter chum, any trouble?"

"Out of gas," said the disgruntled writer.

Well, you can guess the end of the story: The cabbie offered to get some gas, invited the driver's "nice friend" to come along with him, and drove off with the Secretary-General of the United Nations in the front seat—leaving the writer to ponder the role of the peacemaker in today's tense society.

I. A World in Flux

No one ever doubted Dag Hammarskjöld's selfless dedication to peaceful settlement of any and all disputes among men and nations. None questioned his deep personal commitment to the principles of the Charter of the United Nations, whose first business is the peaceful settlement of disputes.

But this can be said of other men: Hammarskjöld was unsurpassed, but he was not alone in his devotion to peace. What distinguished his service to the United Nations is that he came to see it for what it is: a specific piece of international machinery whose implicit capabilities can only be realized by the action of the members and the Secretariat working within its constitutional framework.

There was no doubt in Dag Hammarskjöld—nor is there in many others—that the United Nations is the most remarkable and significant international institution ever conceived. But Hammarskjöld also understood that the machinery not only needs lofty goals and high principles but it has to work in practice—that it has limited, not unlimited functions; that it has finite, not infinite capabilities under given circumstances at a given time.

He saw that the effectiveness of the organization is measured by the best consensus that can be reached by the relevant majority of the relevant organ—and that reaching that consensus is a highly pragmatic exercise.

Understanding all this, Dag Hammarskjöld—himself a key part of the machinery—helped make the machinery more workable, more adaptable, more relevant to the immediate political needs. By doing so, he helped expand the capacity of the machinery to act effectively. This, I think, was his greatest contribution to the United Nations, and thus to world peace.

His was dedicated service—backed by diplomatic skill, by administrative talent, and by a sharp sense of political reality.

The overwhelming political reality of Hammarskjöld's day was the division of the world into opposing and rigid military alliances, led by two incomparable centers of power and influence—with the two halves of this bipolar world engaged in a cold war paced by an uncontrolled and seemingly uncontrollable nuclear arms race—while everyone else held his breath lest the "balance of terror" get too far out of balance.

Many came to accept this as a continuing—almost natural—state of affairs which would continue until one side collapsed or the two sides collided in World War III. We now know that it was a transitory and unhealthy condition of the world body politic.

The cold war has not sunk out of sight, but the field of contest may be shifting radically—and for the better.

The nuclear arms race has not passed into history, but at least it has, for the first time, been brought within a first stage of control.

From Containment to Cease-Fire

For these and a large variety of other reasons, the world is a very different world from that which existed when Dag Hammarskjöld went down to his death in that cruel crash in Africa two and a half years ago. We therefore will be wise to tailor our thinking about the role of the United Nations he served so well not to his world of 1961 but to our world of 1964 — which is to say:

- a world which is no longer bipolar but in which multiple centers of power and influence have come into being;
- a world which at long last is approaching the end of the historic struggle for military superiority — by acquiring absolute military power;
- a world in which the myth of monolithic blocs is giving way to a bewildering diversity among nations;
- a world in which realities are eroding the once rigid political dogmas;
- a world in which not only imperialism but paternalism is dying;
- a world in which old trading systems, monetary systems, market systems, and other elements of the conventional wisdom are being challenged and changed;
- a world which at once makes breath-taking new discoveries and is crippled by ancient feuds — which is both fabulously rich and desperately poor — which is making more progress than ever before and seeing much of it wiped out by an explosive population growth;
- and finally, a world in which fundamental issues of human rights — which have been hidden in closets down the long corridor of history — are out in the open and high on the agenda of human affairs.

For the first time in history the world is being changed radically within the span of an average lifetime: we enter one world and leave quite a different one. As E. B. White once said of New York, "the miracle is that it works at all."

Not even the sloganeers have caught the full essence of these times; we do not yet know what to call this particular passage of history. Since the end of the Second World War we have spoken of the "atomic age" and the "jet age" — of the era of "rising expectations" and the "epoch of the common man" — of

the "first age of space" and the "first age of mass politics." Each
of these labels identifies at least one of the swirling phenomena
of our times, but none of them will do as an over-all title.

II. CONTAINMENT

We should try to come to grips with the central theme of our
times — with that aspect of current affairs which gives them their
characteristic stamp and flavor — with that label which may not
tell all but puts its finger on the most important thing that is
going on.

You will recall that back in 1947 a certain "Mr. X" — who
turned out to be my friend George Kennan — wrote an article for
Foreign Affairs in which he introduced the famous label, the
"Policy of Containment." He invented the phrase but he did not
invent the doctrine; the United States already was busily,
heavily, expensively, and dangerously involved in containing the
ruthless, heavy-handed outer thrust of Stalin's Russia —
wherever he might strike or lean.

This was the main pattern of world events for a number of
years and "Containment" was a meaningful description of the
main purpose of United States policy. It was therefore a great
public service, for in the free world effective foreign policy is
difficult without the understanding and appreciation of the
public. How can one rally support for a policy if one can't even
describe it? In the absence of a suitable description, each individual action of government is dangerously exposed to attack
and suspicion, but if it is known to be part of a larger and well-
understood design, it becomes less difficult to act quickly and
coherently. However, this is not a lecture on the glorious virtues
and crippling vices of sovereign public opinion in a genuine
democracy.

When we look back with pride on the great decisions that
President Truman made, we see now that he had the inestimable
advantage of public understanding. He could react to Korea
quickly because he didn't have to stop to explain, to pull public
opinion up alongside. It was quite clear to all that this was but
another phase of Containment, just like the Berlin airlift and the
guerrilla war in Greece, and NATO.

Up until the postwar years, Americans had been brought up

From Containment to Cease-Fire

on the idea of fighting every conflict to a decisive finish — to total victory, to unconditional surrender. But when the nuclear age revealed the hazards of this course, it was neither easy nor popular to introduce the concept of limited action, primarily to preserve the status quo. This nuclear necessity went against the American grain; it was (and to some still is) both confusing and frustrating. It took patient explaining, and all of us can be grateful that Mr. X gave identification and illumination to a policy that was already being practiced. He showed us why the Greeks thought it so important to have "a word for it."

We can, as I say, be proud of our performance under the Containment policy. Above all we can be proud that the tendency once noted by Lord Acton did not operate in our case: the possession of great power — unprecedented and overwhelming power — did not corrupt the American government or the American people.

But as unquestioned leader of an alliance constantly threatened by external military pressure, we had to stand up and be counted for more; we had to stand firm; we had to confront force with force until the tanks faced each other gun barrel to gun barrel, along Friedrichstrasse in Berlin — until the Korean invaders had been thrown back across the 38th Parallel — until the Navy drew an armored noose around Soviet missile sites in Cuba — and until, at long last, Soviet leaders became convinced that free men will answer steel with steel.

During this whole period the positions and actions taken by the United States Government to contain aggression had broad public understanding and support. In a sense the policy of containment was too easy to understand. It tended to reinforce a simplistic view of a black-and-white world peopled by Good Guys and Bad Guys; it tended to induce a fixation on military borders to the exclusion of other things; and it tended to hide deep trends and radical changes which even then were restructuring the world.

And, of course, the policy of containment — being a reaction to Soviet Communist aggressiveness — necessarily had a negative and static ring to it. This had the unfortunate effect of partially obscuring the positive and progressive purposes of United States policies in support of the United Nations, in support of regional

37

unity in Europe and elsewhere and in support of economic and social growth throughout most of the world where poverty was a centuries-old way of life.

Nevertheless, the doctrine of containment was relevant to the power realities of the times—to the struggle to protect the independent world from Stalinism—and to the defense of peace —which is quite a lot!

Indeed, the doctrine may not yet have outlived its usefulness. If the present Soviet leaders have come to see that expansion by armed force is an irrational policy, it is by no means clear that the Chinese Communists—pretending to read out of the same book—have yet come to the same conclusion.

No doubt we shall have to stand firm again—and face danger again—and run risks again in the defense of freedom.

We cannot and will not resign from whatever degree of leadership is forced upon us by the level of threat used against us, our allies, and our friends.

But as anyone willing to see clearly already knows, the current course of world affairs calls for something more than a "policy of containment."

III. LIMITED PEACE

What, then *is* the dominant theme that marks the character of contemporary world affairs?

I would suggest that we have begun to move beyond the policy of containment; that the central trend of our times is the emergence of what, for lack of a better label, might be called a Policy of Cease-Fire, and Peaceful Change. I would suggest, further, that we may be approaching something close to a world consensus on such a policy.

No analogy is ever perfect, but if the Policy of Containment stands for "limited war," then the Policy of Cease-Fire perhaps stands for "limited peace." I believe this mutation is occurring simply because the H-bomb has made even "limited" war too dangerous.

Cease-Fire and Peaceful Change may strike some as a curious way to describe a period so jammed by violence, by disorder, by quarrels among the nations—an era so lacking in law and order. But I do not speak wistfully; I speak from the record.

From Containment to Cease-Fire

It is precisely the fact that so much violence and so many quarrels *have not led to war* that puts a special mark on our times.

Only a few decades ago, if a street mob organized by a government sacked and burned the embassy of another government—if rioters tore down another nation's flag and spit upon it—if hoodlums hanged or burned in effigy the head of another state—if ships or planes on lawful missions were attacked—you would expect a war to break out forthwith. Lesser excuses than these have started more than one war before.

And only a few decades ago, once hostilities broke out between the armed forces of two nations, it was assumed with good reason that since the war was started, the war would proceed until one nation or one side had "won" and the other had "lost"—however foolish or futile the whole thing might be.

It also was assumed that the only way fighting could be stopped was by surrender—unconditional or negotiated—confirmed by signatures on a document and ritualized by the presentation of swords by the vanquished to the victors. That was in the nature of the institution called war. This is how it was.

But this is *not* the way it has been for well over a decade now and I think we should begin to notice that fact. Scores and scores of what used to be called "incidents"—far too many of them—have occurred around the world without leading to hostilities or even ultimatums. The fact is that in the last decade, nearly every war, partial war, incipient war, and threat of war, has either been halted or averted by a cease-fire.

It is still a very foolish and dangerous thing to insult another nation or desecrate its property or take pot shots at its citizens or equipment. But there are other forms of penalty than mass slaughter and, happily, the world is beginning to avail itself of them. Firing has started and then stopped—organized hostilities have been turned on and then called off—without victory or defeat, without surrender or peace treaty, without signatures or swords.

This is what seems to be happening. If so, it is perhaps the most important and certainly the most hopeful news for many a moon. As Al Smith kept saying, let's look at the record.

Just after the last war, the Soviet Union sent two armored divisions through northern Iran toward the Turkish and Iraqi frontiers while Bulgaria massed troops on its southern frontier to

39

form the other prong of a huge pincers movement against Turkey. Then the Security Council of the United Nations met in London for the first time, and presently the Soviet troops went back into the Soviet Union. Not a shot had been fired.

Since that time there have been some twenty occasions on which the armed forces of two or more nations engaged in more or less organized, formal hostilities, which in another day would have been accompanied by declarations of war—wars to be fought until "victory" was attained by one side or the other. Eight of these could be classified as outright invasions, in which the armed forces of one nation marched or parachuted into the territory of another; only one of them—the mismatched affair between India and Goa—was settled in the traditional way in which wars have been settled in the past.

On at least another twenty occasions there has been minor fighting on disputed frontiers, or armed revolts which usually involved the national interests of an outside state. Any of them would have qualified as a *causus belli* in another day.

At this very moment [in 1964] the agenda of the Security Council of the United Nations lists fifty-seven international disputes. Some of them have been settled, some are quiescent, and others could flare again at any moment. The point here is that more than half a hundred international quarrels have been considered by somebody to be enough of a threat to the peace to take the case to the court of last resort.

This is not exactly peace—at least not the kind of peace that people have dreamed and hoped and prayed for. But the record suggests that if fighting breaks out somewhere tomorrow, the chances are good that the next step will not be the sound of trumpets but the call to cease-fire.

And the chances are good that the step after that will not be an exchange of swords but an exchange of words at a conference table. This is no guarantee that a way will be found to remove the root of the trouble: in the Middle East, Southeast Asia, and the Far East there are temporary armistice lines that have been temporary now for more than a decade. But in these affairs there are no victors and no vanquished—and in this sense we are all winners.

This record of violence-without-war suggests, then, that we

may have slipped almost imperceptibly into an era of peaceful settlement of disputes—or at least an era of cease-fires while disputes are pursued by other than military means.

Without making light of life-and-death matters, one can conclude that it has become distinctly unfashionable to march armies into somebody else's territory. I can think of no better evidence than the fact that the Organization of African Unity—an institution hardly out of its swaddling clothes—quickly arranged cease-fires when fighting broke out on the borders between Morocco and Algeria and again between Somalia and Ethiopia.

How has all this come about? I shall not attempt anything like a definite answer. I would only suggest in passing that *perhaps* Korea was the end of the road for classical armed aggression against one's next-door neighbor; that *perhaps* Suez was the end of the road for colonial-type military solutions; and that *perhaps* Cuba was the end of the road for nuclear confrontation.

Perhaps man is adjusting once again to his environment—this time the atomic environment. *Perhaps* the leaders of nations around the world—small as well as large nations—have absorbed the notion that little wars will lead to big wars and big wars to annihilation. *Perhaps* we are edging toward a consensus on the proposition that nobody can afford an uncontrolled skirmish any more—that the only safe antidote to escalation is cease-fire.

I emphasize *"perhaps"*—for we must work and pray for that historical judgment on these times.

Yet skirmishes will occur—and will have to be controlled. Countless borders are still in dispute. Nationalism and rivalry are rampant. Ethnic and tribal and religious animosities abound. Passions and hatreds—ignorance and ambition—bigotry and discrimination—are all still with us.

IV. Peacekeeping and Peaceful Change

The question is what can be done to make sure that this is in fact an era of peaceful settlement of disputes among nations.

For one thing, we can pursue this consensus on recourse to nonviolent solutions. Most of the world is in agreement right now—though there are a few who would make a small exception for his own dispute with his neighbor. Yet there is reason to hope that the aggressors are extending their doctrine of no-nuclear-war to a broader doctrine of no-conventional-war—on the grounds that you cannot be sure there will be no nuclear war unless you are sure there will be no conventional war either.

For another thing, we can get on with the urgent business of expanding and improving the peacekeeping machinery of the United Nations. Most of the cease-fires I have been speaking about have been arranged by the United Nations and the regional organizations. Most of the truces and negotiations and solutions that have come about have come about with the help of the United Nations. Even if the will had existed, the way would not have been found without the machinery of the United Nations.

Violence—which there will be—without war—which there must not be—is unthinkable without an effective and reliable system of peacekeeping.

How should we and how can we improve the peacekeeping machinery of the United Nations?

The Cyprus crisis has vividly exposed the frailties of the existing machinery: The Security Council, by an impressive unanimous vote, first saved the situation with a cease-fire resolution providing for a United Nations peacekeeping force, but shortly afterward war nearly broke out again before the United Nations could put the resolution into effect.

There were no troops immediately available, and the Secretary-General could not marshal the United Nations force with the speed so urgently required. Then there was no assurance of adequate funds to pay for the operation. While these handicaps were overcome, the Secretary-General has not yet found a mediator of the conflict. While I am confident that he will soon be designated, it took over two weeks (instead of two days or two hours) to get the peacekeeping operation going, and then only because armed intervention appeared imminent.

In short, when time is of the essence, there is a dangerous vacuum during the interval while military forces are being assembled on a hit-or-miss basis.

And we further risk an erosion in the political and moral authority of the United Nations if troops trained only for national forces are thrust without special training into situations unique to the purpose and methods of the United Nations. For a United Nations soldier in his blue beret is like no other soldier in the world—he has no mission but peace and no enemy but war.

Time and again, we of the United States have urged the creation of a United Nations International Police Force, trained specifically for the keeping of the peace.

Perhaps it is too early to contemplate a fixed United Nations international force which would be permanently maintained for use for any and all purposes—for the world's emergencies differ one from another, and there can hardly be one treatment for all of them. But surely it would make sense for member countries of the United Nations to indicate what forces, equipment, and logistic support they would be willing to train for peacekeeping service, and to supply on a moment's notice. And surely it would make sense for the United Nations itself to add to its military and planning staff so that peacekeeping operations can be set in motion with the utmost speed and effectiveness.

There are some encouraging signs of progress. Recently it was announced that Scandinavia would create a permanent force for use on United Nations peacekeeping Missions. This would include Denmark, Sweden, Norway and Finland, although it is not yet clear if Finland would join in an integrated command or form an independent unit. Other nations, such as Canada and the Netherlands, have also shown interest in creating a United Nations stand-by force. So things are moving.

There is also movement on the fiscal front. In 1963 it seemed hopeless that the United Nations General Assembly would be able to agree on a financing formula which would permit its vital Congo operations to continue. But it did, and in the process paved the way for further developments in this all-important area. . . .

It is true that every United Nations peacekeeping effort is and probably always will be different from any other, and that no simple financing formula can fit them all, but agreement on certain principles and improvements in mechanisms should be possible and useful for the future. The United States will join wholeheartedly in the search for such agreements. . . .

Not many members would agree with the Soviet Union's

contention that the General Assembly has no right to recommend a peacekeeping operation and that the Security Council should have the exclusive right to initiate such operations. Nor would many agree to abolish the General Assembly's exclusive right, under the Charter, to apportion and assess expenses.

But it should be possible to give new emphasis to the position of the Security Council by providing that all proposals for initiating a peacekeeping operation should first be presented to the Council, and that the General Assembly should not have the right to initiate such an operation unless the Council had shown that it was unable to act.

Also when it comes to the apportionment of the costs among the members by the General Assembly, we are exploring possible arrangements whereby the viewpoints of the major powers and contributors to the cost could be assured of more adequate consideration, and also the possibility of more flexible methods of distributing the cost.

I mention the fact that these possibilities are being discussed to make clear that the United States is using every effort to reach agreement as to future peacekeeping arrangements, in the hope that agreement as to the future will facilitate solution as to the past and provide a. more firm foundation for a peacekeeping structure that has already proved itself so valuable. . . .

We hope and believe that these efforts to preserve the peacekeeping function will have the support of all members, and certainly of all members who believe in the efficacy, indeed the indispensability, of the United Nations as a force for peace in the world.

Finally, if we are going to get the nuclear genie back in the bottle and keep it there, we shall have to improve our techniques for arriving at basic solutions to problems which remain even when a cease-fire has gone into effect.

I referred earlier to the point that the doctrine of containment was essentially a negative and static concept—as it had to be for its purpose. But a simple cease-fire is static, too; it is a return to the status quo. And that is not good enough for a world in which the only question is whether change will be violent or peaceful.

The world has known periods of relative peace and order

before. Always the order was assured by a system designed to preserve the status quo. And this is precisely why the system of order broke down—because the status quo is indefensible in the long run.

What the world needs is a *dynamic* system of order—a system capable of bringing about not just a precarious halt to hostilities, but a curative resolution of the roots of hostility. This is to say that a dynamic system of order must be one which helps parties to a dispute to break out of rigid stalemates—to adapt to new times—to manage and absorb needed change.

It is easier to write this prescription than to fill it. But if conflicts are to be resolved and not just frozen, it is manifest that only through the United Nations, the community of nations, can the workable system of peaceful change evolve. The United Nations is a shared enterprise; it speaks for no nation, but for the common interest of the world community. And most important, the United Nations has no interest in the status quo.

V. The Challenges to Come

To conclude: I believe there is evidence of new beginnings, of evolution from containment to cease-fire, and from cease-fire to peaceful change. We have witnessed the first concerted and successful effort to avoid the confrontation of naked force. The [1962] Cuban crisis has been followed by the [1963] nuclear test ban treaty and a pause in the arms race. We see growing up in the interstices of the old power systems a new readiness to replace national violence with international peacekeeping. The sheer arbitrament of force is no longer possible, and less lethal methods of policing, controlling and resolving disputes are emerging. Do we perceive, perhaps dimly, the world groping for, reaching out to the fuller vision of a society based upon human brotherhood, to an order in which men's burdens are lifted, to a peace which is secure in justice and ruled by law?

As I have said, I believe that now, as in the days of the Founding Fathers, even the faintest possibility of achieving such an order depends upon our steadfast faith. In their day, too, democracy in an age of monarchs and freedom in an age of empire seemed the most remote of pipe dreams. Today, too, the dream of a world which repeats at the international level the

45

solid achievements — of law and welfare — of our domestic society must seem audacious to the point of insanity, save for the grim fact that survival itself is inconceivable on any other terms.

And once again we in America are challenged to hold fast to our audacious dream. If we revert to crude nationalism and separatism, every present organ of international collaboration will collapse. If we turn in upon ourselves, allow our self-styled patriots to entice us into the supposed security of an impossible isolation, we shall be back in the jungle of rampant nationalisms and baleful ambitions and irreconcilable conflicts which — one cannot repeat it too often — have already twice in this century sent millions to their death, and next time would send everybody.

I believe, therefore, that at this time the only sane policy for America — in its own interests and in the wider interests of humanity — lies in the patient, unspectacular, and if need be lonely search for the interests which unite the nations, for the policies which draw them together, for institutions which transcend rival national interests, for the international instruments of law and security, for the strengthening of what we have already built inside and outside the United Nations, for the elaboration of the further needs and institutions of a changing world for a stable, working society.

If we in the United States do not carry these burdens, no one else will. If we withdraw, retreat, hesitate, the hope of today, I believe without rhetoric or exaggeration, will be lost tomorrow.

We have called this land the "last best hope" of men — but "last" now has overtones of disaster which we would do well to heed. With Churchill, I can say that "I do not believe that God has despaired of His children." But I would say also, in the words of the Scriptures: "Let us work while it is yet day."

WALTER MILLIS

•

INTERNATIONAL CONFLICT IN THE ABSENCE OF WAR

Those of us who have become interested in the possibility of an international order without organized war all begin, I think, with the realization that this does not—and cannot—mean an international order without conflict. Conflict, of course, is inherent in the nature of man. The hope held out by a demilitarized world is not that it will eliminate conflict from the international order but that it will structure or institutionalize conflict in some manner less totally disastrous than that at which we have now arrived.

This institutionalization of conflict into nondestructive and so far as possible nonviolent forms is, after all, the basic function of any system of "law and order." The "law" provides accepted general rules under which conflict will be carried on; the "order," imposed by government's police power, ensures that the rules will normally be observed. The law in any system may be far from just and the order may admit of much casual violence; but the basic purpose of the system, the organization or structuring of conflict among those subject to it, is fulfilled. For this structuring of conflict throughout the world we have relied in modern times upon the developing nation-state system of organization. I think we should recognize that in many ways it has been remarkably successful. As the nation-state has gradually unified its citizens, improved its legal structures, and established a firm monopoly over the domestic police power, it has brought ever larger areas of the globe under a "reign of law." It has, that is to say, structured domestic conflicts within the community into increasingly nonviolent forms; until today there is actually far less violence and bloodshed in our world, in

47

proportion to the size of its population and the difficulty of its problems, than ever before in history.

Unfortunately, individuals, groups, and communities have interests and suffer from ambitions which transcend the national frontiers. However successful a national political system may be, there remains the larger international world, with its threats and opportunities, from which neither the national community as a whole nor those who comprise it can be isolated. It is on this larger stage that the nation-state system has recorded its great failure. As the nation-state monopolized the police power to structure conflict at home, it monopolized the community's military power in the hope of structuring international conflict. All modern wars have been fought in the name of "law and order" — either in defense of an existing order or to establish a new one, commonly thought of as an order in which law of some kind would prevail and violent conflict would be eliminated. The armed nation-state has failed tragically as an instrument to achieve such a global order. But it has contributed more in this direction than is always realized.

By gradually drawing monopoly control over international, as well as national, force into its own hands — by suppressing the freebooter, the privateer, or the private army, like those of the great military trading companies — it has done much to structure even international conflict into nonviolent forms and to reduce the general savagery, sloppiness, and irrelevance of human activity in the international field. In its beginnings, the nation-state still drew a large part of its "military posture" abroad (as, indeed, of its domestic police power) from the ill-regulated activities of private men. There was a great outpouring of British national energies to meet the onset of the Great Armada in 1588; but the riposte delivered against Cadiz in 1589 was mounted as a joint-stock enterprise (in which the Queen took shares along with the London merchants) and delivered by Sir Francis Drake on a kind of cost-plus contract. This kind of thing was to prove ultimately incompatible with the basic idea of the nation-state. Foreign war was to become a problem only for the whole people; the state was more and more to organize it only in the interests of the whole, and thereby to suppress many of the particularist and parochial interest which had led to international turmoil. It absorbed the freebooters and the private armies into its military monopoly. It turned an increasingly cold shoulder upon the entrepreneurs and investors who claimed its support for their operations abroad. It is a long time now since any major military power has called out the soldiery to protect foreign investments, collect debts, or even to protect its trade or acquire markets. All such international problems are better handled now by nonmilitary means.

The nation-state system has produced a very considerable corpus of international law which, while technically unenforceable, does in fact channel a great deal of the normal friction and conflict in the international area into nonviolent modes of resolution. The nation-state system has provided a firm base for an international economic order — not only as manifested in such striking developments as the European Common Market, but for the whole nexus of international trade and monetary relations which today gives us a substantially global economic system. This system involves, like any national economic system, conflicts of interest, differences, and frictions of many kinds, but these are resolved substantially by nonviolent means. In this global economic system developed by the nation-state form of organization, war — as Norman Angell demonstrated half a century ago — simply does not "pay"; and it is, I think, a fact that no significant war since then can be successfully explained on economic grounds. Where economic factors have played a part in modern war situations it has not been for economic but for strategic reasons.

The nation-state system has thus laid very powerful foundations on which to build a generally nonviolent resolution of international conflict. The great tragedy is, of course, that the several nation-states, in gathering not only the internal police power but a monopoly of the community's external force firmly into their own hands, developed an international threat system in which every threat became a total one. In suppressing international violence for private, casual, or trivial ends — for anything less, that is to say, than a total and "vital" national interest — they structured international conflict into a form in which, when violence did come, it was total violence. War ceased to be an instrument of policy; one could only with the greatest difficulty

49

limit it to rational political ends, and every major war tended to become inevitably a total war for "unconditional surrender." The now fully militarized nation-state has created a situation in which any attempt to make good the threats on which it has balanced the world order must probably be a prelude to that order's total destruction.

There seem only two possible exits from this frightful dilemma. One is to abolish the nation-state. The other — simpler, less drastic, and more promising — is to demilitarize it: that is to say, to leave it with all its internal police powers, to continue to profit by the great contributions it has made through them to the nonviolent resolution of human conflict, not only within its own territories but, as I have suggested, in the international world as well; but at the same time to deprive it of its military power to destroy the order which it has done so much to make. The first alternative — entailing the absorption of the nation-state in a federal global state — seems to me quite impossible today and, indeed, to entail so colossal and cumbersome a reorganization of the world's power structures that it may never come about. It is the second which is here under examination.

In asking how international conflict will be resolved in a warless world, we must attempt to envisage the practical situation we are discussing. As I see it, the peoples of the globe will be organized into something over a hundred national units. These will differ extravagantly in size, stability, wealth, and form of government; each will, however, have at its command a national police force, capable by definition of maintaining domestic law and order, controlling its frontiers, enforcing its emigration and customs laws, and providing against border forays. Some of these national police forces will doubtless carry rather heavy weapons — up to tanks, light artillery, light airplanes — but the nations will have divested themselves entirely of the apparatus of military threat — from nuclear and BCR weaponry on down. They will have the armed force necessary to control their land frontiers and coastal waters; but they will be powerless to levy military threat against each other, and certainly powerless to hurl such threats far beyond contiguous territories or beyond the seas.

In addition to these hundred-odd national police forces of

all kinds and sizes, there will have to be what is usually called an "international police force." It should better be called a supranational force, for it must, I believe, be free of national veto within the limits of its mandate. Its primary task, as I see it, will be to ensure that the undertaking to demilitarize is everywhere being honored and, once completed, that remilitarization nowhere takes place. It is unnecessary here to go into the question of how it will be weaponed and organized to accomplish this; the main point is that it will be a police and not a supranational army. It is not the business of a police to make the law; its basic function is to ensure that what law is available is observed and applied with a minimum of violence. One way in which a domestic police does this is by depriving gunmen of their weapons. The main business of the supranational police will be to relieve the nation-states of their weapons of organized international war, and to see that they do not create new ones.

In speaking of "international conflict" in such an order what do we really mean? It will already have been brought to a very high degree of organization. Among the hundred-odd nation states there will be some four or five giant power systems — the United States, the Soviet Union, the Western European coalition, China — with developed systems of law and order, internally stable, with no serious territorial or economic claims upon each other, and each having brought the private or particularist interests of its own constituent individuals and groups to be content with the nonviolent settlement of such conflicts as they become involved in beyond the national frontiers. There will be many other nation-states, far less powerful, but no less stable and well-ordered within their borders, who have already structured such conflicts as arise in the external world into nonviolent patterns. Most of them are not even capable today of making international war except as minor partners in a coalition with one of the giants; and even now it is almost impossible to see a Sweden, a Turkey, an Argentina, a Philippines, making foreign war under anything less than the most dire military attack upon its national existence. There will remain a good many more much less well-ordered, much less stable, but also vastly less powerful, national units. These comprise the presently turbulent areas of the world, where conflict —

of individuals, of groups, of classes, of races, and of the nations themselves — is anything but structured into nonviolent forms. Here is where one might expect conflict to continue to be violent and often bloody even in a world demilitarized. Here, moreover, is where one might expect the demilitarized great states to contend most strongly with each other for "power," for "dominance," or simply for ideological reasons, by those methods of subversion, of fomenting and supporting civil and guerrilla war, which would still, undoubtedly, be open to them.

But over vast areas of our world as it is presently ordered, "indirect aggression" has in fact fallen on only barren ground. Even more, where it has seemed to yield more concrete results, it has done so largely because of the militarization of the world. It is the existence of the great military threats, themselves unusable directly, which has nourished the indirect aggressions, has weaponed and supported them and provided them with their propagandist battle cries.

In a general demilitarization the strategic factor is eliminated; and I believe that "indirect aggression" would be the first victim. A world deprived of its massive military threat power would not thereby be laid open to conquest by "indirect aggression." It would, rather, render indirect aggresssion pointless; it would shut off most of the steam by which this sort of violent conflict is now impelled.

In a world so ordered, what would be the remaining content of conflict across international boundaries, and to what extent would it be structured into nonviolent forms of expression? Kenneth Boulding has pointed to the numerous "strains" which would arise in a demilitarized world economy. He has discussed such things as differential population growths, differential growth in productivity, differential racial opportunity, differential capital formation and access to raw materials. That such factors must produce strains, and perhaps very heavy strains, upon our ever more subtly integrated global system is, I think, quite probable. But that they will, in a world once demilitarized, lead ineluctably back to a revival of military threat and organized war is by no means clear since war is no solution for them. The multimegaton bombs might do something about population growth, but hardly constitute a recommended solution even for this problem. For the others, it is already too obvious to everybody that organized war offers no solution at all. These factors will remain as a source of conflict and struggle in the world; they may remain as a source of conflict between nations as such, but I do not believe that they will drive the nations to a revival of a military threat system which, by their general act of disarmament, they will have agreed to be useless in the modern world.

By demilitarizing the nation-state we leave to it its powerful (or, in the presently more chaotic states, its potentially powerful) ability to structure internal conflict into nonviolent forms. The conflict which continues to transcend the national boundaries must, it seems to me, fall into two general categories. The first includes the conflict generated by individuals, groups, special corporate or party interests, who believe that their aims and ambitions can be satisfied only on the international stage. The nation-state has already successfully structured most of the international conflict arising in this way into nonviolent forms — as I have said, it no longer collects debts for its corporations or puts its soldiery behind its missionaries — and in a demilitarized world would continue to do so. Most conflict of this kind would be dealt with, as it is now, through the instrumentalities of international law and diplomatic negotiation.

Unfortunately, however, there is the special case here of the private interest or private man who grasps for power within the nation by fomenting foreign war, or, having seized the internal police power, employs it to put the whole nation at the service of his private ambition on the international stage. Hitler and Mussolini are the great modern examples; I believe that many more are arising and will arise in the less ordered parts of the world. The military nation-state organization has promoted rather than suppressed their violent and destructive potentialities. A world demilitarized would initially close to them these avenues to power and ambition; but I believe their kind would remain, and would constitute the greatest single threat to the survival of the demilitarized system. It would be from such interests or such people that the pressures would come for cheating on the disarmament agreement, for expanding the national police into a military threat abroad, for reviving organized war. All that one can say here is that the supranational police force should be capable of dealing with them. If it is not, the world without war probably could not survive. But it seems to me the chance is rather good.

The second category of international conflict which will remain will be that in which the total interests of the national community, as such, are involved. This is the kind of conflict usually envisaged when one thinks of the "strains" that the future is certain to impose on our global system. Conflicting interests of the nation-states as such have led to war in the past; the interests of the several national units are bound to conflict in the future; when they do, what other resolution will be possible in a world still based on the nation-state system, except through organized and armed combat? There is plenty of international law and order today to control the ordinary conflicts and frictions of international life; there is no law—and no foreseeable possibility of it—to control in the problems raised, for example, by the overpopulation of China, the undercapitalization of India and Africa, or the rise of an embittered African nationalism. In its absence must we assume that the only recourse for a world demilitarized will be to revive its armaments and return to war?

I think the assumption is over-hasty. At least in modern times, the irresolvable national conflicts ending in major wars have been overwhelmingly strategic in character. They have not reflected any basic strains in the development of the global system; they have, rather, reflected the fears and ambitions flowing from the growth of the military threat system itself. For example, the immediate cause of the Japanese attack in the Pacific in 1941 was the imposition, in July, of the embargo on her Indonesian oil supplies. But neither the embargo nor the war had much if anything to do with the appropriate distribution of oil among the Far Eastern peoples. Both resulted from strategic calculations that in a demilitarized world would be pointless. A largely demilitarized Japan is now getting all the Indonesian oil her people require, and would doubtless continue to do so in a demilitarized world. In such a world the strategic factors that are dominant in situations of this kind— and that actually account for more than nine-tenths of the serious international conflict that arises today—will be removed.

Conflict in the Absence of War

The conflicts of genuinely national interest which will remain as between the several national organizations are not readily discernible. In fact, one of the worst difficulties I have had with this whole subject is to imagine, not how the demilitarized states will fight each other, but what they will have left to fight about. The large issues of human organization and economy cannot be determined by adversary proceedings, whether in the form of the organized warfare which has always prevailed or in the form of pleadings in a court of law. The lesser issues are already resolved, in general, by nonviolent means. But if there remains, as there well may, a middle area of international conflict which can be resolved, under a nation-state system of global organization, only by adversary proceedings by the states themselves (not by their citizens) against each other, it seems to me that the mighty power organizations represented by the developed modern states will have many other means of contesting with each other besides that of organized war.

In addition to its terrible and already unusable military threats, the modern state has at its command the instruments of prestige, of propaganda, of economic power, of technical capacity, even of ideology, which it can deploy against an adversary with dramatic effect. Even when demilitarized, the great modern nation-state will retain large powers to control, or at least to influence, its international environment. It will have its police forces to protect its frontiers and conserve its internal system; it will have its consolidated economic and psychological power to defend its international interests. The great state will still have means to fight, even in the absence of war. But it is difficult to see what the fighting (conflict) will be about and how, therefore, one can expect that it will be structured.

There is the possibility of border warfare, like the recent conflicts between China and India. There does not seem to be here the makings of a great war; it is a situation which can be confined by the police posts involved and which would, in a demilitarized world, be met by the national-police forces. There is the remaining possibility of "indirect aggression." Already our present world has gone far, beneath the horrible umbrella of all-out nuclear war, to reduce this to manageable proportions. The whole present tendency toward the development of instruments of "limited" war, toward the preparation of police-type operations rather than all-out war for use in such special situations as that in Vietnam, toward the development of a United Nations police force to suppress violence in complicated issues like those of the Congo or Palestine, points the way to the manner in which a demilitarized world will deal with international conflict and international power relations on this level.

A world generally demilitarized will still be full of conflict. Most of it will be susceptible then, as now, to management by nonviolent institutions. What remains will not be organized so exclusively around the great, threatening, military state. Insofar as the nation-states as such come in conflict with each other, they will have neither the means nor the impulses to put the issues to total and suicidal decision. Yet there will continue to be violence, bloodshed, mob riot, civil and guerrilla war in the world. How far a supranational police should be empowered to go toward their suppression is, I think, a doubtful question. Once the system of nation-states is effectively demilitarized the great peril will not come, I think, from the conflicts of one national interest against another; it will come, rather, from the possible break-up of the national systems themselves under a too rigid imposition of the domestic and of the supranational police power. Too much order is as great a danger as too little. The nation-state has introduced into our global society a high degree of order; and in curbing its powers for destruction we dare not go too far toward undermining its capacity for regulation. At the same time, in upholding its regulatory capacities, we dare not go too far in the opposite direction of making it the mold for a completely static world society. The intellectual problem is a difficult one. Practically, it seems to me that we are already far on the way toward a generally nonviolent structuring of the conflict inherent in our natures; that a general demilitarization of the nation-state system would introduce no drastically new problems in this development, and that it would, on the contrary, represent little more than a continuation of tendencies which have long been at work in the global society.

FRED WARNER NEAL

•

POLITICAL PREREQUISITES
FOR DETENTE

Few would question that disarmament is an absolute prerequisite for a warless world. But disarmament is a process as well as a
goal, and whether or not there can be real progress toward it
depends above all on political factors. Pope John, in *Pacem in
Terris,* prescribes "mutual trust" as a prerequisite for disarmament. He did not mean the kind of mutual trust that might, for
instance, permit general and complete disarmament—or perhaps disarmament of any kind—without inspection. What he
had in mind was the kind of minimum trust necessary to set the
disarmament process in motion.[1]

Practically speaking, this means primary concern with the
great powers capable of waging such a war, first of all the United
States and the Soviet Union, and secondly other powers which
bid well to join these extant thermonuclear giants in being able
to cause unlimited and uncontrolled destruction.

It is impossible to see how the minimum trust necessary for
real progress toward disarmament can be achieved, therefore,
without a general understanding, a détente, between the United
States and the U.S.S.R. The term "détente" is used to mean more
than simply relaxation of tension, which is not enough, and less
than a formal entente, or alliance, which is too much. What the
term implies here is a joint though informal arrangement for
peaceful—although not necessarily friendly—relations between
the two major powers. There have been signs of interest in such

[1]Pope John XXIII, *Pacem in Terris,* Encyclical letter of April 11, 1963. Cf.
English translation, New York: Paulist Press, 1963, paragraph 113. See also
commentary on Encyclical by Father Peter Riga, *Peace on Earth,* New York:
Herder & Herder, 1964.

a détente on the part of both the Soviet Union and the United States, but thus far it has not been achieved. The signs—hot line, partial test ban treaty, prohibition of bombs in orbit, etc.—may be hopeful, but it would be dangerous to confuse them with the détente itself. For this, more fundamental matters must be involved.

If disarmament is a prerequisite for a warless world, and if a United States-Soviet détente is a prerequisite for disarmament, then what are the prerequisites for a détente? There are two principal ones. First, an awareness on each side that the other genuinely sees its own interest served by making progress toward disarmament, which of course implies a mutual conviction that neither will use armed force against the interest of the other; and, second, the settlement of existing major disputes between them by negotiation. Involved in both is an agreement on the status quo.

COEXISTENCE

The first—which is basic—may be more simply expressed as coexistence. Because the Communists employ this term so much, many in the West don't like it. In spite of this, it is a useful and expressive term, and should be good enough here.[2] But it is altogether inadequate—indeed it is little if anything—for both sides simply to state that they are for coexistence. For coexistence to be a meaningful concept, both sides must (a) understand and agree on what it means and (b) accept the fact that each does believe in it.

One of the main difficulties posed in securing a mutual acceptance of an agreed-upon coexistence concept is the moral aura of opposing ideologies of the Communist and non-Communist worlds. Some in both camps feel a moral repugnance in accepting the idea of coexisting with societies having "false" ideologies. Nothing better testifies how modern technology has welded morality and practicality than the manner in which Khrushchev, for the greater part of the Communist community, and Pope John, for those grounded in Western idealism, got around this point. Both of them, generally speaking, have declared that under coexistence neither side accepts

[2]Cf. Riga, *op. cit.,* pp. 136, 181-182.

the ideology of the other; that both sides continue vigorously to work for the triumph of their own special ideas; but that both also renounce the use of armed force as a means to that end. Indeed, in one sense, both the Kremlin and the Vatican agree that the reason for such coexistence is to ensure the survival necessary for the hoped-for future philosophical triumph. Khrushchev calls it "competitive coexistence."[3] Pope John does not use this term but expresses the same concept in his separation of fixed "philosophical teachings" from "historical movements [which] cannot . . . avoid being subject to changes, even of a profound nature."[4] However different the methods by which they arrived at the same conclusion, on this point the positions of Khrushchev and Pope John are identical: to agree on the idea of coexisting, that is, not trying to destroy each other by military means, does not require agreement on ideology. While this does not necessarily make it unanimous — we shall, for example, discuss the Chinese demurrers later — it does provide ground for disposing of the moral issue in coexistence as far as the immediate issues of practical international politics are concerned.

A more important difficulty about coexistence is concerned with the nature of early Soviet theoretical formulations which gave rise to it and Western understanding — and misunderstanding — about it.[5] As Lenin interpreted Marx, capitalism inevitably led to war.[6] Originally, this meant war between or among capitalist states. Then, when the capitalist powers intervened in the Russian Civil War after the Bolshevik revolution, there was also postulated the inevitable hostility of capitalist states and, along with it, conflict with them.[7] The naive and beleaguered Bolshe-

---

[3]Cf. Khrushchev's "Concluding Remarks" at the 21st Congress of the Communist Party of the Soviet Union, in Leo Gruliow (ed.), *Current Soviet Policies III*, New York: Columbia University Press, p. 202.

[4]Pope John XXIII, *op. cit.*, paragraph 159.

[5]For a general discussion, see my *U.S. Foreign Policy and the Soviet Union*, Santa Barbara, Calif.: Center for the Study of Democratic Institutions, 1961, especially pp. 8-11.

[6]Lenin initially and most forcefully advanced this thesis in 1916 in *Imperialism, the Highest State of Capitalism*.

[7]The distinction between the concepts of inevitability of war (1) among capitalist states and (2) between the Soviet Union and capitalist states is noted by F. S. Burin, "The Communist Doctrine of the Inevitability of War," *American Political Science Review*, June 1963, pp. 334-354. Burin, however, sees the two concepts as contradictory rather than, as it seems to the present writer, linked by the theory of inevitability of capitalist hostility.

59

viks, already at war with the capitalists and feeling that capitalism was about to collapse all over the world, tended to see the future triumph of communism as coming from military efforts.[8] The capitalist efforts to do in the new Soviet regime failed. At the same time it became apparent to Lenin that the anticipated collapse of capitalism was to be delayed. Until that time arrived, he decreed, the Communists would devote their main efforts to building up the Soviet Union which would, meanwhile, "coexist" with capitalist regimes.

The basic doctrine never held that war against capitalism was inevitable or that war should be launched to establish communism. Rather, it held that the capitalists would inevitably make war, and since the capitalist states were by nature — according to the theory — hostile to the U.S.S.R., it was not unlikely that the inevitable conflict would in one way or another be directed against Moscow. A part of Lenin's theory was based on the idea that revolution could not succeed unless "objective conditions" for it were present. In the postrevolutionary period of temporary capitalist stability, these conditions were absent, and therefore, according to Lenin, the Communists should bide their time instead of engaging in overt revolutionary activity.

Lenin's concept of coexistence, in any event, was altogether tactical. Coexistence would continue until the objective conditions for revolution should appear. Meanwhile war — some kind of war — was still posited as the ideal method for revolution. The capitalists might begin it, but the workers, once armed, would turn the imperialist conflict into a class conflict, just as happened in Russia. Moreover, wars for the defense and extension of socialism, along with "wars of national liberation" were considered "just wars."[9]

Presented with this doctrine, and with the Comintern pe-

[8]Lenin's famous statement on this score, made in 1919, while capitalist powers were invading, was: "... the existence of the Soviet Republic next to a number of imperialist states for a long time is unthinkable. In the end either the one or the other must triumph. Until that end comes, a series of most terrible conflicts between the Soviet Republic and the bourgeois states is inevitable ..." "Otchet Tsentral'nogo Komiteta 18 Marta" [Report of the Central Committee, March 18], *Sochineniya (Works)*, vol. XXIV, p. 122.

[9]Cf. "Theses of the Sixth World Congress of the Communist International," *International Press Correspondence,* No. 84, November 28, 1928, especially p. 150.

riodically issuing shrill if ineffectual revolutionary propaganda, it was not unnatural that Western observers who were not altogether ignorant of the new theory of coexistence either misunderstood it or refused to accept it as meaningful.

For the Russians, the theory of temporary coexistence also spelled confusion. The U.S.S.R. had to practice its foreign policy in a hostile capitalist world where it knew war would inevitably break out sooner or later. Thus, even if Moscow did not actively seek the destruction of its capitalist adversaries, it felt it had to deal with them on the basis of a truce rather than peace. Meaningful long-term agreements were therefore out of the question. Continued manifestations of capitalist hostility, as Moscow interpreted the trend of international affairs, seemed to justify this wary approach to the outside world, which as often as not took a querulous chip-on-shoulder attitude that in turn generated hostility not always there before.

World War II spelled only a respite in this state of affairs. Although in fact Moscow's rather negative attitude toward "world revolution" continued until at least 1952, the Cold War emphasized anew the clear hostility of the two camps. Indeed, this hostility was intensified because Western fears of the U.S.S.R., whose power and influence now extended to Eastern Europe, had increased. On top of this, Stalin, at the 19th Congress of the Soviet Communist Party, proclaimed a favorable shift in the revolutionary tide. Although the old dictator scouted the likelihood of a war with the capitalists—but reiterated his belief in the inevitability of a war generally—he did call for Soviet foreign policy to end its defensive, almost isolationist stance and take the offensive.[10] Ironically, the West was so convinced that Soviet foreign policy was already aggressive that this decreed shift went almost unnoticed outside the Communist world. It did have the effect, however, of adding confusion to the already unclear concept of coexistence. Although Stalin stressed the inevitability of war between capitalist countries—as

[10]Offensive in the sense that it would now actively engage in diplomatic and other efforts—collaborating with neutralist countries, non-Communist nationalist movements, etc.—to break down the American-led Western coalition and further the movement toward socialism and communism. For Stalin's pronouncements, see account of 19th Congress of CPSU, in Leo Gruliow (ed.), *Current Soviet Policies,* New York: Praeger, 1953.

opposed to war between socialist and capitalist states — there was no doubt that in the Soviet lexicon peace over any prolonged period was seen as impossible as long as capitalism existed.

Between the 19th Congress of the Soviet Communist Party and the 20th Congress in 1956, two significant things happened. First, there was the development of thermonuclear bombs. Second, increasing Soviet might, economic development at home and in Eastern Europe, plus — or so it seemed at the time — the addition of China to the Communist world meant that the U.S.S.R. for the first time was equal to the West in basic military strength. The combination of these factors led Khrushchev to undertake a far-reaching revision and — ultimately — clarification of the doctrine of coexistence.

The new theory as stated in 1956 was essentially this: war was no longer inevitable, even though capitalism existed in the world. Capitalist states were still hostile and warlike by nature, but whereas in the past the weaker Soviet Union could only react to capitalist initiatives, now it was sufficiently strong to be able to take the initiative itself and might in this way prevent war from breaking out. In addition, the thermonuclear nature of modern war was such that no society could escape destruction, and communism could not possibly be built on the ruins of what, if anything, was left. Therefore, avoidance of thermonuclear war not only was possible but, in order to ensure the final triumph of communism, was essential. Also, the nature of thermonuclear conflict meant that the capitalists themselves might now be less eager to wage war.[11]

In subsequent years, the Soviet concept of coexistence developed further. Khrushchev ruled out initiating the use of force "in any form." Avoidance of war was now the prime task.[12] Even local wars were proscribed because they might escalate into thermonuclear war.[13] "Wars of national liberation" were proba-

[11]For Khrushchev's statement of the new theory, see Leo Gruliow (ed.), *Current Soviet Policies II,* New York: Praeger, 1957, especially pp. 29-63.

[12]See "Program of the Communist Party of the Soviet Union," adopted at 22nd Congress, in Leo Gruliow (ed.), *Current Soviet Policies IV,* New York: Columbia University Press, p. 14. See also N. S. Khrushchev, *To Avert War, Our Prime Task,* New York: Crosscurrents Press, 1962, p. 93.

[13]*Statement of the Soviet Government, September 21, 1963,* New York: Crosscurrents Press, 1963, p. 38. But the Soviet attitude toward local wars — of which that

bly unavoidable and were "just," deserving Soviet sympathy and support. But as long as wars of national liberation remained internal affairs, i.e., not crossing boundaries and not involving intervention from others, the Soviet Union would not necessarily engage in them militarily.[14] Nor would Moscow interfere to stir them up.[15] Thus the old idea that war could be a vehicle for world revolution was repudiated. Revolutions might still occur, and in some cases be necessary to overthrow capitalism by force, but modern conditions created sweeping new possibilities for Communists coming to power without violent revolution. The U.S.S.R. has not condemned violent revolutions as such, but it has de-emphasized them significantly and has advised Communists to try to avoid them if possible.[16] Meanwhile, the development of socialism and communism would now come by demonstrating superiority through peaceful competition.[17]

On the other hand, the Soviet Union would extend military protection to "countries friendly to it." While the U.S.S.R. would not "export revolution," it saw its "international duty" as combating "interference of the imperialists in . . . any country that has risen in revolution."[18]

Thus elaborated, this concept of coexistence goes a long way toward meeting many requirements for acceptance by the West, although, of course, it does not satisfy those who feel that the Soviet Union should give up its goal of world communism and

over the Suez Canal in 1956 is identified as one — is not necessarily neutrality. Cf. Khrushchev on the Conference of Representatives of Communist and Workers' Parties, *Pravda,* January 25, 1961.

[14]*Statement, ibid.* See also Khrushchev, *To Avert War, Our Prime Task, op. cit.,* pp. 92-95.

[15]See 22nd Party Congress Program, *op. cit.,* and discussion in Leonard Schapiro (ed.), *The USSR and the Future: An Analysis of the New Program of the CPSU,* New York: Praeger, 1963, especially p. 273. The extent of anticipated Soviet involvement in national wars of liberation, however, would appear to be greater than in the case of local wars. Cf. Khrushchev in *Pravda,* January 25, 1961.

[16]*Current Soviet Policies IV, op. cit.,* p. 9. See also *Current Soviet Policies II, op. cit.,* p. 38.

[17]*Current Soviet Policies III, op. cit.,* p. 57, p. 202.

[18]*Fundamentals of Marxism-Leninism,* second revised edition, Moscow: Foreign Languages Publishing House, 1963, p. 471. See also Program adopted by the 22nd Congress, *Current Soviet Policies IV, op. cit.,* p. 14; and Khrushchev, "On Peaceful Coexistence," *Foreign Affairs,* October, 1959, p. 8.

cease support for Communist movements even by nonmilitary means. On this latter score, the Soviet position is emphatic: the U.S.S.R. still expects and will work for the ultimate triumph of communism. But this should not obscure the immediate significance of this new stance for Soviet policy. The significance is essentially this: the U.S.S.R. regards coexistence no longer only as a short-term tactic but as a long-term strategic policy. Freed of the dogma that war is inevitable, the Soviet Union could now think and act in terms of long-run, meaningful agreements with capitalist countries. Indeed, such agreements, especially those regarding disarmament, were not only possible but necessary to ensure the avoidance of war, which itself is necessary to ensure the triumph of communism. Further, such agreements, far from impeding this triumph—as the Chinese suggest—would accelerate it, because it would permit the Communist countries to devote less resources to armaments and more to internal development and thus enable them to compete with capitalism more advantageously.

That the Soviet Communists assert such a policy would foster their interests, rather than deterring the West from crediting it, should only help convince the West that it is a stance adopted wholeheartedly and sincerely. The fact is, however, that the West is still a long way from accepting the new Soviet concept at face value. One reason for this is that, despite the lengths the Russians have gone to make it specific, the Soviet position still has confusions and ambiguities about it which, if not faced up to, could conceivably contradict the basis of the whole position. On the other hand, these doubtless appear less significant in Moscow than in Washington, and it is not unlikely that the U.S.S.R. has difficulty comprehending that the West either does not understand or does not accept its new coexistence posture.

The main point of confusion involves the question of under what circumstances the Soviet Union might feel its military intervention justified. Khrushchev has made it clear that he will extend Soviet military assistance to a Socialist *government* threatened by the "imperialists." But what about *revolutions* in progress? What about "wars of national liberation?" These, in the Soviet definition, are essentially revolutionary wars, inside the boundaries of a nation. The U.S.S.R. admittedly and not unnaturally has "sympathies" for them. Khrushchev has almost said, but not quite, that the U.S.S.R. will not intervene militarily in such wars, at least provided the capitalists also stay out, and, in some cases, possibly, even if the capitalists don't stay out.[19] But what does nonintervention mean, and what do sympathies mean? They cannot reasonably be expected to mean no propaganda, but do they exclude arms shipments to revolutionaries? If the United States were to send armaments to a revolt-ridden *government,* would this mean the U.S.S.R. would feel entitled to send armaments to the *revolutionary forces?* Does nonintervention exclude "volunteers," à la China? Does it exclude "military advisers," à la South Vietnam? These are troublesome questions to the West, and they should be cleared up. An informal understanding between the United States and the Soviet Union on some "rules of the road" of coexistence—rules, at least, of what not to do—might go far toward gaining mutual acceptance of the concept.

What is at issue here, in one sense, is a definition of the status quo. In 1959, Walter Lippmann understood Khrushchev's definition of the status quo to mean the Soviet Union could work to bring about communism in underdeveloped areas, for example, while the West could do nothing about it.[20] As the Soviet coexistence concept stands now, this is not correct, for while it means both sides would refrain from military intervention, it also means both sides could work in nonmilitary ways for and against communism. The term "status quo," however, implies acceptance not only of existing boundaries but also of existing national power relationships.

The Soviet position, in this connection, is understandable enough applied to, say, an outbreak of revolution in Nigeria. Here is a country not a core interest—that is, not within the clear strategic interest zone—of either the United States or the U.S.S.R. The Soviet position here appears to be that it would not intervene militarily on the side of the revolutionaries if the

[19]Because imperialist intervention against revolutionary movements could not succeed in any event. Cf. Schapiro, *op. cit.,* p. 270. But, on the other hand, see Khrushchev in *Pravda,* January 25, 1961. The Soviet attitude here is, at best, most unclear.

[20]Walter Lippmann, *The Communist World and Ours,* Boston: Little, Brown, 1959, pp. 12-13.

United States did not intervene against them. Although one may question equating support of an existing *government* with support of an antigovernment *revolution,* still strong arguments could be raised against American intervention in such a case. But suppose the revolution broke out in Costa Rica. Here is an area of the highest strategic importance to the United States, a clear core interest. Does coexistence mean that the United States could not intervene to help the Costa Rica *government* without expecting that this would bring Soviet intervention on behalf of the *revolutionaries?* There is some indication that the Soviet Union would not necessarily feel called on to intervene in such a situation. But it is not clear.

Another related question is perhaps even more troublesome. Whether or not the Soviet Union would intervene on the side of *revolution* in an American-sphere country, Moscow's clearly declared policy is that if the revolution succeeds and if a Socialist *government* is then established, it will intervene to protect such a government from "imperialist" intervention, regardless of where the situation occurs. This means the possibility of Soviet military involvement in core interests of the United States, and this is exactly what happened in Cuba. If one assumes that a nation will respond with warlike measures to defend its core interests — as the United States did in Cuba — then this Soviet policy *could* result in risking the very thing that the whole coexistence policy is designed to circumvent.

It is, of course, true that Soviet doctrine of extending military protection to Socialist regimes is in one sense only a counterpart to a United States policy of extending military protection to non-Socialist regimes. There is no reason why United States military intervention to strengthen Iran or Turkey against Soviet aggression should be any less offensive to Moscow than Soviet military intervention to strengthen Cuba against American aggression was to Washington. But in terms of practical international politics, two additional factors must be considered: First, it may be more likely that new pro-Communist regimes will come to power in the area of American core interests than it is that new anti-Communist regimes will come to power in the area of Soviet core interests. Thus the likelihood of Soviet involvement in American core interests may be greater than the likelihood of United States involvement in Soviet core interests. Secondly, a policy of protecting new governments achieving power by revolution lends itself to connivance not present in one of protecting established governments against revolution. It is always possible, for example, for a revolutionary movement that has in fact not succeeded to claim as a tactic that it has become the government and then appeal for military intervention.[21] This is not to suggest that the Soviet Union necessarily has this in mind, but in the suspicious milieu created by the Cold War it is enough to cause concern on both sides.

Clarification of these ambiguities of coexistence does not lend itself to formal agreement, but informal official discussions, focused on just these problems, could accomplish much. Actually, the basic need doubtless is for the Soviet Union to persuade the United States that its policy is actually grounded in a form of coexistence Americans can accept. The Soviet position is certainly more acceptable now than it was, say, prior to 1956, and it is altogether possible that the Russians could make it still more acceptable by further clarification. As noted above, one present difficulty may be that Moscow is unaware of the extent of either Western doubts or the ambiguities involved in its own position.

Agreement on coexistence as a workable framework for United States-Soviet relations would mean, of course, that the United States would have to limit its role as a sort of international anti-Communist gendarme. Since this policy has not been startlingly successful, in any event, exploration of such a policy revision should commend itself. The extent of the revision would depend in part on the definition of nonintervention mutually agreed upon. Ideally, the United States would want to be free to intervene in areas of prime American security interest, e.g., Latin America — even against a Socialist government — without Soviet intervention, in the same way the U.S.S.R. was free to march into Hungary in 1956 without American intervention.[22] Such an arrangement would require some revisions of the

[21]Both have, indeed, utilized versions of this tactic—the Soviet Union in the 1940 Winter War against Finland, the United States in connection with Panama in 1903 and, to some extent, Guatemala in 1954.

[22]The 1956 Soviet intervention in Hungary is not an exact parallel but it illustrates the point. Khrushchev has denied any parallel between Hungary and the Suez in 1956. Cf. *Pravda,* January 25, 1961.

present Soviet position. At minimum, the United States would want to have it clear that it could come to the aid of beleaguered Latin American governments without having to worry about Soviet military intervention. It is possible the U.S.S.R. would agree to this, given clear reciprocity for its own core interests. Even a discussion which would simply raise the issues could, if it were sufficiently dispassionate, be of great mutual benefit.

THE GERMAN QUESTION

We have thus far concerned ourselves only with the prerequisite of coexistence. We must now take up the closely related second prerequisite for a United States-Soviet détente, the settlement by negotiation of existing major disputes between the two countries. In the mid-1960's there was really only one—Germany. However, this dispute blocks, almost absolutely, progress toward disarmament, not only by preventing achievement of détente but by barring the most promising next steps in the disarmament process, i.e., the freezing of nuclear weapons strength in Central Europe and then establishing a nuclear free zone there.

Here again the problem involves defining an acceptable status quo. The existing situation is challenged by both the United States and the Soviet Union. The United States challenges it by refusing, along with West Germany, to accept East Germany and the Oder-Neisse frontier with Poland. The Soviet Union challenges it by demanding changes in the situation in Berlin. More fundamentally, however, the German problem reflects a lack of Western faith in Soviet professions of coexistence. It follows, therefore, that agreement on the latter may be a prerequisite for agreement on the former.

Actually, the Western position is a more clear and serious challenge to the status quo than the Soviet position. The realities of the German situation—the status quo, as it were—include the existence of two German states, one in the Western alliance, the other in the Eastern, with a divided Berlin containing Western troops, deep in East Germany. The United States position is to challenge the status quo presented by two German states—i.e., we refuse to recognize East Germany or its boundaries—but demand that the Soviet Union accept the status quo presented by Berlin. The Soviet position, on the other hand, while it calls for changes in the Berlin set-up, does not insist on eliminating the status quo factors there which Washington seems to consider most important—the maintenance of West Berlin's free status and the continued presence of Western troops there. What the Russians do insist on—a "neutralized" status for West Berlin in which it would no longer be used as a base for Western or West German cold war operations—in principle is not necessarily objectionable to the United States. In fact President Eisenhower at one point more or less agreed to it. The details of the Soviet proposals may not be acceptable as presently formulated, but they are negotiable. On the other hand, the United States-West German position of demanding reunification of Germany on Western terms could not be agreed to by the Soviet Union in principle or in any conceivable form and thus is not negotiable.[23]

There has been a lot of diplomatic talking about the German question, but to date no real negotiations in the sense of discussions about realistically possible compromises. The reason for this is not so much the Soviet proposals on Berlin as the concomitant Soviet demands for recognition of East Germany and its borders. Although the Soviet Union has not insisted on de jure recognition, with diplomatic relations and exchange of ambassadors, but only de facto recognition, recognition in any form is exactly what the United States and its allies refuse to give. Even the fact that a United States-Soviet agreement might actually enhance the weak Western position in Berlin has not been sufficient to budge the West.[24]

The rationale of the Western position is to be found in its relations with West Germany and in West Germany's relations

[23]For a discussion of the German question, see my *War and Peace and Germany*, New York: W. W. Norton & Co., Inc., 1962, and "The Unsolved German Settlement," *Annals of the American Academy of Political and Social Science*, vol. CCCLI, January, 1964, pp. 148-156. The negotiability of the Soviet proposals on Berlin and non-negotiability of Western demands for reunification stem from the fact that the former do not necessarily and directly challenge Western core interests, while the latter do represent a clear challenge to Soviet core interests.

[24]Cf. Arthur Krock in the *Los Angeles Times*, July 4, 1961, part III, p. 5. United States Senator Claiborne Pell of Rhode Island is also of the opinion that an agreement on Berlin involving recognition of East Germany would enhance the United States position. See his *Report to the U.S. Senate on the Berlin Situation*, April, 1963, Washington, D.C.: United States Government Printing Office, 1963.

with NATO. West Germany is adamantly opposed to recognition of East Germany and up to now, encouraged by the United States, has insisted that German reunification could be achieved without recognition through a policy of strength in NATO. West Germany is the kingbolt of NATO, and NATO is the kingbolt of American policy in Europe. The fear in Washington is that if the United States recognizes East Germany, the reaction in Bonn would be such as to jeopardize seriously if not actually destroy NATO. And in official American thinking, NATO cannot be jeopardized because it is vital for Western European defenses against the Soviet Union. Thus we come back to the question of coexistence. To put the German question another way, no negotiation of this dispute has been possible primarily because the United States does not accept the Soviet renunciation of war at face value. Obviously, origins of the American idea that NATO is necessary for Western European defense are grounded in the idea that the Soviet Union might launch an attack. Whether such a danger in fact ever existed or not is beside the point here. The point is that the Americans thought it existed and that the impact of this idea still colors their general approach to foreign policy, particularly in Europe. If they could now be persuaded that this danger were groundless, obviously their fears of how West Germany might react to recognition of East Germany would be lessened, if not obviated, and they could proceed to negotiate the German dispute.

At one time, reunification might have been possible in either of two ways: the United States could have "given up" West Germany and permitted a reunified German state neutralized and in neither NATO or the Warsaw Pact; or the Soviet Union could have "given up" East Germany and permitted a reunified Germany inside NATO. Neither side was willing to accept the other's position because both feared aggression from each other. If both sides had accepted the idea of coexistence and believed that each other accepted it, one or the other of these solutions would have been possible. But today the situation is different. Even assuming agreement on coexistence, reunification is an impossibility in any foreseeable future. For regardless of what the West may think, the Ulbricht regime in East Germany is an established entity, and it is extremely doubtful if the Soviet

Union could compel it to commit suicide even if Moscow desired. In addition, given the Soviet quarrel with the Communist Chinese over leadership and direction of the Communist movement as a whole, the Soviet Union could not, even if it wanted to, act so as to diminish the bounds of the Communist world, which is what it would be doing if it sought to "give up" East Germany.

Reunification of Germany, assuming it were desirable, can, therefore, come, if at all, only through a slow process of agreement between the two German states. For this, obviously, both states must be accepted. Moreover, the process would be meaningful only in the context of détente between the United States and the Soviet Union. What we have now is the United States agreeing with West Germany in the name of reunification to a policy that prohibits even the possibility of reunification.

Meanwhile, the unstable and dangerous situation in Berlin continues, with the troops of both sides, armed with tactical atomic weapons, juxtaposed under conditions of constant tension. This in itself illustrates why a real détente depends on a German settlement. In addition, however, not only does the continuing German dispute thus block progress toward détente and disarmament but it could reverse whatever progress has been made thus far. Convinced that strong military defense of Western Europe is necessary, the United States is tempted to repair the sorely rent NATO unity by such gimmicks as the Multilateral Nuclear Force.[25] Whether it is workable or not, MLF would give the West Germans some say in disposal of thermonuclear weapons and could well lead to West German control of them. There is no reason to doubt the solemn Soviet warnings that if such a situation develops, it will have to revalue its entire position on disarmament. In such event, any type of German settlement would be virtually impossible. Under conditions that might develop from such a policy, chances for a United States-

---

[25]Cf. *New York Times,* May 15, 1964, p. 16. The MLF proposal is one for turning over to NATO surface vessels armed with thermonuclear bombs and ICBMs, manned by mixed national crews, under mixed command. The nuclear weapons could be fired when and if unanimity of decision was reached, thus giving the United States a veto as long as American representatives were involved. Alone among the other NATO members, West Germany is strongly supporting MLF.

Soviet détente, and with them disarmament and, consequently, a warless world, might well be reduced to the vanishing point.

CHINA

A United States-Soviet détente is the first prerequisite for disarmament, but it is not the only one. It is obvious that a disarmament agreement that did not include China would not be meaningful. Therefore, we must now turn briefly to the Chinese role in the international arena.

The Chinese position on coexistence is far more ambiguous than that of the Soviet Union and includes elements that would seem to preclude Western acceptance of it.[26] The Chinese have accepted, somewhat hesitantly, the idea that war may not be inevitable, but they believe it is likely. And they are opposed to a United States-Soviet détente not because they are necessarily warlike but because they fear it would mean accepting the status quo not only in Europe but in Asia as well. To accept the status quo and to agree to disarmament under existing conditions in Asia would consign them to an inferior position. It could mean, for example, accepting continuation of American support for Chiang Kai-shek on Formosa and American efforts at containment in Southeast Asia and elsewhere.

In Chinese eyes, it is primarily the Americans who refuse to accept the status quo in Asia since it is the Americans who refuse to accept the reality of the Communist regime in mainland China and deny to it the kind of geopolitical core interests accepted in the case of the U.S.S.R. and other countries. This is not to say that the Chinese might not under certain conditions join in a general disarmament agreement, but not under present conditions of what they feel is an inferior position.

How much a bar the Chinese stance is to achievement of conditions necessary for a warless world may depend in large part on the course of United States-Soviet relations. At least, if the United States and the U.S.S.R. should be able to work out their détente soon, the situation in Asia might be less of a barrier

[26]For a good summary of the Chinese position, see "The Proletarian Revolution and Khrushchev's Revisionism," *Peking Review,* April 3, 1964. See also my "U.S. China Policy and Disarmament," *Bulletin of Atomic Scientists,* November, 1963, pp. 5-8.

to disarmament than now appears to be the case. Ultimately, one may expect, the present American policy toward China will give way to one more based on reality. In the interim, as long as the United States does not actually invade a Communist state, e.g., North Vietnam, it is quite possible that Moscow may make noises but in fact more or less ignore United States military intervention elsewhere in Asia on the theory that it cannot succeed in the long run and in the short run may serve a purpose by worrying the Chinese. If also in the interim the framework of a United States-Soviet disarmament agreement could be worked out, there would exist something the Chinese could affiliate with later. Assuming a change in United States Asian policy, it is not at all impossible that the Chinese would decide to do so, which would, of course, involve a change in their own position.[27]

Achievement of a real United States-Soviet détente should help relax American fears about communism generally and, hopefully, produce an atmosphere more conducive to a reconsideration of United States China policy. While the Chinese reaction to a more conciliatory American posture is far from certain,[28] it can be safely said that without some change in United States policy the Chinese are extremely unlikely to join in any disarmament agreement. And, as we have said, without China no disarmament agreement would be meaningful.

SOME DANGERS

In all of this, time is of the essence. Meanwhile, one should note at least two dangers. The most obvious one, and the most serious, is that United States military intervention in Asia could blow up into a big war despite American hopes to the contrary. The second danger stems from pressure of the Chinese "hard" position on the Soviet Union. Thus far, the new Soviet coexistence policies have not resulted in the détente with the United States the Russians appear to be seeking, and meanwhile the Chinese position is not without its supporters in the Communist

[27]See A. Doak Barnett, "The Inclusion of Communist China in an Arms Control Program," in Donald G. Brennan (ed.), *Arms Control, Disarmament and National Security*, New York: George Braziller, 1961, pp. 282-305.
[28]*Ibid.* See also perceptive analysis by Oscar Gass in *Commentary*, November, 1962.

movement, including some in the U.S.S.R. At some point in the future, if the United States response is not such that a détente has been achieved, or looks more likely than it does now, it is not impossible that the pressures on the Soviet Union may produce policies closer to the "hard" Chinese position. This would herald a dim future for a warless world.

There is also another and more obvious reason for trying to achieve the prerequisites for disarmament with all possible speed. At present, for all practical purposes, thermonuclear weapons are limited to the United States and the Soviet Union. But this will not always be the case. Within ten years, in the absence of a disarmament agreement, it is more than likely that a number of countries will have their own thermonuclear weapons and the means of delivering them. In such an "nth country" situation, disarmament would be infinitely more difficult to arrange than at present. By the same token, however, should the United States and the U.S.S.R. reach a general disarmament agreement before the "nth country" situation is too far advanced, the chances are good that all countries — China, France and others — whether they are striving to have their own H-bombs or actually have them — would come in to it. The fact that some of these countries, France and China, for example, refuse to sign the test ban treaty does not mean that they would not sign a treaty for actual disarmament. On the other hand, of course, it is not certain that they would. But what is certain is that no countries can join a disarmament agreement unless one exists in the first place for them to join.

CONCLUSIONS

This brief discussion has not pretended to touch on all the political prerequisites for a warless world. Possibly it has not included even the major ones; certainly this is true insofar as institutional changes in the nation-state system are concerned. One of the functions of war has been to act as an agent of change. Since change will always be with us, in a warless world some mechanisms for peaceful change will certainly have to be found. But such institutional alterations, to be meaningful, must evolve over a long time, and we do not have a long time. The need for a warless world is now, and what is imperative, first of all, is to deal with the political realities at hand to try to make sure that the world as it now exists does not blow itself to bits while the slow process of social adaptation to the new era of thermonuclear power proceeds. There is no certainty of success in this endeavor. But for even the hope of success, we must be concerned with minimum, first-step prerequisites that are at the same time sufficiently fundamental to make a difference. These lie in the realm of international politics and diplomacy of the nation-state system with all its grave imperfections and limitations.

From the foregoing discussion of some of these factors, one may draw the following conclusions:

1. Disarmament is necessary to a warless world, and a United States-Soviet détente is a prerequisite to disarmament.

2. Agreement on coexistence and settlement of the German dispute by negotiation are prerequisites for a United States-Soviet détente.

3. To achieve these prerequisites, the Russians must clarify their concept of coexistence; both Soviet and American policies must be modified, but United States policies must be modified somewhat more than Soviet policies, at least in regard to the German question.

4. Chinese adherence to a disarmament agreement is necessary to make it meaningful.

5. For the Chinese to come into a disarmament agreement, modification of American Far Eastern policies is necessary.

6. The whole process—détente, disarmament, and warless world—may be jeopardized if tangible progress is not made soon.

EDITORIAL DEPARTMENTS OF
Jen-min jih-pao AND *Hung-ch'i*

•

THE FANTASY OF A WARLESS WORLD

COMMENT ON THE OPEN LETTER OF THE CENTRAL COMMITTEE OF THE C.P.S.U. (5)

The whole world is discussing the question of war and peace.

The criminal system of imperialism has brought upon the people of the world numerous wars, including two disastrous world wars. Wars launched by imperialism have caused the people heavy suffering, but have also educated them.

Since World War II, people everywhere have been vigorously demanding world peace. More and more people have come to understand that to defend world peace it is imperative to wage struggles against the imperialist policies of aggression and war.

Marxist-Leninists throughout the world are duty-bound to treasure the peace sentiments of the people and to stand in the forefront of the struggle for world peace. They are duty-bound to struggle against the imperialists' policies of aggression and war, to expose their deceptions and defeat their plans for war. They are duty-bound to educate the people, raise their political consciousness and guide the struggle for world peace in the proper direction.

In contrast to the Marxist-Leninists, the modern revisionists help the imperialists to deceive the people, divert the people's attention, weaken and undermine their struggle against imperialism and cover up the imperialists' plans for a new world war, thus meeting the needs of imperialist policy.

Fantasy of a Warless World

The Marxist-Leninist line on the question of war and peace is diametrically opposed to the revisionist line.

The Marxist-Leninist line is the correct line conducive to the winning of world peace. It is the line consistently upheld by all Marxist-Leninist parties, including the Communist Party of China, and by all Marxist-Leninists.

The revisionist line is a wrong line which serves to increase the danger of a new war. It is the line gradually developed by the leaders of the C.P.S.U. since its 20th Congress.

On the question of war and peace many lies slandering the Chinese Communists have been fabricated in the open letter of the Central Committee of the C.P.S.U. and in numerous statements by the leaders of the C.P.S.U., but these cannot conceal the essence of the differences.

In what follows we shall analyse the main differences between the Marxist-Leninist and the modern revisionist lines on the question of war and peace.

THE LESSONS OF HISTORY

Ever since capitalism evolved into imperialism, the question of war and peace has been a vital one in the struggle between Marxism-Leninism and revisionism.

Imperialism is the source of wars in modern times. The imperialists alternately use a deceptive policy of peace and a policy of war. They often cover their crimes of aggression and their preparations for a new war with lies about peace.

Lenin and Stalin tirelessly called upon the people of all countries to combat the peace frauds of the imperialists.

Lenin said that the imperialist governments "pay lip-service to peace and justice, but in fact wage annexationist and predatory wars." (Lenin, *Selected Works*, F.L.P.H., Moscow: 1952, vol. II, part 1, p. 332.)

Stalin said that the imperialists "have only one aim in resorting to pacifism: to dupe the masses with high-sounding phrases about peace in order to prepare for a new war." (Stalin, *Works*, F.L.P.H., Moscow: 1953, vol. VI, p. 297.) He also said:

> Many think that imperialist pacifism is an instrument of peace. That is absolutely wrong. Imperialist pacifism is an instrument for the preparation of war

77

and for disguising this preparation by hypocritical talk of peace. Without this pacifism and its instrument, the League of Nations, preparation for war in the conditions of today would be impossible. (*ibid.,* vol. XI, p. 209.)

In contrast to Lenin and Stalin, the revisionists of the Second International, who were renegades from the working class, helped the imperialists to deceive the people and became their accomplices in unleashing the two world wars.

Before World War I, the revisionists represented by Bernstein and Kautsky endeavoured by hypocritical talk about peace to paralyse the revolutionary fighting will of the people and cover up the imperialist plans for a world war.

As World War I was breaking out, the old revisionists speedily shed their peace masks, sided with their respective imperialist governments, supported the imperialist war for the redivision of the world, voted for military appropriations in parliament, and incited the working class of their own countries to plunge into the war and slaughter their class brothers in other countries under the hypocritical slogan of "defending the motherland."

When the imperialists needed an armistice in their own interests, the revisionists typified by Kautsky tried to poison people's minds and to oppose revolution by such glib talk as "nothing would make me happier than a conciliatory peace based on the principle, 'Live and let live.' "[1]

After World War I, the renegade Kautsky and his successors became still more brazen trumpeters of the imperialists' peace fraud.

The revisionists of the Second International spread a pack of lies on the question of war and peace.

1. They prettified imperialism and turned the minds of the people away from their struggles. Kautsky said, " . . . the danger to world peace from imperialism is only slight. The greater danger appears to come from the national strivings in the East and from the various dictatorships."[2] Thus people were asked to believe that the source of war was not imperialism but the

[1] Kautsky, *National Problems,* Russian ed.
[2] Kautsky, *The Question of Defence and Social-Democracy,* in German.

oppressed nations of the East and the Soviet state, the great bulwark of peace.

2. They helped the imperialists cover up the danger of a new war and blunted the fighting will of the people. Kautsky said in 1928, "If today you keep on talking loudly about the dangers of imperialist war, you are relying on a traditional formula and not on present-day considerations."[3] Old revisionists of this brand described those believing in the inevitability of imperialist wars as "committed to a fatalistic conception of history."[4]

3. They intimidated the people with the notion that war would destroy mankind. Kautsky said, ". . . the next war will not only bring want and misery, but will basically put an end to civilization and, at least in Europe, will leave behind nothing but smoking ruins and putrefying corpses."[5] These old revisionists said, "The last war brought the entire world to the brink of the precipice; the next one would destroy it completely. The mere preparation for a new war would ruin the world."[6]

4. They made no distinction between just and unjust wars and forbade revolution. Kautsky said in 1914:

> . . . in present-day conditions, there is no such thing as a war which is not a misfortune for nations in general and for the proletariat in particular. What we discussed was the means by which we could prevent a threatening war, and not which wars are useful and which harmful.[7]

He also said:

> The yearning for perpetual peace increasingly inspires the majority of cultured nations. It temporarily pushes the essentially great problem of our times into the background. . . .[8]

5. They propagated the theory that weapons decide ev-

[3]*ibid.*

[4]Haase's speech on the question of imperialism at the Congress of the German Social-Democratic Party in Chemnitz, 1912, published in the *Handbook of the Congress of the Social-Democratic Party in 1910-1913,* vol. II, in German.

[5]Kautsky, "Preface to *War and Democracy*," in German.

[6]Resolution on the League of Nations, adopted by the Berne Conference of the Socialist International in 1919, Russian ed.

[7]Kautsky, *Social-Democracy in War,* in German.

[8]Kautsky, "Preface to *War and Democracy*," in German.

erything and they opposed revolutionary armed struggle. Kautsky said:

> As has been often stated, one of the reasons why the coming revolutionary struggles will more rarely be fought out by military means lies in the colossal superiority in armaments of the armies of modern states over the arms which are at the disposal of "civilians" and which usually render any resistance on the part of the latter hopeless from the very outset.[9]

6. They spread the absurd theory that world peace can be safeguarded and equality of nations achieved through disarmament. Bernstein said:

> Peace on earth and good will to all men! We should not pause or rest and must attend to the unhindered advance of society towards prosperity in the interests of all, towards equality of rights among nations through international agreement and disarmament.[10]

7. They spread the fallacy that the money saved from disarmament can be used to assist backward countries. Kautsky said:

> . . . the lighter the burden of military expenditures in Western Europe, the greater the means available for building railways in China, Persia, Turkey, South America, etc., and these public works are a far more effective means of promoting industrial development than the building of dreadnoughts.[11]

8. They submitted schemes for the "peace strategy" of the imperialists. Kautsky said:

> The nations of civilized Europe (and likewise the Americans) can maintain peace in the Near and Far East more effectively through their economic and intellectual resources than through ironclads and planes.[12]

9. They extolled the League of Nations which was controlled by the imperialists. Kautsky said:

[9]Kautsky, "A Catechism of Social-Democracy," in German.
[10]Bernstein's speech on the question of disarmament at the Congress of the German Social-Democratic Party in Chemnitz, 1912, published in the *Handbook of the Congress of the Social-Democratic Party in 1910-1913,* vol. II, in German.
[11]Kautsky, "Once More on Disarmament," in German.
[12]Kautsky, *The Question of Defence and Social-Democracy,* in German.

The mere existence of the League of Nations is itself already a great achievement for the cause of peace. It represents a lever for the preservation of peace such as no other institution can offer.[13]

10. They spread the illusion that reliance could be placed on United States imperialism to defend world peace. Kautsky said:

Today the United States is the strongest power in the world and will make the League of Nations irresistible as soon as it works inside it or with it to prevent war.[14]

Lenin ruthlessly exposed the ugly features of Kautsky and his ilk. He pointed out that the pacifist phrases of the revisionists of the Second International were only "a *solace* to the people, a means which makes it easier for the governments to bring about the docility of the people in further imperialist slaughter!" (Lenin, *Collected Works,* 4th Russian ed., Moscow: vol. XXIII, p. 224.)

Stalin pointed out:

And the most important thing in all this is that Social-Democracy is the main channel of imperialist pacifism within the working class—consequently, it is capitalism's main support among the working class in preparing for new wars and intervention. (Stalin; *op. cit.,* vol. XI, p. 210.)

Even a cursory comparison of Comrade Khrushchov's statements on the question of war and peace with those of Bernstein, Kautsky and others shows that there is nothing new in his views, which are a mere reproduction of the revisionism of the Second International.

On the question of war and peace, which has a vital bearing on the destiny of mankind, Khrushchov is following in the footsteps of Bernstein and Kautsky. As history shows, this is a road extremely dangerous to world peace.

In order effectively to defend world peace and prevent a

[13]*ibid.*
[14]Kautsky, *Socialists and War,* in German.

81

new world war, Marxist-Leninists and peace-loving people all over the world must reject and oppose Khrushchov's erroneous line.

THE GREATEST FRAUD

There is no bigger lie than the designation of the arch enemy of world peace as a peace-loving angel.

Since World War II, United States imperialism, stepping into the shoes of the German, Italian and Japanese fascists, has been endeavouring to set up a vast world empire such as has never been know before. The "global strategy" of United States imperialism has been to grab and dominate the intermediate zone lying between the United States and the Socialist camp, put down the revolutions of the oppressed peoples and nations, proceed to destroy the socialist countries, and thus to dominate the whole world.

In the 18 years since the end of the World War II, in order to realize its ambition of world domination, United States imperialism has been carrying on aggressive wars or counter-revolutionary armed interventions in various parts of the world and has been actively preparing for a new world war.

It is obvious that imperialism remains the source of modern wars and the United States imperialism is the main force of aggression and war in the contemporary world. This has been clearly affirmed in both the 1957 Declaration and the 1960 Statement.

Yet the leaders of the C.P.S.U. hold that the chief representatives of United States imperialism love peace. They say that a "reasonable" group has emerged capable of soberly assessing the situation. And Eisenhower and Kennedy are representatives of this "reasonable" group.

Khrushchov praised Eisenhower as one who "enjoys the absolute confidence of his people," who "has a sincere desire for peace" and who "also worries about ensuring peace just as we do."

Now Khrushchov praises Kennedy as even better qualified to shoulder the responsibility of preserving world peace than was Eisenhower. He showed "solicitude for the preservation of peace," and it is reasonable to expect him to "create reliable conditions for a peaceful life and creative labour on earth."

Khrushchov works as hard as the revisionists of the Second International at telling lies about imperialism and prettifying it.

The open letter of the Central Committee of the C.P.S.U. asks those who do not believe in these lies: "Do they really think that all bourgeois governments lack all reason in everything they do?"

Obviously, the leaders of the C.P.S.U. ignore the ABC of Marxism-Leninism. In a class society there is no reason that can transcend class. The proletariat has proletarian reason and the bourgeoisie bourgeois reason. Reason connotes that one must be good at formulating policies in the fundamental interests of one's own class and at taking actions according to one's basic class stand. The reason of Kennedy and his like lies in acting according to the fundamental interests of United States monopoly capital, and it is imperialist reason.

At a time when the international balance of class forces is becoming increasingly unfavourable to imperialism and the United States imperialist policies of aggression and war are meeting with constant setbacks, the United States imperialists have to disguise themselves more frequently under the cloak of peace.

It is true that Kennedy is rather clever at spinning words about peace and employing peace tactics. But as with his war policy, Kennedy's deceptive peace policy serves the "global strategy" of United States imperialism.

Kennedy's "strategy of peace" aims at unifying the whole world into the "world community of free nations" rooted in United States imperialist "law and justice."

The main points of Kennedy's "strategy of peace" are:

To promote United States neo-colonialism in Asia, Africa and Latin America by peaceful means;

To penetrate and dominate other imperialist and capitalist countries by peaceful means;

To encourage by peaceful means the Socialist countries to take the Yugoslav road of "peaceful evolution";

To weaken and undermine by peaceful means the struggle of the people of the world against imperialism.

In his recent speech at the United Nations General Assembly, Kennedy arrogantly announced the following conditions for peace between the United States and the Soviet Union:

1. The German Democratic Republic must be incorporated into West Germany.

2. Socialist Cuba must not be allowed to exist.

3. The Socialist countries in Eastern Europe must be given "free choice," by which he means that capitalism must be restored in these countries.

4. The Socialist countries must not support the revolutionary struggles of the oppressed peoples and nations.

To attain their aims by "peaceful means" wherever possible has been a customary tactic of imperialists and colonialists.

Reactionary classes always rely on two tactics to maintain their rule and to carry out foreign aggrandizement. One is the tactic of priest-like deception, the other that of butcher-like suppression. Imperialism always employs its deceptive policy of peace and its policy of war to reinforce each other, and they are complementary. The reason of Kennedy, who is the representative of United States monopoly capital, can express itself only in a more cunning use of these two tactics.

Violence is always the main tactic of reactionary ruling classes. Priest-like deception plays only a supplementary role. Imperialists always rely on positions of strength to carve out their spheres of influence. Kennedy has made this point very clear. He said, "In the end, the only way to maintain the peace is to be prepared in the final extreme to fight for our country— and to mean it." Since Kennedy took office, he has followed the "strategy of flexible response," which requires the speedy building of "versatile military forces" and the strengthening of "all-round power" so that the United States will be able to fight any kind of war it pleases, whether a general war or a limited war, whether a nuclear war or a conventional war, and whether a large war or a small war. This mad plan of Kennedy's has pushed United States arms expansion and war preparations to an unprecedented peak. Let us look at the following facts published by official United States sources:

1. The military expenditures of the United States Government have increased from 46,700 million dollars in the fiscal

year 1960 to an estimated 60,000 million dollars in the fiscal year 1964, the highest total ever in peace time and greater than during the Korean war.

2. Kennedy recently declared that in the past two years and more there has been a 100 per cent increase in the number of nuclear weapons of the United States strategic alert forces and a 45 per cent increase in the number of combat-ready army divisions, the procurement of airlift aircraft has been increased by 175 per cent and there has been an increase by nearly five times in the "special guerrilla and counter-insurgency forces."

3. The United States Joint Strategic Target Planning Staff has mapped out plans for nuclear war against the Soviet Union and other Socialist countries. Robert S. McNamara, the United States Secretary of Defence, declared at the beginning of this year:

> ... we have provided, throughout the period under consideration, a capability to destroy virtually all of the "soft" [above-ground] and "semi-hard" [semi-protected] military targets in the Soviet Union and a large number of their fully hardened missile sites, with an additional capability in the form of a protected force to be employed or held in reserve for use against urban and industrial areas.

The United States has strengthened its network of nuclear missile bases directed against the Socialist camp and has greatly strengthened the disposition of its missile-equipped nuclear submarines abroad.

At the same time, the troops of the NATO bloc under United States command have pushed eastward this year and approached the borders of the German Democratic Republic and Czechoslovakia.

4. The Kennedy Administration has reinforced its military dispositions in Asia, Latin America and Africa and made great efforts to expand the "special forces" of its land, sea and air services in order to cope with the people's revolutionary movement in those areas. The United States has turned southern Viet Nam into a proving ground for "special warfare" and increased its troops there to more than 16,000.

5. It has strengthened its war commands. It has set up a

"United States Strike Command" which controls a combined land and air force maintaining high combat readiness in peace time, so that it can be readily sent to any place in the world to provoke wars. It has also set up national military command centres both above and below ground, and organized an Emergency Airborne Command Post operating from aircraft and an Emergency Sea Command Post operating from warships.

These facts demonstrate that the United States imperialists are the wildest militarists of modern times, the wildest plotters of a new world war, and the most ferocious enemy of world peace.

It is thus clear that the United States imperialists have not become beautiful angels in spite of Khrushchov's bible-reading and psalm-singing; they have not turned into compassionate Buddhas in spite of Khrushchov's prayers and incense-burning. However hard Khrushchov tries to serve the United States imperialists, they show not the slightest appreciation. They continue to expose their own peace camouflage by fresh and numerous activities of aggression and war, and thus they continue to slap Khrushchov in the face and reveal the bankruptcy of his ridiculous theories prettifying imperialism. The lot of the willing apologists of United States imperialism is indeed a sorry one.

The Question of the Possibility of Preventing a New World War

It is a fact that the imperialists headed by the United States are actively preparing a new world war and that the danger of such a war does exist. We should make this fact clear to the people.

But can a new world war be prevented?

The views of the Chinese Communists on this question have always been quite explicit.

After the conclusion of World War II, Comrade Mao Tse-tung scientifically analysed the postwar international situation and advanced the view that a new world war can be prevented.

Back in 1946, in his well-known talk with the American correspondent Anna Louise Strong, he said:

> But the fact that the U.S. reactionaries are now trumpeting so loudly about a U.S.-Soviet war and creating a foul atmosphere, so soon after the end of

Fantasy of a Warless World

World War II, compels us to take a look at their real aims. It turns out that under the cover of anti-Soviet slogans they are frantically attacking the workers and democratic circles in the United States and turning all the countries which are the targets of U.S. external expansion into U.S. dependencies. I think the American people and the peoples of all countries menaced by U.S. aggression should unite and struggle against the attacks of the U.S. reactionaries and their running dogs in these countries. Only by victory in this struggle can a third world war be avoided: otherwise it is unavoidable. (Mao Tse-tung, *Selected Works,* Peking: Foreign Languages Press, 1961, vol. IV, p. 100.)

Comrade Mao Tse-tung's remarks were directed against a pessimistic appraisal of the international situation at the time. The imperialists headed by the United States, together with the reactionaries in various countries, were daily intensifying their anti-Soviet, anti-Communist and anti-popular activities and trumpeting that "war between the United States and the Soviet Union is inevitable" and that "the outbreak of a third world war is inevitable." The Chiang Kai-shek reactionaries gave this great publicity in order to intimidate the Chinese people. Frightened by such blackmail, some comrades became faint-hearted in the face of the armed attacks launched by the Chiang Kai-shek reactionaries with U.S. imperialist support and dared not firmly oppose the counter-revolutionary war with a revolutionary war. Comrade Mao Tse-tung held different views. He pointed out that a new world war could be prevented provided resolute and effective struggles were waged against world reaction.

His scientific proposition was confirmed by the great victory of the Chinese revolution.

The victory of the Chinese revolution brought about a tremendous change in the international balance of class forces. Comrade Mao Tse-tung pointed out in June 1950:

The menace of war by the imperialist camp still exists, the possibility of a third world war still exists. But the forces thwarting the danger of war and preventing a third world war are rapidly developing, and the political consciousness of the broad masses of the people of the world is rising. A new world war can be

87

prevented provided the Communist Parties of the world keep on uniting and strengthening all the forces of peace and democracy that can be united. (*Jen-min jih-pao,* June 13, 1950.)

In November 1957, at the meeting of fraternal Parties, Comrade Mao Tse-tung made a detailed analysis of the changes in international relations since the end of World War II and showed that the international situation had reached a new turning-point. He vividly depicted the situation with a metaphor from a classical Chinese novel—"The East wind prevails over the West wind." He said, "It is characteristic of the situation today, I believe, that the East wind is prevailing over the West wind. That is to say, the forces of socialism are overwhelmingly superior to the forces of imperialism." (*On Imperialism and All Reactionaries Are Paper Tigers.*)

He arrived at this conclusion by an analysis of international class relations. He explicitly placed on the side of "the East wind" the Socialist camp, the international working class, the Communist Parties, the oppressed peoples and nations and the peace-loving people and countries, while confining "the West wind" to the war forces of imperialism and reaction. The political meaning of this metaphor is very lucid and definite. The fact that the leaders of the C.P.S.U. and their followers are twisting this metaphor into a geographical or ethnical or meteorological concept only shows that they want to squeeze themselves into the ranks of the "West" in order to please the imperialists and to stir up chauvinism in Europe and North America.

Comrade Mao Tse-tung's main aim in stating that "the East wind prevails over the West wind" was to point to the growing possibility that a new world war could be prevented and that the Socialist countries would be able to carry on their construction in a peaceful environment.

These propositions of Comrade Mao Tse-tung's have been and are the consistent views of the Communist Party of China.

It is thus clear that the leaders of the C.P.S.U. are deliberately concocting a lie in alleging that the Chinese Communist Party does "not believe in the possibility of preventing a new world war."

Again, it is clear that the thesis on the possibility of preventing a third world war was advanced by Marxist-Leninists long ago; it was not first put forward at the 20th Congress of the C.P.S.U., nor is it Khrushchov's "creation."

Is it then true that Khrushchov has created nothing at all? No. He has created something. Unfortunately, these "creations" are by no means Marxist-Leninist, but revisionist.

First, Khrushchov has wilfully interpreted the possibility of preventing a new world war as the only possibility, holding that there is no danger of a new world war.

Marxist-Leninists hold that while pointing to the possibility of preventing a new world war, we must also call attention to the possibility that imperialism may unleash a world war. Only by pointing to both possibilities, pursuing correct policies and preparing for both eventualities can we effectively mobilize the masses to wage struggles in defence of world peace. Only thus will the Socialist countries and people and other peace-loving countries and people not be caught unawares and utterly unprepared should imperialism force a world war on the people of the world.

However, Khrushchov and others are against exposing the danger of a new war which the imperialists are plotting. According to them, imperialism has actually become peace-loving. This is helping the imperialists to lull the masses and sap their fighting will so that they will lose their vigilance against the danger of the new war the imperialists are plotting.

Second, Khrushchov has wilfully interpreted the possibility of preventing a new world war as the possibility of preventing all wars, holding that the Leninist axiom that war is inevitable so long as imperialism exists is outmoded.

The possibility of preventing a new world war is one thing; the possibility of preventing all wars, including revolutionary wars, is another. And it is completely wrong to confuse the two.

There is soil for wars so long as imperialism and the system of exploitation of man by man exist. This is an objective law discovered by Lenin after abundant scientific study.

Stalin said in 1952 after indicating the possibility of preventing a new world war, "To eliminate the inevitability of war, it is necessary to abolish imperialism." (Stalin, *Economic Problems of Socialism in the U.S.S.R.*, Moscow: F.L.P.H., 1952, p. 41.)

89

Lenin and Stalin are right and Khrushchov is wrong.

History shows that while the imperialists have succeeded in launching two world wars, they have waged numerous wars of other kinds. Since World War II, by their policies of aggression and war the imperialists headed by the United States have brought about ceaseless local wars and armed conflicts of every description in many places, and especially in Asia, Africa and Latin America.

It is clear that national-liberation wars are inevitable when the imperialists, and the United States imperialists in particular, send their troops or use their lackeys to carry out sanguinary suppression of the oppressed nations and countries fighting for or upholding national independence.

Lenin said:

> To deny all possibility of national wars under imperialism is wrong in theory, obviously mistaken historically, and in practice is tantamount to European chauvinism. (Lenin, *Selected Works,* Moscow: F.L.P.H., 1950, vol. I, part 2, p. 571.)

It is equally clear that revolutionary civil wars are inevitable when the bourgeois reactionaries suppress the people in their own countries by force of arms.

Lenin said:

> . . . civil wars are also wars. Whoever recognizes the class struggle cannot fail to recognize civil wars, which in every class society are the natural, and under certain conditions, inevitable continuation, development and intensification of the class struggle. All the great revolutions prove this. To repudiate civil war, or to forget about it, would mean sinking into extreme opportunism and renouncing the Socialist revolution. (Lenin, *Selected Works,* Moscow: F.L.P.H., vol. I, part 2, p. 571.)

Nearly all the great revolutions in history were made through revolutionary wars. The American War of Independence and Civil War are cases in point. The French revolution is another example. The Russian revolution and the Chinese revolution are of course examples too. The revolutions in Viet Nam, Cuba, Algeria, etc., are also well-known examples.

In 1871, summing up the lessons of the Paris Commune

in his speech commemorating the seventh anniversary of the founding of the First International, Marx mentioned the conditions for the elimination of class domination and class oppression. He said, ". . . before such a change can be consummated, a dictatorship of the proletariat is necessary, and its first premise is an army of the proletariat. The working class must win the right to its emancipation on the battlefield." (Marx and Engels, *Works*, German ed., Berlin: Verlag Dietz, 1962, vol. 17, p. 433.)

In accordance with Marxist-Leninist theory, Comrade Mao Tse-tung advanced the celebrated thesis that "Political power grows out of the barrel of a gun," when discussing the lessons of the Russian and Chinese revolutions in 1938. This thesis, too, has now become a target of attack by the leaders of the C.P.S.U. They say it is evidence of China's being "warlike."

Respected friends, slanders like yours were refuted by Comrade Mao Tse-tung as far back as 25 years ago:

> According to the Marxist theory of the state, the army is the chief component of state power. Whoever wants to seize and retain state power must have a strong army. Some people ridicule us as advocates of the "omnipotence of war." Yes, we are advocates of the omnipotence of revolutionary war; that is good, not bad, it is Marxist. (Mao Tse-tung, *Selected Military Writings*, Peking: F.L.P., 1963, p. 273.)

What is wrong with Comrade Mao Tse-tung's remark? Only those who reject all the historical experience gained in the bourgeois and proletarian revolutions over the last few hundred years would reject this view of his.

With their guns, the Chinese people have created Socialist political power. All except imperialists and their lackeys can readily understand that this is a fine thing and that it is an important factor in safeguarding world peace and preventing a third world war.

Marxist-Leninists never conceal their views. We wholeheartedly support every people's revolutionary war. As Lenin said of such revolutionary war, "Of all the wars known in history it is the only lawful, rightful, just, and truly great war." (Lenin, *Collected Works*, Moscow: F.L.P.H., vol. VIII, p. 107.) If we are accused of being warlike simply because of this, it only goes to prove that we genuinely side with the oppressed peoples and nations and are true Marxist-Leninists.

The imperialists and revisionists always denounced the Bolsheviks and revolutionary leaders like Lenin and Stalin for being "warlike." The very fact that today we are likewise abused by imperialists and revisionists shows that we have been holding aloft the revolutionary banner of Marxism-Leninism.

Khrushchov and others vigorously propagate the view that all wars can be prevented and "a world without weapons, without armed forces and without wars" can be brought into being while imperialism still exists. This is nothing but Kautsky's theory of "ultra-imperialism" which has long been bankrupt. Their purpose is all too clear; it is to make the people believe that permanent peace can be realized under imperialism and thereby to abolish revolution and national-liberation wars and revolutionary civil wars against imperialism and its lackeys, and in fact to help the imperialists in their preparations for a new war.

NUCLEAR FETISHISM AND NUCLEAR BLACKMAIL ARE THE THEORETICAL BASIS AND GUIDING POLICY OF MODERN REVISIONISM

The heart of the theory of the leaders of the C.P.S.U. on war and peace is their thesis that the emergence of nuclear weapons has changed everything including the laws of class struggle.

The open letter of the Central Committee of the C.P.S.U. says, "The nuclear rocket weapons that were created in the middle of our century changed the old notions about war." In what way were they changed?

The leaders of the C.P.S.U. hold that with the appearance of nuclear weapons there is no longer any difference between just and unjust wars. They say, "the atomic bomb does not adhere to the class principle" and that "the atomic bomb does not distinguish between the imperialists and working people, it hits big areas and therefore millions of workers would be destroyed per one monopolist."

They hold that with the appearance of nuclear weapons the oppressed peoples and nations must abandon revolution and refrain from waging just popular revolutionary wars and wars of national liberation, or else such wars would lead to the destruction of mankind. They say, ". . . any small 'local war' might spark off the conflagration of a world war" and "Today, any sort of war, though it may break out as an ordinary non-nuclear war, is likely to develop into a destructive nuclear-missile conflagration." Thus, "We will destroy our Noah's Ark — the globe."

The leaders of the C.P.S.U. hold that the Socialist countries must not resist but must yield to imperialist nuclear blackmail and war threats. Khrushchov said:

> There can be no doubt that a world nuclear war, if started by the imperialist maniacs, would inevitably result in the downfall of the capitalist system, a system breeding wars. But would the Socialist countries and the cause of socialism all over the world benefit from a world nuclear disaster? Only people who deliberately shut their eyes to the facts can think so. As regards Marxist-Leninists, they cannot propose to establish a Communist civilization on the ruins of centres of world culture, on land laid waste and contaminated by nuclear fall-out. We need hardly add that in the case of many peoples, the question of socialism would be eliminated altogether because they would have disappeared bodily from our planet.

In short, according to the leaders of the C.P.S.U., with the emergence of nuclear weapons, the contradiction between the Socialist and the imperialist camps, the contradiction between the proletariat and the bourgeoisie in the capitalist countries, and the contradiction between the oppressed nations and imperialism have all disappeared. The world no longer has any class contradictions. They regard the contradictions in the contemporary world as boiling down to a single contradiction, that is, their fictitious contradiction between the so-called common survival of imperialism and the oppressed classes and nations on the one hand and their total destruction on the other.

As far as the leaders of the C.P.S.U. are concerned, Marxism-Leninism, the Declaration and the Statement, and socialism and communism have all been cast to the winds.

How frankly *Pravda* puts it! "What is the use of principles if one's head is chopped off?"

This is tantamount to saying that the revolutionaries who died under the sabres of the reactionaries for the victory of the Russian revolutions and the October Revolution, the warriors who bravely gave up their lives in the anti-Fascist war, the heroes who shed their blood in the struggle against imperialism and for national independence and the martyrs to the revolutionary cause through the ages were all fools. Why should they have given up their heads for adherence to principle?

This is the philosophy of out-and-out renegades. It is a shameless statement, to be found only in the confessions of renegades.

Guided by this theory of nuclear fetishism and nuclear blackmail, the leaders of the C.P.S.U. maintain that the way to defend world peace is not for all existing peace forces to unite and form the broadest united front against United States imperialism and its lackeys but for the two nuclear powers, the United States and the Soviet Union, to co-operate in settling the world's problems.

Khrushchov has said:

> We [the U.S.A., and the U.S.S.R.] are the strongest countries in the world and if we unite for peace there can be no war. Then if any madman wanted war, we would but have to shake our fingers to warn him off.

It is thus apparent to everybody how far the leaders of the C.P.S.U. have gone in regarding the enemy as their friend.

In order to cover up their error, the leaders of the C.P.S.U. have not hesitated to attack the correct line of the C.P.C. by lies and slanders. They assert that by advocating support for the peoples' wars of national liberation and revolutionary civil wars the Communist Party of China wants to provoke a nuclear world war.

This is a curious lie.

The Communist Party of China has always held that the Socialist countries should actively support the peoples' revolutionary struggles, including wars of national liberation and revolutionary civil wars. To fail to do so would be to renounce their proletarian internationalist duty. At the same time, we hold that the oppressed peoples and nations can achieve liberation only by their own resolute revolutionary struggle and that no one else can do it for them.

We have always maintained that Socialist countries must not use nuclear weapons to support the peoples' wars of national liberation and revolutionary civil wars and have no need to do so.

94

Fantasy of a Warless World

We have always maintained that the Socialist countries must achieve and maintain nuclear superiority. Only this can prevent the imperialists from launching a nuclear war and help bring about the complete prohibition of nuclear weapons.

We consistently hold that in the hands of a Socialist country, nuclear weapons must always be defensive weapons for resisting imperialist nuclear threats. A Socialist country absolutely must not be the first to use nuclear weapons, nor should it in any circumstances play with them or engage in nuclear blackmail and nuclear gambling.

We are opposed both to the wrong practice on the part of the leaders of the C.P.S.U. of withholding support from the revolutionary struggles of the peoples and to their wrong approach to nuclear weapons. Instead of examining their own errors, they accuse us of hoping for a "head-on clash" between the Soviet Union and the United States and trying to push them into a nuclear war.

Our answer is: No, friends. You had better cut out your sensation-mongering calumny. The Chinese Communist Party is firmly opposed to a "head-on clash" between the Soviet Union and the United States, and not in words only. In deeds too it has worked hard to avert direct armed conflict between them. Examples of this are the Korean war against United States aggression in which we fought side by side with the Korean comrades and our struggle against the United States in the Taiwan Straits. We ourselves preferred to shoulder the heavy sacrifices necessary and stood in the first line of defence of the Socialist camp so that the Soviet Union might stay in the second line. Have the leaders of the C.P.S.U. any sense of proletarian morality when they concoct such lies?

In fact, it is not we but the leaders of the C.P.S.U. who have frequently boasted that they would use nuclear weapons to help the anti-imperialist struggle of one country or another.

As everyone knows, the oppressed peoples and nations have no nuclear weapons and they cannot use them to make revolutions; nor is there any need for them to do so. The leaders of the C.P.S.U. admit that there is often no clear battle line between the two sides in national-liberation wars and civil wars, and therefore the use of nuclear weapons is out of the question. We should then like to ask the leaders of the C.P.S.U.: What need is there for a Socialist country to support the peoples' revolutionary struggles by nuclear weapons?

We should also like to ask them: How would a Socialist country use nuclear weapons to support the revolutionary struggle of an oppressed people or nation? Would it use nuclear weapons on an area where a war of national liberation or a revolutionary civil war was in progress, thereby subjecting both the revolutionary people and the imperialists to a nuclear strike? Or would it be the first to use nuclear weapons against an imperialist country which was waging a conventional war of aggression elsewhere? Obviously, in either case it is absolutely impermissible for a Socialist country to use nuclear weapons.

The fact is that when the leaders of the C.P.S.U. brandish their nuclear weapons, it is not really to support the people's anti-imperialist struggles.

Sometimes, in order to gain cheap prestige, they just publish empty statements which they never intend to honour.

At other times, during the Caribbean crisis for instance, they engage in speculative, opportunistic and irresponsible nuclear gambling for ulterior motives.

As soon as their nuclear blackmail is seen through and is countered in kind, they retreat one step after another, switch from adventurism to capitulationism and lose all by their nuclear gambling.

We wish to point out that the great Soviet people and Red Army have been and remain a great force safeguarding world peace. But Khrushchov's military ideas based on nuclear fetishism and nuclear blackmail are entirely wrong.

Khrushchov sees only nuclear weapons. According to him, "The present level of military technique being what it is, the air force and the navy have lost their former importance. These arms are being replaced and not reduced."

Of course, those units and men having combat duties on the ground are even less significant. According to him, "In our time, a country's defensive capacity is not determined by the number of men under arms, of men in uniform. . . . a country's defence potential depends in decisive measure on the firepower and the means of delivery that country commands."

As for the militia and the people, they are still more inconsequential. Khrushchov has made the well-known remark that for those now having modern weapons at their disposal, the militia is not an army but just human flesh.

Khrushchov's whole set of military theories runs completely counter to Marxist-Leninist teachings on war and the army. To follow his wrong theories will necessarily involve disintegrating the army and disarming oneself morally.

Obviously, if any Socialist country should accept Khrushchov's erroneous military strategy, it would inevitably place itself in a most dangerous position.

Khrushchov may confer on himself such titles as "a great peace champion," award himself a peace prize and pin heroes' medals on himself, but no matter how much he may praise himself, he will not be able to cover up his dangerous practice of recklessly playing with nuclear weapons or his fawning before imperialist nuclear blackmail.

FIGHT OR CAPITULATE?

World peace can be won only through struggle by the people of all countries and not by begging the imperialists for it. Peace can be effectively safeguarded only by relying on the masses of the people and waging a tit-for-tat struggle against the imperialist policies of aggression and war. This is the correct policy.

Tit-for-tat struggle is an important conclusion drawn by the Chinese people from their prolonged struggle against imperialism and its lackeys.

Comrade Mao Tse-tung said:

> Chiang Kai-shek always tries to wrest every ounce of power and every ounce of gain from the people. And we? Our policy is to give him tit for tat and to fight for every inch of land. We act after his fashion. (Mao Tse-tung, *Selected Works,* Peking: F.L.P., 1961, vol. IV, p. 14.)

He added:

> He always tries to impose war on the people, one sword in his left hand and another in his right. We take up swords, too, following his example. (*ibid.*)

Analysing the domestic political situation in 1945, Comrade Mao Tse-tung said:

> How to give "tit for tat" depends on the situation. Sometimes, not going to negotiations is tit-for-tat; and sometimes, going to negotiations is also tit-for-tat. . . . If

they start fighting, we fight back, fight to win peace. Peace will not come unless we strike hard blows at the reactionaries who dare to attack the Liberated Areas. (*ibid.,* p. 56.)

He drew the following historical lesson from the failure of China's revolution of 1924-27:

Confronted by counter-revolutionary attacks against the people, Chen Tu-hsiu did not adopt the policy of giving tit for tat and fighting for every inch of land; as a result, in 1927, within the space of a few months, the people lost all the rights they had won. (*ibid.,* p. 16.)

The Chinese Communists understand and adhere to the policy of giving tit for tat. We oppose both capitulationism and adventurism. This correct policy ensured the victory of the Chinese revolution and the Chinese people's subsequent great successes in their struggle against imperialism.

All revolutionary people approve and welcome this correct fighting policy put forward by the Chinese Communists. All imperialists and reactionaries fear and hate it.

The policy of giving tit for tat as put forward by the C.P.C. is virulently attacked by the leaders of the C.P.S.U. This only goes to show that they do not in the least want to oppose imperialism. Their sole purpose in attacking and smearing the policy of tit for tat is to cover up their wrong line of catering to the needs of imperialism and surrendering to it.

The leaders of the C.P.S.U. assert that a tit-for-tat struggle against imperialism will lead to international tension. How terrible!

According to their logic, the imperialists are allowed to commit aggression and make threats against others but the victims of imperialist aggression are not allowed to fight, the imperialists are allowed to oppress others but the oppressed are not allowed to resist. This is a naked attempt to absolve the imperialists of their crimes of aggression. This is a philosophy of the jungle, pure and simple.

International tension is the product of the imperialist policies of aggression and war. The peoples should of course wage a firm struggle against imperialist aggression and threats. Facts have shown that only through struggle can imperialism be compelled to retreat and a genuine relaxation of international tension be achieved. Constant retreat before the imperialists cannot lead to genuine relaxation but will only encourage their aggression.

We have always opposed the creation of international tension by imperialism and stood for the relaxation of such tension. But the imperialists are bent on committing aggression and creating tension everywhere, and that can only lead to the opposite of what they desire.

Comrade Mao Tse-tung said:

> The U.S. imperialists believe that they will always benefit from tense situations, but the fact is that tension created by the United States had led to the opposite of what they desire. It serves to mobilize the people of the whole world against the U.S. aggressors. (*Jen-min jih-pao*, Sept. 9, 1958.)

Further, "If the U.S. monopoly groups persist in their policies of aggression and war, the day is bound to come when the people of the world will hang them by the neck." (*ibid.*)

The Declaration of 1957 rightly says, "By this policy these anti-popular, aggressive imperialist forces are courting their own ruin, creating their own grave-diggers."

This is the dialectic of history. Those who revere the imperialists can hardly understand this truth.

The leaders of the C.P.S.U. assert that by advocating a tit-for-tat struggle the Chinese Communist Party has rejected negotiations. This again is nonsense.

We consistently maintain that those who refuse negotiations under all circumstances are definitely not Marxist-Leninists.

The Chinese Communists conducted negotiations with the Kuomintang many times during the revolutionary civil wars. They did not refuse to negotiate even on the eve of nationwide liberation.

Comrade Mao Tse-tung said in March 1949:

> Whether the peace negotiations are overall or local, we should be prepared for such an eventuality. We should not refuse to enter into negotiations because we are afraid of trouble and want to avoid complications, nor should we enter into negotiations with our minds in a haze. We should be firm in principle;

we should also have all the flexibility permissible and necessary for carrying out our principles. (Mao Tse-tung, *Selected Works*, Peking: F.L.P., 1961, vol. IV, p. 372.)

Internationally, in struggling against imperialism and reaction, the Chinese Communists take the same correct attitude towards negotiations.

In October 1951, Comrade Mao Tse-tung had this to say about the Korean armistice negotiations:

We have long said that the Korean question should be settled by peaceful means. This still holds good now. So long as the U.S. Government is willing to settle the question on a just and reasonable basis, and will stop using every shameless means possible to wreck and obstruct the progress of the negotiations, as it has done in the past, success in the Korean armistice negotiation is possible; otherwise it is impossible. (*Jen-min jih-pao*, Oct. 24, 1951.)

Resolute struggle against the United States imperialists compelled them to accept the Korean armistice agreement in the course of negotiations.

We took an active part in the 1954 Geneva Conference and contributed to the restoration of peace in Indo-China.

We are in favour of negotiations even with the United States, which has occupied our territory of Taiwan. The Sino-United States ambassadorial talks have been going on for more than eight years now.

We took an active part in the 1961 Geneva Conference on the Laotian question and promoted the signing of the Geneva agreements respecting the independence and neutrality of Laos.

Do the Chinese Communists allow themselves alone to negotiate with imperialist countries while opposing negotiations by the leaders of the C.P.S.U. with the leaders of the imperialist countries?

No, of course not.

In fact, we have always actively supported all such negotiations by the Soviet Government with imperialist countries as are beneficial and not detrimental to the defence of world peace.

Comrade Mao Tse-tung said on May 14, 1960:

Fantasy of a Warless World

We support the holding of the summit conference whether or not this sort of conference yields achievements, or whether the achievements are big or small. But the winning of world peace should depend primarily on resolute struggle by the people of all countries. (*Jen-min jih-pao*, May 15, 1960.)

We favour negotiations with imperialist countries. But it is absolutely impermissible to pin hopes for world peace on negotiations, spread illusions about them and thereby paralyse the fighting will of the peoples, as Khrushchov has done.

Actually, Khrushchov's wrong approach to negotiations is itself harmful to negotiations. The more Khrushchov retreats before the imperialists and the more he begs, the more the appetite of the imperialists will grow. Khrushchov, who poses as the greatest devotee of negotiations in history, is always an unrequited lover and too often a laughing stock. Countless historical facts have shown that the imperialists and reactionaries never care to save the face of the capitulationists.

THE ROAD IN DEFENCE OF PEACE AND THE ROAD LEADING TO WAR

To sum up, our difference with the leaders of the C.P.S.U. on the question of war and peace is one between two different lines —whether or not to oppose imperialism, whether or not to support revolutionary struggles, whether or not to mobilize the people of the world against the imperialist war plots and whether or not to adhere to Marxism-Leninism.

Like all other genuine revolutionary parties, the Communist Party of China has always been in the forefront of the struggle against imperialism and for world peace. We hold that to defend world peace it is necessary constantly to expose imperialism and to arouse and organize the people in struggle against the imperialists headed by the United States, and it is necessary to place reliance on the growth of the strength of the Socialist camp, on the revolutionary struggles of the proletariat and working people of all countries, on the liberation struggles of the oppressed nations, on the struggles of all peace-loving peoples and countries and on the broad united front against United States imperialism and its lackeys.

This line of ours is in keeping with the common line for all

Editorial Departments of Jen-min jih-pao and Hung-ch'i

Communist Parties laid down in the 1957 Declaration and the 1960 Statement.

With this line, it is possible ceaselessly to raise the political consciousness of the people and to expand the struggle for world peace in the right direction.

With this line, it is possible constantly to strengthen the forces for world peace with the Socialist camp as their core and strike at and weaken the imperialist forces for war.

With this line, it is possible constantly to expand the peoples' revolutions and manacle imperialism.

With this line, it is possible to turn to account all available factors, including the contradictions between United States imperialism and the other imperialist powers, and to isolate United States imperialism to the fullest extent.

With this line, it is possible to smash the nuclear blackmail practised by United States imperialism and defeat its plan for launching a new world war.

This is the line for the people of all countries to win both victory in revolution and world peace. It is the sure and effective road in defence of world peace.

But the line pursued by the leaders of the C.P.S.U. is diametrically opposed to our line, to the common line of all Marxist-Leninists and revolutionary people.

The leaders of the C.P.S.U. direct the edge of their struggle not at the enemy of world peace but at the Socialist camp, thus weakening and undermining the very core of strength which defends world peace.

They use nuclear blackmail to intimidate the people of the Socialist countries and forbid them to support the revolutionary struggles of the oppressed peoples and nations, thus helping United States imperialism to isolate the Socialist camp and suppress peoples' revolutions.

They use nuclear blackmail to intimidate the oppressed peoples and nations and to prohibit them from making revolution, and they collaborate with United States imperialism in stamping out the "sparks" of revolution, thus enabling it freely to carry on its policies of aggression and war in the intermediate zone lying between the United States and the Socialist camp.

They also intimidate the allies of the United States and

forbid them to struggle against the control it has imposed on them, thus helping United States imperialism to enslave these countries and consolidate its position.

By this line of action the leaders of the C.P.S.U. have altogether relinquished the struggle against the imperialist policies of aggression and war.

This line of action denies the united front against United States imperialism and its lackeys and in defence of world peace.

It tries to impose the greatest isolation not on the arch enemy of world peace but on the peace forces.

It means the liquidation of the fighting task of defending world peace.

This is a line that serves the "global strategy" of United States imperialism.

It is not the road to world peace but the road leading to greater danger of war and to war itself.

Today the world is no longer what it was on the eve of World War II. There is the powerful Socialist camp. The national-liberation movement in Asia, Africa and Latin America is surging forward. The political consciousness of the people of the world has been very much raised. The strength of the revolutionary peoples has been very much enhanced. The people of the Soviet Union, of the Socialist countries and of the whole world will never allow their own destiny to be manipulated by the imperialist forces for war and their trumpeters.

The aggression and war activities of the imperialists and reactionaries are teaching the people of the world gradually to raise their political consciousness. Social practice is the sole criterion of truth. We are confident that as a result of such teaching by the imperialists and reactionaries, many people now holding wrong views on the question of war and peace will change their minds. We have high hopes on this score.

We firmly believe that the Communists and the people of the world will surely smash the imperialist plan for launching a new world war and safeguard world peace provided they expose the imperialist frauds, see through the revisionist lies and shoulder the task of defending world peace.

III

•

COMMON INTERESTS OF
THE UNITED STATES
AND SOVIET UNION

ARTHUR I. WASKOW

•

ADVANCING THE AMERICAN
NATIONAL INTEREST WITHOUT WAR

The essence of the "American national interest" is that it is
dynamic, not stable; that it encourages change in the world, not
the status quo; that it seeks both the expansion of American
power and the advancement in other countries of the sorts of
liberty that Americans understand. It is sometimes argued that
Americans should change this definition of the national interest,
should stop "playing busy-body" in the world, should give up the
"adolescent illusion of omnipotence" and abandon the dream of
manifest destiny. Indeed, it is sometimes argued that only if
Americans do this can a warless world be attained.

I do not agree with this prescription. I do not want the
United States to give up the attempt to win more power and
influence in the world, nor do I think it probable that most
Americans will be willing to change their definition of the
national interest, as prescribed. And I do not believe such a
change will be needed in order to achieve the warless world.
Certainly America is not and cannot be omnipotent, but in a
warless world she need not be impotent either, though she often
seems to be impotent today. The ways in which American
potency might be restored and used in a warless world are what I
should like to discuss.

In doing so I shall be describing a warless world that is not
utopia, but a world in which much the same national conflicts
and distrusts that exist now would persist. (In fact, some of my
suggestions may sound so unpleasant as to be almost anti-

Reprinted with permission from *Bulletin of the Atomic Scientists*, February
1964, pp. 23-25.

utopian, in the style of *Brave New World*.) We need to look at such a world because national governments will not abolish war until they know how they could pursue their traditional aims and cope with persistent international conflicts and distrusts without using war. The strategy I propose is based on the advancement of current American interests, and the tactics I suggest can be based on experience or on solid research.

I am using the phrase "warless world" to mean something quite limited: that all national governments have agreed to disarm and to give up organized international violence, and have created an institution that will attempt to enforce their agreement. I will not assume the establishment of a stable peace based on shared values, nor even the continued adherence of every nation to the original agreement.

The first requirement of American national interest is that this nation be protected from attack or invasion. The primary means of achieving this end in a warless world would probably be the prevention of rearmament and aggression by an international institution. But the self-interest of the United States would probably require that such an institution be made incapable of coercing us into changing our society. In other words, our national interest would require the creation of an institution that would have enough power to prevent rearmament by any nation, but not enough power to impose its policies and values on great powers like the United States.

We can sketch some possible characteristics of such an institution, but many more possibilities would have to be explored through historical research and small-group experiments. We can imagine that the size of such an institution might range considerably closer to that of the U.S. marine corps than to that of the U.S. army. It would probably attempt to act on individuals actually engaged in rearmament, rather than upon national officials who ordered it. It would concentrate on trying to enforce disarmament, rather than on punishing the rearmers: for example, it might drop 50 men with helicopters on a factory that was turning out tanks, knock out the workers with a temporary paralytic gas, smash up the key electrical machinery in the plant, and leave without even arresting anyone for trial. The force might well be commanded by a series of graduated votes, so that, for example, the sending of ten men armed with tear gas to enforce a cease-and-desist order might be ordered by a two-ninths vote of a nine-nation commanding board, the sending of 100 men armed with rifles would have to be approved by a five-ninths vote, and the sending of 5000 men armed with tanks and machine guns would require unanimous agreement of the four Great Powers—say the United States, the Soviet Union, Europe, and China—plus one other vote. Again, the internal organization of the force might be structured in such ways—judicious combinations of national units and units drawn from a specially trained transnational civil service, for example—that it would be unlikely that an effective portion of the force could act like the Praetorian Guard or the French paratroops and turn itself into a political army. If safeguards like these were built into the international institution, the United States could probably feel reasonably secure either from attack by a foreign army secretly prepared or from attack by the international force itself.

It might be, however, that the United States would not want to leave protection of its most vital national interest—the safety of this continent—in international hands. One can imagine that as a last-ditch defense against invasion—the only last-ditch defense that could legitimately be prepared in a warless world—the United States could train its citizens for personal resistance to an occupying force, resistance perhaps by a combination of guerrilla and Gandhian methods. Such training might create other problems—it might add to the difficulty of keeping internal order, for example—but historical cases of guerrilla and Gandhian resistance do exist, and more research on them might lead to more understanding of their applicability in the future.

Beyond its interest in protecting this continent, the United States can be said to have two basic interests in the world: the expansion of that area in which the writ of freedom runs, and the increase of its national power and that of its citizens over the future of other nations and peoples. These two aims—the advancement of liberty and of American power—may seem, and indeed may be, contradictory. The debate as to which aim should be that of the national government is an old debate between Americans, at least as old as the debate over annexing Hawaii. Undoubtedly this internal debate would continue in a warless world. In fact, one of the major advantages of a world without war would be that such internal conflicts could actually be fought out politically. As things stand now in the armed world, the pressures to unite behind official policy inhibit the expression of serious political disagreements over the goals of foreign policy, and fear of the H-bomb freezes Americans into not pursuing *either* goal of foreign policy—liberty or power—with verve and vigor.

Let us look first at the means of advancing liberty. There are two major threats to liberty in the world today: the readiness in many underdeveloped countries to squeeze every possible ounce of energy out of most of the citizens in order to invest the savings in scientific and industrial developments; and the readiness in some developed nations to use the advanced techniques of natural and social science to control most of the citizens and keep the rulers in power. Since Jefferson called America "the last hope of earth," we have thought a crucial part of our national interest to be the encouragement of liberty and the undermining of tyranny, whether of the sort that squeezes the last drop of blood from a peasant so that his grandchildren may manage a steel mill, or of the sort that silences a dissenter so that the party or the army may stay in control. It should be clear that neither of these sorts of tyranny is necessarily Communist, although the Communists have used both of them. Both sorts exist among our present friends and allies as well as among our present enemies.

The tyranny that results from hunger for economic progress can be resisted if the United States will multiply by many times its aid to underdeveloped nations. In some cases, this could be accomplished by relieving the squeeze on the hungry peasant by providing enough food to feed both him and his jobless cousin in the big city, who would like to work on a dam but must stay in town to beg scraps of food. Certainly the United States is peculiarly able to supply such food, especially if it would reverse its present policy of reducing the farm surplus and instead would deliberately encourage its expansion, would encourage farmers to grow the crops and breed the animals most needed for food in specific underdeveloped countries, and would have the government buy the resulting special surplus for delivery overseas.

In other cases, the most effective action would be the provision of skilled labor both to work with and to train the citizens of an underdeveloped country. Now we do this in a tiny way with the Peace Corps; in a warless world, we could use the entire manpower now swallowed up in our armed forces, and very possibly the extra manpower that is being disemployed by the advance of automation. New techniques of teaching languages make it possible, for example, to hire or draft ten thousand mechanics for two years' technical service overseas, teach them all Urdu or Swahili or Arabic, and send them to teach Africans and Indians how to run and maintain a cheap and simple tractor. They could be organized and commanded in quasi-military fashion, and operate the way the Army Corps of Engineers did in the United States during the nineteenth century as the crucial cadre for economic development. Simply because automation is more advanced here than anywhere else in the world, we could afford the drain on our trained labor supply better than any other nation.

Or we might do the job another way through private enterprise. If disarmament savings on military goods were channeled into specialized tax reductions, we could encourage the myriad forms of American private enterprise to invest in overseas development. For example, we could provide major tax rebates for any company that would set up a joint American-African enterprise intending to put all the capital and most of the skilled labor and training, to take out half the profits for ten years, and then to get out entirely. Israel and Ghana have found this kind of approach most useful, and with governmental help many American firms might try it. Certainly the fantastic flexibility of American enterprise, ranging from General Motors to the Rand Corporation to the family grocery to the New York Port Authority to the local telephone company to the farm cooperative to the Federal Reserve System, and on and on, suggests that the United States could easily bring economic development in the context of pluralism to the hungry nations. Our national interests in this sphere would best be accomplished by bringing in our capital in such diverse ways and from such different sources that accepting it would inevitably create a pluralist profusion of enterprises in the developing country. Once such a cluster of institutions is created, they would be hard for a totalitarian government to stamp out.

Advancing American Interests Without War

What about the advancement of political liberty in a country where the army or a bureaucratic party is trying to impose totalitarian controls? Especially with the increase of communication satellites and the possibilities of highly miniaturized radio receivers, one could imagine the United States making available to citizens of a totalitarian state the whole spectrum of proscribed ideas, in ways the government could not stop or penalize. Such information could even include sophisticated suggestions on how to tie the bureaucracy up in its own red tape. For example, several years ago British postmen protected their salary scale not by striking but by following all the regulations. They stopped the entire postal system. Recently in the United States, a northern Negro integrationist warned that if a governor would not pay attention to Negro protests over school segregation, thousands of Negroes would telephone the Governor's Mansion and the State House. That would stop all telephone business with the state government, and probably choke many other long-distance telephone services as well. Details on such techniques could easily be told to the citizens of a totalitarian nation, and the ruling party or army might find itself hard put to establish control.

There might be many occasions on which the United States would decide to try to exert its power over other nations, or to support the power of some private groups of Americans as part of its definition of advancing the national interest. For example, we might see a repetition of the Mossadegh affair, in which the United States government determined that the control of Iranian oil by a consortium that included some American oil companies was in the national interest of the United States. Various techniques, none of them involving the use or the threat of armed force, were then used in helping certain Iranian political groups oust Mossadegh. Certainly in a warless world one can imagine that American control over the government, the business, the labor unions, or the newspapers of another country might seem to be in the national interest. Bribery, blackmail, espionage, the provision of financial help or political advice to an internal clique, might well be used in such a situation. So might such more public techniques as the use of a sort of "international credit rating" to threaten a country with withdrawal of certain investment credits if it did not agree to certain political requests or, conversely, to offer a country new credits if it took an agreeable line.

The United States might not only pursue the kinds of policies I have sketched out here in order to advance its national interest without war, but also might explore wholly new lines of action not now apparent. In fact, another crucial element of American policy would be the intensive pursuit of research to develop new strategies and tactics for advancing the national interest without war. The Rand Corporation would get bigger, and its job more subtle and difficult, in a disarmed world. For the development of new means of waging war is relatively simple. All men have the same sort of body, and all can be killed in the same ways—ways that are constantly getting simpler and cheaper. But fighting for the national interest without war means knowing the enemy's society and psychology, how to convert him or coerce him or trick him, not simply how to destroy him. That characteristic of nonlethal means of carrying on conflict will require our future Rands in the warless world to have far more knowledge than they do now of what kinds of skilled labor Brazil can use, what sorts of bribes will work with an Englishman that will not with an Indonesian, what the peculiar vulnerabilities of the Soviet Communist Party are as against the Chinese Communist Party, what forms of organization would allow a tribal society to make effective use of large amounts of capital, and what points of information flow might be most easily affected in various authoritarian societies.

There is another characteristic of nonlethal as against thermonuclear strategy that will increase the importance of strategic research. Thermonuclear strategizing is not science; the finespun theories of controlled thermonuclear war cannot be checked against reality, at least not until we have a thermonuclear war. But the process of advancing the national interest without war can always be checked against the strategists' predictions. As the various techniques are used, they can be assessed and changed. As strategy research changes from the status of astrology to that of science, the magical aura may disappear but the practical utility will increase. Since the subtlety of the work will be increasing at the same time, the United States will find that in its national interest the quality and quantity of political research must be increased.

I emphasize the word "political." For what will distinguish the warless world is that politics will again be possible. Just as the abolition of war will revive political disagreement within the United States as to what the national interest is, so it will revive the clash of national interests in the world that is now constrained within very narrow limits by the fear of war. The unorthodox methods I have mentioned of advancing national interests without war will be countered by the unorthodox methods of other countries. American victories will not be automatic in such a world. But the dynamism and pluralism that have characterized the United States until very recently in its history are exactly what we need, if we are to move forward in a warless world.

For move we shall. What characterizes a political world is change, and the world will not stay frozen forever in the pattern of conflict I have described. For example, there might sooner or later be a crisis of rearmament, when some nation were losing an intense nonmilitary conflict and decided to resort to arms. At that point, either the minimal world disarmament-enforcing institution that I have described would move somewhat closer toward being a government, or it would collapse. Or let us take another case: what if the findings of much more intensive political research were used by one group within a nation against another internal group? Would the nation tend to dissolve into its industrial, professional, and ethnic components? And what would the impact of those changes be on the rest of the world? Again, what would the effect of a generation of increasing prosperity be on the old conflicts between East and West, North and South?

But these are problems and questions for the second generation after disarmament. Every generation has its own task, and ours is to eliminate war and the weapons to fight it with. Having done that, we may well find ourselves in an unruly world, one in which only one regulation—no war—is rigidly enforced, and all other regulations on how to advance the national interest have been removed. It would be for later generations to decide how they would use the new chaotic politics to build their future.

Mikhail A. Suslov

•

QUESTIONS OF WAR, PEACE, AND REVOLUTION

Comrades, the fortunes of our great cause, and of the peoples, depend in decisive measure on the Communist movement employing the correct strategy and tactics on questions of war, peace and revolution. It is particularly important to take account of the interconnection and interdependence of these questions today, for never before have the revolutionary achievements of each particular country been so directly bound up with the development of the international situation as a whole, with the world revolutionary process.

The Marxist-Leninist parties see their consistent struggle for peace as fulfilment of their historical responsibility to mankind, which is to prevent the extermination of peoples in the flames of a thermonuclear war. Furthermore, they see it as a most important condition for the successful construction of socialism and communism and for the expansion of the revolutionary struggle of the proletariat of the capitalist countries and of the liberation movement of the peoples oppressed by imperialism.

An all-round analysis of the balance of world forces enabled the Communist and Workers' parties to draw the cardinal conclusion that world war can be averted even before socialism triumphs throughout the world, and to re-emphasise that the Leninist principle of the peaceful coexistence of countries with different social systems is the unshakable basis for the foreign policy of the Socialist countries.

Source: "The Struggle of the C.P.S.U. for Unity of the World Communist Movement," speech to the Plenary Meeting of the Central Committee of the C.P.S.U., February 14, 1964. Published in *Information Bulletin* (Prague: Peace and Socialism Publishers), 1964, Nos. 8-9, pp. 275-348.

War, Peace, and Revolution

As we know, these propositions were laid down in the 1957 Declaration and 1960 Statement adopted in Moscow. The experience of recent years, far from shaking belief in the vital necessity of the policy of peaceful coexistence, has, in fact, fully borne it out. It is due to the Socialist countries' consistent implementation of this policy, which is supported by hundreds of millions of people all over the world, that we have been able to foil the imperialist reactionaries' schemes against peace. The blessings of peace which mankind enjoys today do not come from the gods. They are a concrete result of the staunch resistance of the peace forces to attempts to unleash a thermonuclear war, a result of the growing power of the Soviet Union and other Socialist countries, as well as of the correct policy of the Communist parties, which have raised aloft the banner of the struggle for peace and rallied the whole of progressive mankind to this banner.

The Chinese leaders, who engaged first in a controversy with the C.P.S.U. and other Marxist-Leninist parties, and then in a political fight against them, showed especial zeal in attacking the conclusions of the Twentieth Congress of the C.P.S.U. and the theses of the Moscow meeting of fraternal parties on questions of war, peace and revolution. They imagined that it was on these points that they would be able to make political capital, and with this aim in view they accused the entire Communist movement of "losing sight of the revolutionary perspective" and "surrendering to imperialism."

To impart at least a semblance of veracity to their infamous charges, the Chinese theoreticians resort to a device that is neither clever nor new. Artificially separating two aspects of a single social process from each other, they contrast the fight for peace to the revolutionary movement, and claim that these two highly important tasks are mutually exclusive. From what they allege it follows that those who fight to maintain peace and ward off world war are against revolution and hamper the revolutionary struggle.

One does not require a special Marxist education to see that the C.P.C. leaders, who pose as grandmasters of dialectics, have in fact killed dialectics, which Lenin described as the "living soul" of Marxism. The Communist parties, which hold aloft the banner of the struggle for peace, are with increasing energy stepping up the class struggle of the proletariat and all working people, and the national liberation movement against imperialism.

In their fight against the Leninist policy of peaceful coexistence, which they counter with the idea of giving revolution a "push" by means of war, the C.P.C. leaders have gone as far as to assert that war is an acceptable and, in fact, the only means of settling the contradictions between capitalism and socialism. They ignore the experience of the world Communist movement and exalt the road of the victorious revolution in China as something absolute, trying to make it an incontrovertible truth for all countries and peoples. On every occasion, whether suitable or not, Chinese propaganda quotes what Mao Tse-tung said about war and peace in the thirties, during the civil war in China.

Among the widely popularised statements of Mao Tse-tung are the following: "the war to be waged by the overwhelming majority of mankind ... will become a bridge over which mankind will pass into a new era in history," "the world can only be reorganised by means of the rifle"; "we stand for abolishing war, we have no use for it, but war can only be abolished through war. If you want rifles to go out of existence, take to the rifle."

Almost three decades have passed since those statements were made. Radical changes have occurred in the world—the world Socialist system has formed and has become a mighty force, the revolutionary movement of the working class has assumed a mass scale, and the national-liberation movement has scored historic victories. Today the alliance of the peace forces can, as the documents of Communist parties point out, overcome the forces of imperialism and prevent them from launching a new world war. The prevention of war has become a particularly pressing task because the most destructive weapon recorded in history has been created and has been stockpiled in quantities that can bring untold calamities to all nations.

The Chinese leaders refuse to take all that into consideration. Plainly showing off their irresponsible attitude, they affirm that the nuclear bomb is a "paper tiger" and in no way affects the issue of war and peace. In keeping with this logic, which runs counter to elementary common sense, Mao Tse-tung, speaking at the Moscow meeting in 1957, argued that the struggle for socialism even stood to gain from a world thermonuclear war. "Can one foresee," he said, "the number of human lives that the future war may take? It may be one-third of the 2,700 million inhabitants of the world, that is, a mere 900 million people . . . I had an argument over this matter with Nehru. He is more pessimistic in this respect than I. I told him that should half of mankind be destroyed, the other half would survive; in return, imperialism would be wiped out completely and there would be only socialism in the world. In half a century or a whole century the population would grow again — even by more than half."

This concept is even more lucidly expressed in the collection of articles *Long Live Leninism!*, which the C.C., C.P.C., has approved and is circulating. "On the ruins of fallen imperialism," it says, "the victorious people will build a thousand times more wonderful future at an extremely rapid rate." That is the kind of ultra-revolutionary verbiage, complete political irresponsibility that is particularly dangerous because it is being demonstrated by people standing at the helm of a large Socialist country.

It is common knowledge that Lenin pointed out as far back as 1918 that a world war in which the mighty achievements of technology are used with such great energy for the mass extermination of human life, apart from being a major crime, can also lead "to the undermining of the very foundations of human society" (*Works*, vol. XXVII, p. 386). In our days, with the production and the development of nuclear missile weapons, this danger has increased still more. How can people, particularly the adherents of the Communist teaching, ignore this fact?

Neither the Socialist countries nor the working people want a world war; it cannot serve the cause of the triumph of socialism. The conclusions drawn by specialists on the possible consequences of another world war are quite unambiguous. For example, the progressive American scientist Linus Pauling gives figures to show that within 60 days after the outbreak of a nuclear war out of 190 million Americans 170 million would perish, 15 million would suffer greatly and only five million would remain relatively unharmed. The situation in other regions drawn directly into the sphere of military operations would evidently be the same. Moreover, account must also be taken of such delayed consequences of a nuclear war as the disorganisation of society due to the destruction of key industrial centres and of the means of transport and communication, and increasing radioactive pollution. Without mincing words, one can say that if a world thermonuclear conflict breaks out it would be the greatest tragedy for humanity and would, of course, deal the cause of communism a heavy blow.

No party that really cherishes the interests of the people can fail to appreciate its responsibility in the struggle for averting another world war. Yet the Chinese leaders, as we have seen, even boast that, allegedly for "the sake of the revolution," they are prepared to agree to the destruction of half of mankind. It does not worry them in the least that the losses in densely-populated countries that would find themselves in the centre of military operations would be so great that for entire peoples there would no longer be any question of the triumph of socialism because they would have disappeared from the face of the earth.

Here it would be appropriate to recall certain facts. When in a conversation with Tao Chu, member of the C.C., C.P.C., a Czechoslovak journalist mentioned that in the event of a thermonuclear war the whole of Czechoslovakia, where 14 million people live, might be destroyed, the answer he received was: "In the event of a war of annihilation the small countries in the Socialist camp will have to subordinate their interests to the common interests of the camp as a whole." Another well-known C.P.R. official told Soviet representatives that Comrade Togliatti, General Secretary of the Italian Communist Party, was wrong when, expressing anxiety for the fate of his people, he said that if a thermonuclear war broke out the whole of Italy would be destroyed. "Other people will remain," declared this official, "and imperialism will be wiped out. . . ."

In an effort to disprove the conclusion of the international Communist movement concerning the possibility of averting war, in Peking it is alleged that in pursuing a policy of peaceful coexistence the C.P.S.U. and other fraternal parties proceed from the assumption that the nature of imperialism has changed, base all their calculations on the "peace-loving and humane nature of the imperialists," and "appeal and beg for" peace from them. On the other hand, the C.P.C. leaders, it is claimed, are waging a determined and relentless struggle against imperialism and exposing its aggressive nature.

But these crude falsifications and distortions can fool no one. The attempts to portray Marxists-Leninists as some kind of pacifists are simply ludicrous. In the 1957 Declaration it is recorded that as long as imperialism exists there will always be the soil for aggressive wars. From this, however, the Communist parties did not draw the conclusion that world war is fatally inevitable. They showed that while the nature of imperialism, its rapacious essence, remains unchanged, there has been a change in the balance of forces in the world, that the place and role of imperialism in the world economy and world politics are not what they were, and that its influence on the course of events is diminishing. All this forces the imperialists to accept peaceful coexistence.

Consequently, it is not that the imperialists have become "peace-loving" or more "tractable," but that they have no alternative but to take the growing strength of socialism into account. They are aware that the Soviet Union, the Socialist countries, possess a formidable weapon and are able to deal any aggressor a crushing blow. They cannot help but take into account the strength of the mighty working-class and democratic movement in the capitalist countries, and the huge scale of the national liberation struggle of the peoples. The fact that capitalism will be wiped out and buried if the imperialist madmen unleash a world war is being more and more clearly apprehended in the camp of our class enemies.

The possibility of averting war, the threat of which remains as long as imperialism exists, does not arise of itself. It requires that the peace-loving forces display the greatest energy in the struggle for peace and show the greatest vigilance with regard to the intrigues of its enemies. It depends to a vast extent on the policy of the Socialist countries, on their defensive might, on the unswerving implementation of the Leninist principles of peaceful coexistence. That is exactly the policy being pursued by the Soviet Union and other Socialist countries that firmly adhere to the positions proclaimed in the Declaration and Statement of the fraternal parties.

However, it is precisely against this, the only sensible policy,

Mikhail A. Suslov

that the Chinese leaders have declared war. Having their own special objectives in mind, they are trying to discredit the principles of peaceful coexistence, assuring the peoples that their efforts to preserve peace are futile. Strange as it may seem, the Chinese leaders have proclaimed this point of view optimistic.

In *Long Live Leninism!* it is asserted: "Wars of one kind or another may break out as long as an end is not put to the imperialist system and the exploiter classes." "Naturally, whether or not the imperialists in the end start a war does not depend upon us for we are not the chiefs of their general staffs." At the Peking session of the World Federation of Trade Unions in June 1960, Liu Ning-yi, member of the C.C., C.P.C., said: "The assertions about the possibility of peaceful coexistence only make the imperialists happy." At the World Peace Council session in Stockholm in December 1961, the same Liu Ning-yi made himself more plain: "Those who think agreement can be reached with the imperialists and peaceful coexistence ensured only delude themselves." It is not difficult to notice that one and the same importunate and gloomy refrain that "war cannot be averted" is repeated in all these statements.

The opposition of the Chinese leaders to the policy of peaceful coexistence is closely tied up with their stand on the question of disarmament, on international negotiations between the Socialist countries and the Western powers. They regard disarmament as an "illusion, an unrealisable slogan" that can only mislead the peoples. For example, speaking at the Peking session of the General Council of the World Federation of Trade Unions in 1960 Liu Chang-sheng, member of the C.C., C.P.C., declared: "Some people think that the disarmament proposal can be carried into effect while imperialism exists. That is an illusion that has nothing to do with reality ... A world without wars and without arms is possible only in an epoch when socialism triumphs throughout the world."

It is not hard to see in these statements the desire of the Chinese leaders to distort the clear stand of the C.P.S.U. and of all the Marxist-Leninist parties and at the same time to undermine the policy of disarmament which is an important condition in the struggle for the prevention of a new world war and for a relaxation of international tensions.

War, Peace, and Revolution

It is absurd to assert that our Party entertains any illusions concerning the military policy of the imperialist powers and their readiness to agree to general and complete disarmament. As long as imperialism exists, the reactionary forces will clutch at armaments as a last resort to retain their domination, and will use these armaments in wars, if they manage to unleash them. All this is quite obvious.

Does this, however, mean that the Communists should drop the struggle for disarmament and admit the inevitability of the arms race and of a new world war? No, such a passive stand would be contradictory to the entire revolutionary spirit of our teaching and to the vital interests of the peoples.

We are convinced that the revolutionary struggle of the working people, the general democratic upsurge, the growing might of socialism and the resolute actions of all the peace-loving forces can and should force the imperialists to comply, contrary to their desire, with the peoples' demands for disarmament. We are not fatalists, we believe in the tremendous capacities of the popular masses. Already 70 years ago Frederick Engels called upon the Communists to fight for disarmament, and this at a time when capitalism held undivided sway in the world.

"It is 25 years already that all Europe has been arming on an unprecedented scale. Each great power endeavours to outstrip the other in military might and preparedness for war. Germany, France and Russia do their utmost to surpass one another," wrote Engels in a series of articles entitled "Can Europe Disarm?" "Is it not foolish to talk of disarmament under such circumstances?" he asked, and replied: "I maintain: *disarmament, and hence a guarantee for peace, is possible*" (*Works*, ed. 2, vol. XXII, p. 387, Russ. ed.).

That is how Engels put the question! Already in those days he saw the vast social forces rising against war. How, then, can one speak of disarmament as of an "unrealisable illusion" today when all progressive mankind is coming out for disarmament and when the forces of peace have the mighty support of the Socialist countries?

The slogan "A World Without Arms, A World Without Wars" — is for the Communist parties a mighty means of uniting and mobilising the popular masses for an active struggle against the inveterate militarist imperialist circles. This slogan is clear to every man, regardless of his political convictions. Disarmament means ending the arms race and, consequently, reducing the tax burden. It conforms to the vital interests of the broadest sections of the population. Not only the Communists, but also many other social forces actively support and propagate this slogan. Then why should we, Communists, discard it? Is it not clear that rejecting this slogan could only weaken the influence of the Communists among the masses, and that this would play into the hands of the reactionary forces.

Are the Chinese leaders so naive as not to realise where their strange logic leads them and how grave a responsibility they are assuming before the peoples of the world by advancing such reckless theses fraught with the direst consequences?

The Chinese leaders not only take a negative stand on such vitally important questions of international policy as disarmament, termination of nuclear weapon tests and relaxation of international tension, but also try to paralyse the efforts of the Soviet Union and other Socialist countries fighting against the threat of world war.

The facts show that time and again the C.P.R. Government has acted in the world arena as a force opposing the peaceful foreign policy of the Socialist countries and disorganising the common antiwar front, that time and again when the world was faced with an acute situation in which unity of action among the Socialist countries and all peace-loving forces was particularly imperative, the Chinese leaders became active. But against whom? Against the Soviet Union and other Socialist countries seeking a relaxation of tension. Moreover, it has been noted that Peking could not conceal its chagrin and annoyance every time the situation was normalised and a military conflict avoided. That was the case, for example, during the Caribbean crisis. The C.P.C. leadership did nothing to help avert a world war and effectively support revolutionary Cuba. They did nothing to support the defensive measures of the Warsaw Treaty powers, adopted to meet possible imperialist aggression, and said nothing about China siding with the Socialist countries in the event of a United States attack against Cuba. It was quite evident that at a time when the Soviet Union was prepared to defend the Cuban revolution with all the means at its disposal, the Chinese leaders strove to benefit from the crisis in the Caribbean region. . . .

Not only Marxists-Leninists but also all friends of socialism and peace noted with alarm that the "bellicose" outpourings from Peking practically border on direct justification and even lauding of war as a means of settling social conflicts.

Hysterically attacking the Moscow partial test ban treaty of July 31, 1963, and thereby finding themselves aligned with the most aggressive circles of imperialism, the Chinese leaders still further exposed themselves as opponents of the policy of peace and peaceful coexistence of states with different social systems. The enemies rejoiced over their actions and friends could not but condemn them.

The Chinese leaders realized that they had gone too far and in order to extricate themselves from this situation they made a complete volte-face in their propaganda. Lately a stream of "peace-loving" statements has suddenly gushed from Peking, while representatives of the Chinese government are hastening to sign documents concerning the struggle for peace and fidelity to the policy of peaceful coexistence. Such was the tenor of many of the statements made by Chou En-lai during his tour in Africa and Asia.

"World war cannot be averted," they were saying plainly in Peking only yesterday. Today they are trying to persuade people to believe that the thesis that war can be averted was put forward by none other than the leaders of the C.P.C. Yesterday they abused peaceful coexistence, today they are posing as practically its only and most zealous supporters. Yesterday they declared that disarmament was a deception of the peoples, today they sign statements in which they undertake to work for disarmament.

This volte-face could only be welcomed if there were signs that the C.P.C. leadership really realizes its mistakes and is taking a correct stand. Unfortunately everything points to the fact that the aims and objectives of the Chinese leaders have not changed. Their "love of peace" is nothing but a screen masking their real intentions, which have received a rebuff and been censured by world public opinion. One cannot fail to see that the "love of peace" now emanating from Peking is in glaring contrast to the actual deeds, to the concrete policy of the Government of the C.P.R.

The obviously adventurist position of the C.P.C. leaders makes itself felt in their attitude to the question of nuclear weapons.

It is well known that the C.P.C. leaders insistently sought to obtain the atomic bomb from the Soviet Union. They expressed their deep mortification when our country did not give them samples of nuclear weapons.

The C.C., C.P.S.U. and the Soviet Government have already explained why we consider it inexpedient to help China produce nuclear weapons. The inevitable reaction to this would be the nuclear arming of powers of the imperialist camp, in particular, West Germany and Japan. Having a higher level of economic, scientific and technological development they could undoubtedly produce more bombs than China and build up a nuclear potential much faster. It should be borne in mind that revanchist aspirations are particularly strong in these countries. These are the countries which in the past were the main hotbeds of military threats and militarism.

The Soviet Union's atomic weapon is a reliable guarantee of the defence not only of our country but also of the entire Socialist camp, including China. The leaders of the C.P.C. are well aware of this fact. Nonetheless, they want to acquire the nuclear weapon at all costs. Very indicative in this respect is the interview given to Japanese journalists in October 1963 by Chen Yi, member of the Politbureau of the C.C., C.P.C., and Deputy Premier of the C.P.R. Saying that China would create her own nuclear weapon whatever the price, he declared, as was reported in the Japanese press, that possibly it would take China several years and perhaps even longer than that to begin the mass production of the bomb. But China, he said, would produce the most modern weapon even if it would cost them their last shirt. And several days later a statement by a Chinese government spokesman, published in *Jen-min jih-pao,* stated that China would adhere to this line "even if the Chinese people will not be able to create the atom bomb in a hundred years . . . ."

It thus turns out that possession of the atom bomb, which the Chinese leaders call a "paper tiger," is their cherished goal.

In a fit of anger, the C.P.C. leaders went so far as to say that the threat of a nuclear war comes not from imperialism but from the "modern revisionists," unambiguously hinting at the Soviet Union and other Socialist countries. In a speech in Pjongyang on September 18, 1963, Liu Shao-chi, Chairman of the C.P.R., stated: "Imperialism did not use the nuclear weapon everywhere and at will and would not dare to do so." He followed this up with the wild assertion that "in agreement with the imperialists" the Soviet Union "has monopolised the nuclear weapon" and organises "nuclear blackmail with regard to the peoples of the Socialist countries and the revolutionary peoples of the whole world." If the "modern revisionists," he pathetically exclaimed, "go so far as to use the nuclear weapon first and will thereby provoke a nuclear world war, they will earn the stern condemnation of the peoples of the whole world."

What touching concern Liu Shao-chi shows to lull suspicion that the imperialists have any intention of unleashing a nuclear war. After this, is it not hypocrisy on the part of the C.P.C. leadership to call for an "adherence to the class approach," for "distinguishing friend from foe," for a struggle against United States imperialism as the chief enemy of peace? In this connection one cannot help but recall the treacherous rule of bourgeois diplomacy, which Palmerston expounded as "We have neither eternal allies nor eternal friends. Only our interests are eternal." All this shows how little significance the Chinese leaders attach to their own statements concerning the aggressive nature of imperialism and their uncompromising attitude to class enemies.

The following example of the discrepancy between what the Chinese leaders say and do must also be pointed out. This concerns the relations between the Socialist countries and the countries of the capitalist world. Here the Chinese leaders have two yardsticks—one for appraising the policy of the U.S.S.R. and other Socialist countries and the other for assessing China's foreign policy. Everyone knows the sharply negative reaction of the Chinese leaders to the efforts the Soviet Union and other Socialist countries are making to normalise and improve economic and other relations with the capitalist countries, including the United States of America. Why, one involuntarily asks, does any normalisation of relations between the U.S.S.R. and the

U.S.A., the two great nuclear powers on whose efforts a relaxation of international tension largely depends, evoke such opposition from the Chinese government? With a persistence worthy of better application, the Chinese leaders are doing their utmost to hinder an improvement of United States-Soviet relations, portraying it as a "conspiracy with the imperialists." At the same time the C.P.R. Government is making feverish efforts to establish better relations with Britain, France, Japan, West Germany and Italy. All the indications are that they would not be averse to an improvement in relations with the U.S.A. if the opportunity presented itself.

Never before has Peking received so many businessmen, political leaders and statesmen from the capitalist countries as now. C.P.R. representatives have talks with them and sign agreements on trade, credits, scientific and technical aid and even on political issues.

Do we want to reproach the C.P.C. leaders for this activity? Of course not. It is a normal and intrinsic element of the policy of peaceful coexistence. All Socialist countries ultimately have to have contacts with people from the bourgeois states and not only with friends but also with representatives of the ruling imperialist circles. But the thing is that the Chinese leaders consider that when they themselves develop such activity it is an expression of the policy of real "revolutionaries," but when other Socialist states do the same thing it is "revisionism" and "treachery."

But the attempts to slander our peace-loving foreign policy will inevitably collapse. Our Party shall continue to wage a struggle to avert a world thermonuclear war, secure lasting world peace and steadfastly pursue the Leninist policy of peaceful coexistence between countries with different social systems. Our peaceful policy, Lenin said, is approved by the overwhelming majority of the world's population. Peace helps to strengthen socialism. The working people of all countries, of all continents desire peace. The Communist Party of the Soviet Union has won deserved glory as the banner-bearer of peace and shall always remain faithful to this banner.

The course of events has shown that the programme of struggle for peace, democracy, national independence and socialism drawn up by the Moscow Meetings is the programme which closely links up the immediate and ultimate goals of the working class and ensures the advance of the world revolution.

At the same time, far from facilitating the development of the world revolutionary process, the theoretical platform and, chiefly, the practical activity of the C.P.C. leadership create additional difficulties for the realisation of the age-old aspirations of the peoples, who are hungering for peace and social progress.

It is absurd to oppose the struggle for peace, for the peaceful coexistence of countries with different social systems, to the revolutionary class struggle of the working class of the capitalist countries and the national liberation struggle of the peoples. For Marxists-Leninists there neither is nor can there be a dilemma of whether to wage a struggle for peace or a revolutionary struggle. The two are inter-related and are, in the final analysis, spearheaded against imperialism. The struggle for peace is one of the main forms of the struggle of the peoples against imperialism, against the new wars being prepared by it, against the aggressive acts of the imperialists in the colonial countries, against the military bases of the imperialists on the territory of other countries, against the arms race, and so on. Surely this struggle expresses the vital interests of the working class and all working people.

We know that peace is a true ally of socialism. The situation created by peaceful coexistence also favourably influences the development of the national liberation movement and the revolutionary struggle of the working class in the capitalist countries.

The working class movement has made particularly great headway in recent years. Experience shows that in many countries the struggle of the working class for democratic and social rights is closely intertwined with the struggle for peace and against the forces of militarism. In the struggle against militarism a political complexion is imparted even to the economic actions of the working class. The efforts of the working class and all working people to avert the threat of another world war help to educate the peoples in a spirit of international solidarity because under present-day conditions the struggle for peace is, as never before, essentially an international struggle.

What, for example, does it mean to work for peace in a country like the Federal Republic of Germany? It means, first and foremost, active opposition to the big monopolies, which are hatching ideas of revenge, opposition to their offensive against the vital rights and political freedoms of the working people. By participating in this struggle, the revolutionary working class, far from "dissolving" in the mass democratic movement, as the Chinese leaders maintain, gets a schooling in revolutionary organisation and discipline, unites its ranks and wins greater influence among the masses.

Naturally, being a general democratic movement the struggle for peace neither sets itself nor can set itself the task of effecting Socialist changes. This, incidentally, is what the C.P.C. leaders, who are trying to foist on the peace movement tasks alien to it, fail to understand. But the struggle for peace is furthering the cause of socialism inasmuch as it is waged against imperialism, the source of the war threat, inasmuch as it is helping the masses better to understand what are their vital interests.

The repudiation of this extremely close bond between the struggle for peace and the struggle for socialism reveals in effect the utter lack of confidence of the C.P.C. leaders in the popular masses, in their ability to take organised action in the class struggle. The essence of the C.P.C. leadership's present concepts regarding revolution lies in rejection of the Leninist precept that the Socialist revolution is the result of the mass struggle, in relying solely on armed uprisings everywhere and in all cases, without taking into account the sentiments of the masses, their preparedness for revolution, without taking into account the internal and external situation.

The immense harm of this line lies in the fact that it rejects painstaking and patient work with the masses and reliance on the maturing of the objective and subjective conditions for a Socialist revolution in favour of revolutionary phrase-mongering, or, what is still worse, in favour of adventurist actions by a handful of men who have no ties with the people. What has this kind of action in common with Marxism-Leninism? Is this not the propagation of Blanquist and Trotskyite ideas that have been rejected long ago?

War, Peace, and Revolution

No matter what the C.P.C. leaders say to the contrary, one of the pivotal points of the polemics in the Communist movement is the problem of "the ways of carrying out the revolution" and not the dilemma of "whether to carry or not to carry on the revolution." If the Communist parties pin all their hopes solely on an armed struggle without taking into consideration whether the masses are prepared to support such a struggle this will inevitably lead only to bitter failures.

In other words, the Chinese leaders have forgotten one of the prime propositions of Marxist-Leninist theory, namely that the revolution cannot be accelerated or made to order, that it cannot be given a push from without. "Some people," Lenin said, "think that revolution in a foreign country can be made to order, by agreement. People who think so are either madmen or provocateurs" (*Collected Works*, vol. XXVII, p. 441, Russ. ed.). Revolution is made by the masses headed by the proletariat and its revolutionary vanguard. Naturally, this does not in any way imply that Marxists-Leninists must passively wait for a favourable situation to arise. The experience of the C.P.S.U. shows that even a relatively small, steeled party that has the support of the proletariat and the advanced section of the peasantry can head the revolution and lead the people. But for this, as Lenin repeatedly emphasised, there must be a revolutionary situation in which the "upper strata" are no longer able to rule and the "lower strata" no longer want to live the old way.

Realistically assessing the present situation, the fraternal parties allow for the possibility of transition from capitalism to socialism either by peaceful or nonpeaceful means.

However, no matter how the transition from capitalism to socialism is achieved, it is possible only through a Socialist revolution, through a dictatorship of the proletariat in its various forms. In each given country the actual possibility for a peaceful or nonpeaceful transition to socialism is determined by concrete historical conditions. The fraternal parties in the capitalist countries are invariably guided by Lenin's proposition that the working class must master all forms and means of revolutionary struggle without exception, that it must be ready to pass from one form of struggle to another in the quickest and most unexpected manner and to utilise it in conformity with the concrete situation. But the Chinese leaders oppose this creative approach to questions of tactics by the fraternal parties and attempt to instruct them from Peking on how and when to carry out a revolution in their countries. Quite understandably these "instructions" are meeting with a unanimous rebuff from Marxists-Leninists.

Our Party has always unswervingly adhered to positions of proletarian internationalism. No slander and no foul fabrications can smear the banner of proletarian internationalism which is sacred to us. Our Party will continue tirelessly to strengthen its solidarity with the working class, with the working masses of the capitalist countries who are struggling to destroy the capitalist system and to reshape society on Socialist lines. This road was charted for us by Lenin and we shall steadfastly follow it. . . .

WALTER C. CLEMENS, JR.

•

PEKING, MOSCOW, AND THE WEST
IN A WARLESS WORLD

Under what conditions might one or both giants of the Communist world consider that its interests could be best promoted in a "warless world"? To begin we shall examine the ideological pronouncements by Peking and Moscow on this point, noticing that China justifies its position by reference mainly to the pre-1917 works of Lenin, while the Soviet leadership quotes Lenin at a later stage in his political outlook. Second we shall endeavor to lift the ideological veil to grasp the key factors of military, political, and economic interest conditioning Soviet and Chinese views on collaboration and conflict with the West. This analysis will set the stage for consideration in a subsequent chapter of the implications for United States policy, assuming the West wished to encourage at least one of the colossi of international communism toward a deeper commitment to collaboration in working out a strategy of peace.

I. CONFLICTING IDEOLOGIES

Peking's attitude toward disarmament was trenchantly stated three years before the open rift accompanying the signing of the "Moscow Treaty" on nuclear testing in July 1963. The editors of *China Youth,* allegedly in response to a reader's query, declared in 1960:

> The so-called "warless world"—if it is not a childish fantasy—can only be a world where there is no imperialism . . . where there is no class. To realize this ideal, the human race must necessarily undergo a long-term, sinuous, complicated and violent struggle to eliminate

imperialism and class. At a time when the imperialists not only still exist but are even armed to the teeth, any thought that there is a short cut to realizing a "warless world" will only disarm the people's vigilance against the imperialists. . . .[1]

This view, which Peking continues to affirm, corresponds directly with the attitude which Lenin expressed toward disarmament prior to the Bolshevik revolution. Thus, during Russia's 1905 revolution he warned:

> Let the hypocritical or sentimental bourgeoisie dream about disarmament. While there is still oppression and exploitation on earth, we must strive not for disarmament, but for universal, popular armament. Only it can entirely assure freedom. Only it can completely overthrow reaction.[2]

And just a year before the Bolshevik *coup d'état* Lenin reaffirmed that "Only *after* the proletariat has disarmed the bourgeoisie will it be able, without betraying its world-historical mission, to throw all armaments on the scrap heap; the proletariat will undoubtedly do this, but only *after this condition has been fulfilled, and under no circumstances before then.*"[3]

The years from 1917 to 1920, however, saw Lenin change his views toward the expediency of arms control and disarmament, just as he compromised a number of radical measures in the Communist program in the face of the realization that, although revolution was not immediately to sweep Europe, it could nevertheless survive for the moment in Russia. Soviet

---

[1]*China Youth,* No. 4, February 16, 1960, in translation in *Red World in Tulmult,* compiled and edited by Devere E. Pentony, San Francisco: Chandler, 1962, pp. 80-81. Lenin's pre-1917 works have been repeatedly cited in Chinese statements since 1960, most notably in the Chinese "Open Letter" of June 14, 1963, given in *Peking Review,* vol. VI, No. 25, June 21, 1963, 6-22, and in "Two Different Lines on the Question of War and Peace—Comment on the Soviet Open Letter," November 18, 1963, in the *Peking Review,* vol. VI, No. 47, November 27, 1963, 6-16.

[2]V. I. Lenin, *Sochineniia,* ed. 2, 30 vols., Moscow: 1926-1932, vol. VIII, pp. 395-397. For additional discussion of Lenin's views, see Walter C. Clemens, Jr., "Lenin on Disarmament," *Slavic Review,* vol. XXIII, No. 3, September 1964, 504-525.

[3]Lenin, *op. cit.,* vol. XIX, pp. 314 *passim* (emphasis in the original).

negotiators from 1917 to 1921 sought what they called "guarantees of peaceful coexistence" in the treaties which Russia signed with her neighbors, but which today might be called arms control measures—for example, demilitarized frontier zones.[4] By 1922 the Soviet Government no longer opposed the principle of disarmament negotiations, but espoused it in order to mount mass propaganda to paralyze the capitalist governments of the West. Lenin even came to argue that Soviet diplomacy should advocate the "broadest pacifist program" in order to strengthen the liberal elements in the Western ruling classes. Lenin advised in 1922 that Soviet diplomacy should announce its desire not only for trade but for agreement with the liberal wing of the bourgeoisie, "as one of the few chances for the peaceful evolution of capitalism to a new structure," a development which Communists could have "little faith in" but which it was their duty to test.[5]

Although Lenin's advocacy of disarmament negotiations aimed primarily at dividing the Western countries internally and among themselves, his wife Krupskaia recounts that in 1918 and again in 1920-1921 the Soviet leader talked earnestly with her about the possibility of an end to all war as a result of the increasing destructiveness of military technology.[6]

The evolution in Lenin's views toward disarmament means that "doctrinal" foundations may be quoted by both the supporters as well as the opponents of moves toward arms control and disarmament. To rebut Chinese attacks on the Soviet peaceful coexistence line the Khrushchev government even published previously unpublished correspondence between Lenin and his Foreign Minister Chicherin which laid the basis for the Soviet campaign for disarmament begun in 1922 and brought from obscurity the recollections of Lenin's wife.[7]

Under Khrushchev the Soviet Government seemed to go even further than the second stage in Lenin's thought. From

---

[4]Clemens, *loc. cit.*, p. 507.
[5]V. I. Lenin, *Leninskii Sbornyk,* Moscow: 1959, vol. XXXVI, pp. 451-454; see also documents published for the first time in *Pravda,* April 12 and 22, 1964.
[6]N. S. Krupskaia, *O Lenine: Sbornyk statei,* Moscow: 1960, p. 41.
[7]See the materials cited in the preceding two notes.

Walter C. Clemens, Jr.

1955 to 1964 Moscow continued to use disarmament propaganda as a tactic, as Lenin had advised, but went on to seek and actually sign arms control agreements with the capitalist adversary. The Soviet Government, Khrushchev often declared, was "sincere" in seeking disarmament,[8] and proved this to some extent by observing a moratorium on nuclear testing from 1958 to 1961, by signing the Antarctica treaty in 1959, by the three agreements of 1963 — the hot line, test ban, and ban on bombs in orbit — and by the pledge in 1964 to reduce the production of fissionable materials.

These moves, especially the test ban, were regarded by Peking as a Soviet-United States plot to keep China from obtaining nuclear weapons. Chinese sources even alleged that Moscow informed Peking in August 1962 that it intended to enter an agreement proposed by Secretary of State Rusk to prevent the transfer of nuclear weapons and know-how to non-nuclear powers.[9]

Moscow's response to the Chinese attacks was to assert in effect that what Lenin foresaw in 1918-1921 in his talks with Krupskaia had become a reality: the nuclear bomb, the Soviets now said, "does not adhere to the class principle — it destroys everybody within the range of its devastating force."[10] Peaceful coexistence with capitalism was therefore dictated by "life itself."

II. Conflicting Interests

Behind these ideological pronouncements lay diverse strategic, political, and economic interests which constitute the driving forces and limitations upon Soviet and Chinese interests in arms control and disarmament. The basic differences between the Soviet and Chinese outlooks arise from the fact that Russia has become a "have" nation — militarily, politically, economically, and psychologically — while China remains a "have-not" in al-

[8]See for example, his speech of January 6, 1961, in *Kommunist,* No. 1, January 1961, 23-24, rendered however in a somewhat "soft" translation in *World Marxist Review,* January 1961.

[9]See the Chinese statement in the *Peking Review,* vol. VI, No. 33, August 16, 1963, 7-15, especially part XI. See also Walter C Clemens, Jr. "The Sino-Soviet Dispute — Dogma and Dialectics on Disarmament," *International Affairs* (London), vol. XLI, No. 2, April 1965, 204-222.

[10]Soviet "Open Letter" of July 14, 1963, document in William E. Griffith, *The Sino-Soviet Rift,* Cambridge, Mass.: The M.I.T. Press, 1964, p. 299.

most every sense but demographic. The gap between the perception of "what is" and "what ought to be" in the Soviet outlook is much narrower than it is for the Chinese.[11] This stark reality means that the Soviet regime has a much greater stake in preserving the present order than China, while Peking has more reason to pursue revolutionary policies involving high risks to bring about the great changes needed to satisfy its interests.

The point is not that the present or any future Soviet Government is absolutely committed to a policy of nonviolence and progress toward a disarmed world, but that its interest in stabilizing the international environment is much greater than Peking's—if less than Washington's. If an opportunity emerged for Moscow to seek and obtain a commanding power position vis-à-vis the West, the Kremlin might well engage in high-risk policies to obtain such a goal, as it did in the Caribbean in 1962. But the present constellation of internal and external factors facing the Kremlin is conducive to a conservative and gradualist policy, whereas Peking is impelled more toward a radical and revolutionary course. Future changes in the Soviet leadership or the international situation could alter the Kremlin's perception of opportunities and constraints, but Khrushchev's successors seem to respond much as he did to the strategic, political, and economic realities of the mid-1960's. An increasingly pragmatic world view in the Soviet elite seems likely to continue this orientation.

A. STRATEGIC FACTORS

Moscow's overriding concern, at least since Stalin's demise, has been to avoid an all-out war with the West that might obliterate in moments the political and economic accomplishments of the Soviet state. This concern therefore leads to a policy of caution toward limited military encounters that could rapidly escalate into great power confrontations. Although we should not take at face value Mao Tse-tung's ostensible faith that a brave new world would arise from the ashes of a nuclear war, the Chinese

[11]For development of this idea, see Robert C. North, "Soviet and Chinese Goal Values: A Study of Communism as a Behavior System," in *Unity and Contradiction: Major Aspects of Sino-Soviet Relations,* Kurt London (ed.), New York: Praeger, 1962, pp. 62-63.

leadership does appear less anxious to prevent such a war than Moscow. And while Peking's policy toward the Nationalist-held islands in the Formosan Strait has shown a healthy respect for the United States Seventh Fleet, the Chinese Government seems much less inhibited than Moscow about sparking limited wars and wars of "national liberation." The Kremlin and Peking, in short, seem to have differed over both the likelihood and the consequences of escalation.[12]

Soviet concern to damp down conflicts that could lead to war has been frequently reflected in Kremlin diplomacy. Moscow has championed the idea of a nonaggression pact between NATO and the Warsaw Pact and Khrushchev proposed on December 31, 1963, a renunciation by all states of the use of force in settling territorial disputes. Attempting to keep his kasha and eat it at the same time, however, Khrushchev qualified his proposal to renounce force by the reservation that it should not keep nations from moving toward national independence or should not apply to the ousting of foreign occupation, e.g., from Taiwan.[13] The immediate aim of such proposals has been to improve Moscow's image and to undermine the political cohesion of NATO, but subsidiary objectives have probably included a desire to inhibit the chances of German "revanchism" and of any future Chinese moves to reclaim territory in Central Asia or Siberia ceded to Tsarist Russia by the Chinese empire. Moscow's concern over its eastern front has no doubt deepened as a consequence of the intermittent clashes along the Sino-Soviet frontier since 1958 and of China's moves since 1959 to gratify her revisionist claims against India. Khrushchev's December 31, 1963, proposals may also have aimed at inhibiting violence among the emerging nations of the third world. This supposition was reinforced by a Soviet proposal in July 1964 for the establishment of a United Nations peacekeeping force com-

[12]These differences were strikingly asserted in the Chinese and Soviet letters of June 14 and July 14, 1963, cited above, and in the subsequent Chinese and Soviet documents reproduced in this book. For additional documentation, see Harry Gelman, "Russia, China, and the Underdeveloped Areas," *Annals of American Academy of Political and Social Science,* September 1963, pp. 130-142.

[13]Text in *New Times* (Moscow) No. 2, January 1964, see p. 36 (Russian edition).

posed of contingents from nonpermanent members of the Security Council but subject to the Security Council. Such a force, obviously, could be of use only against smaller states.[14]

Because the Soviet Union enjoys a credible deterrent to inhibit any foreign aggressor, it can contemplate freezing the existing military balance far more readily than Peking. While the United States has a tremendous lead over Russia in numbers of long-range delivery systems, Moscow's ICBMs are tipped with much larger warheads than United States missiles and huge numbers of Soviet MRBMs continue to hold Europe hostage against Washington. A quick-fix such as could be achieved by emplacing Soviet MRBMs in Cuba may again tempt Moscow, but economic and other factors militate against any present attempt to outproduce the United States in the arms race. Soviet strategic interests might well be served by the variant of general and complete disarmament which Moscow has advocated since September 21, 1962. The Soviet Government accepted in 1962 and expanded in 1963 the principle that the two superpowers should retain a "nuclear umbrella" until the process of general and complete disarmament (GCD) had been completed. While Soviet diplomats have been vague about the details of this proposal, they seem to have in mind a force of about 100 missiles to be retained by Moscow and Washington. United States forces would thus be reduced by a much greater factor than Soviet, while nuclear-rocket forces for other states (such as China) would be prohibited or severely limited.[15]

Short of achieving such a protected position in a generally disarmed world, the Soviet Government has endeavored to inhibit the spread of nuclear weapons to China and other countries by advocacy of a nuclear test ban, of nuclear free

[14]*The New York Times,* July 5, 1964, section IV, p. 9; for United States and British comment, see *ibid.,* July 8, August 7, and August 30, 1964.

[15]A revised version of the March 1962 Soviet draft incorporating this and other modifications was circulated by the United Nations Secretariat on September 24, 1962, as U.N. Doc. A/C.1/867. Whereas the September 1962 proposal would have extended a nuclear umbrella for the United States and Soviet Union into the second stage of GCD, Gromyko proposed on September 19, 1963, that the umbrella be retained until the end of the third and final stage. Text, e.g., in *Bulletin of Atomic Scientists,* vol. XIX, No. 9, November 1963, 43.

zones, and — some evidence suggests — by a nonproliferation agreement.[16] Chinese sources state that Moscow specifically refused in 1959 to turn over to China nuclear weapons or technological data necessary for their production.[17] And Peking responded quite coolly to Soviet proposals in 1959 for an atom-free zone in the Far East. The test ban signed in 1963, as we have seen, was termed by Peking a "plot" against Chinese interests.

The Soviet GCD proposals introduced since 1959 have also envisioned drastic cuts in the conventional forces that would compel the withdrawal of United States forces from Europe and neutralize the manpower advantages of states like China vis-à-vis the nuclear umbrella to be retained by Moscow. Moscow's proposals specify that military training of civilians should be prohibited as well, a measure aimed perhaps in part at destroying China's militia system rooted in the farm and factory.

Not surprisingly the Chinese response to such Soviet proposals has been quite negative. Peking refuses any measure that would foreclose its hopes of overcoming present strategic inferiority. General and complete disarmament that eliminated the nuclear advantages of other states would be quite acceptable, Chinese sources have stated, but not a test ban or nonproliferation agreement designed to freeze the strategic balance to China's disfavor.[18] Soviet efforts to keep Britain from testing hydrogen bombs in 1956 and France from testing atomic weapons in 1960 were greeted with a similar response by London and Paris.[19] Like the de Gaulle government, Peking refused to sign the test ban treaty in 1963 and proceeded in 1964 to join the nuclear club with tests that showed great technological sophistication and promised great political repercussions. Power, as Mao Tse-tung said, grows out of the barrel of a gun — especially, he could add, an atomic cannon.

[16]See above, note 9.

[17]*Peking Review,* vol. VI, No. 33, August 16, 1963, pp. 7-15, part XI.

[18]This position was affirmed by Peking not only after the 1963 "Moscow Treaty," but also after China entered the atomic club in 1964. See *Peking Review,* vol. VI, No. 31, August 2, 1963, 7-8 and *ibid.,* vol. VII No. 43, October 23, 1964, 5.

[19]Ciro Elliot Zoppo, "The Test Ban: A Study in Arms Control Negotiation," unpublished Ph.D. dissertation, Columbia University, 1963, pp. 429, 446, 449.

B. POLITICAL FACTORS

The divergent political requirements of the Soviet and Chinese governments also account for their conflicting views on the utility of moving toward accommodation with the West. For China today as for Stalin's Russia the image of a hostile external foe — Western imperialism — serves as a justification for imposing economic sacrifice and dictatorial controls upon the population. The Soviet Government under Khrushchev, in contrast, staked the success of its foreign policy upon the possibility and desirability of coming to terms with moderate groups in the West. Khrushchev promised the Soviet people peace as well as prosperity, while Mao Tse-tung has called for a "struggle" against imperialism and for self-abnegation in Communist labor. The Soviet regime has seen that limited and gradually increasing amounts of contact with "bourgeois" culture is not disastrous to political stability but serves perhaps as a necessary release for mounting internal pressure. The Chinese Government however is much more xenophobic when dealing with Westerners or, for that matter, with Soviets. Internal political restraints in China, therefore, much more than in the Soviet Union, militate against relaxation of East-West tensions and steps toward arms control.

Similarly, China's external political interests are much more opposed to détente with the West than is the case for the Soviet Union. Moscow seems to value the preservation of security and peace over revolutionary considerations that might be undermined by accommodation with the adversary. Naturally the Soviet regime wants to retain its influence in Eastern Europe, but it appears since 1959 to have come close to conceding the impossibility of keeping Asian communism under Soviet direction. Further, Moscow seems since 1961 to have grown quite pessimistic about the possibility of reaping any great rewards by influencing the nonaligned nations toward Soviet positions.

The Soviet Government has opted, as it were, to put priority on maintenance of security on its western front, but it has continued to do what it can to promote its interests on the eastern and southern fronts. To this end Moscow has endeavored to create a virtue out of a necessity — avoidance of war — by arguing, *contra* Peking, that peaceful coexistence is the policy best suited to bring revolution as well as peace and prosperity to the third world. It is not a betrayal of revolutionary interests, as Peking says, but the best and most necessary vehicle for their realization.

Moscow and Peking slant their propaganda line to the emerging nations in different terms. China argues that the main revolutionary front lies in the struggle of the oppressed against the imperialist nations. Being a have-not nation in most senses of the term, China aspires to lead this struggle, appealing to accumulated anti-white and anti-imperialist sentiments and identifying them with Russia. The Soviet Union, in contrast, argues that the main "contradiction" in present-day politics is between the Socialist camp (led by Moscow) and the capitalist. The outcome of this conflict will be settled by the growing economic might of socialism, a victory that will automatically redound to the political and economic benefit of the emerging nations.[20]

C. ECONOMIC FACTORS

At the basis of Moscow's general interest in upholding the existing order is the fact that the Soviet Union has already become an industrialized power on the threshold of an age of relative consumer abundance. Soviet economic might has built the minimum nuclear deterrent that guarantees Russian security. This economic power has finally reached the stage where, after a half-decade of sacrifice, the foundations have been laid for a rapid march into relatively affluent "goulash" communism. The ability of the Soviet economy to perform this march, however, depends in an absolute sense on the maintenance of peace, and the rate of progress hinges in part on a limitation and reduction of allocations to defense. All these considerations heighten the Soviet interest in the reduction of East-West tensions and a downturn in the arms race.

There are sound reasons to argue that the economic development of the Soviet Union is converging in a pattern similar to

[20]These divergencies are set out in the Chinese and Soviet statements of June 14 and July 14, 1963, and are analyzed in Robert A. Scalapino, "The Sino-Soviet Conflict in Perspective," *Annals of American Academy of Political and Social Science,* January 1964, pp. 7-11.

the path taken in the West. If so, this would undercut at least one cause for international tension—dogmatic assertions on both sides that coexistence between "opposite" systems cannot endure. Both capitalism and communism may be seen as attempts at mastering the challenges of the industrial revolution. As these challenges are mastered, the similarities between the two systems may tend to outweigh the differences, and in fact, the differences may diminish. The West comes more to appreciate the need for economic planning and welfare programs—state or private—while Russia and the Eastern European countries recognize increasingly the inefficiency of excessive centralization and suppression of initiative and living standards. This sort of convergence may be expected to enhance the prospects of peace, because the growth of free enterprise and private property in the East should inhibit the totalitarian rule conducive to aggression, while the growth of planning and welfare programs in the West should contribute to stable economic growth and the tempering of egotistic drives.[21]

Red China, by contrast, has a lean and hungry look that portends at the minimum a strong desire for change and probably a willingness to gamble to obtain such change. The Chinese economy is just beginning to industrialize and offers the rapidly growing population little imminent prospect of improved living standards. The mellowing process known as *embourgeoisement* may already have vitiated revolutionary *élan* in Russia but has little base to do the same in China. Despite or because of the Great Leap Forward, China remains a basically agrarian and underdeveloped country with less in common with Russia than Russia has with the West.

While the Soviet Union is relatively developed economically and China still quite backward, both countries share a common interest in reducing the burden of defense expenditures, in

[21]See Cyril A. Zebot, *The Economics of Competitive Coexistence: Convergence Through Growth,* New York: Praeger, 1964, especially pp. 138 ff.; for an argument that parallel evolution rather than political convergence may be expected in the *political* development of the United States and Soviet Union, see Zbigniew Brzezinski and Samuel P. Huntington, *Political Power: USA/USSR,* New York: Viking Press, 1964; for a Soviet attack on the theory of "convergence," see *Kommunist,* No. 13, September 1962, 110-119.

obtaining long-term credits to permit imports from the West, and in collaboration with the West in science and technology. Whether these objective interests can become operative, however, depends on the Soviet and Chinese leaderships' perceptions of the military-political situation. For this reason the West has an opportunity to shape the perceived interest of Peking as well as of Moscow in moving toward a warless world. The opportunity will require a most skillful orientation of the West's military, political, and economic posture toward the Soviet Union and China.

Anatol Rapoport

•

THE NEEDS OF AMERICAN AND SOVIET SCIENCE

In a warless world we would expect more of man's energy to be directed to constructive ends. In particular, science would be cleansed of its guilt of contributing to crimes against humanity. So much is clear. What the constructive functions of a truly humane science would be, however, is not as clear as seems at first thought. Technological magic, emancipation from drudgery, conquest of disease—all of these are always cited as the blessings which science bestows upon us. But once the obvious sources of suffering are removed, is it not possible (an irreverent thought!) that more and more of the same magic might turn man into a dullard, bored to disgust with his effortless, challengeless existence?

As science satisfies man's physical needs, its emancipating spiritual functions ought to be brought more into focus. If science is not to turn man into a slothful sensualist, man must give of himself to science and its ideals as well as take the material gifts which science bestows. In other words, man must not be content to be nurtured by science. He must also administer to the needs of science.

When we speak of the "needs" of science, we personify science. Men have always personified the important factors in their lives: forces of nature, animals, diseases. We do the same. The national state, to give one other example, and science are both important entities in our lives, and accordingly we personify them.

In personifying something, we endow it with our own needs. For example, those who identify with the national state ascribe to this entity the appetite which they themselves probably feel most keenly, namely the appetite for power. Those of us who live with science and identify emotionally with it tend to ascribe to it two vital needs, namely freedom and responsibility.

Are the strivings for power and for freedom compatible? I believe not, because I believe that a commitment to the accumulation of power inhibits a commitment to the enlargement of freedom. A more difficult question is whether the strivings for freedom and for responsibility are compatible. I think the answer to this question is yes. Although freedom and responsibility sometimes seem antithetical, they are actually complementary. Failure to realize this is, in my opinion, at the root of the ideological component of the cold war, which is popularly represented by one side as a struggle between freedom and slavery and by the other as a struggle between social responsibility and greed.

This sort of good-evil dichotomy in the minds of the participants has characterized all major power struggles in history: Christian against Moslem, Catholic against Protestant, nation-state against nation-state. In the present version of the polarized struggle, there would seem to be no prospect but slaughter, if it were not for some restraining influences. One of these restraining factors is, of course, a partial realization even on the part of the power-oriented elite that violence in the nuclear age spells their doom as well as everyone else's. In addition there is another restraining influence, namely the much more important role played by science in modern life. Here I mean not science as it is popularly understood in the sense of magic-bearing gadgetry but the scientific outlook. True, the people committed to this outlook are numerically a pitiful minority. But this fraction is many times larger today than it was a generation or two ago, and their influence is probably greater in relation to their numbers than it has ever been. This international, intercultural, self-critical outlook, which was not able to prevent World War I nor the mass psychosis of Naziism, may now have recruited a critical mass of adherents sufficient to prevent World War III. This view may be unjustifiably optimistic, but it cannot be definitively refuted, and I think it is a wholesome exercise to pursue its consequences.

Needs of American and Soviet Science

THE IDEOLOGICAL GAP

Can the scientific outlook bridge the ideological gap between East and West? Perhaps it can, precisely because the ideological foci of the two worlds are complementary in the same way that the two great needs of science, namely freedom and responsibility, are complementary.

The catchword of Western liberal ideology used most often to marshal support for the cold war struggle is Freedom. In the Communist world, this catchword is also not infrequently used. This word has two separate connotations. One is the everyday obvious connotation, the same in both worlds, namely independence from constraints. The other connotation of freedom is deeper, and it points up a crucial ideological difference between the two worlds.

Let us first look at the everyday meaning of freedom. In the propaganda war between East and West denigration of the others' science has been frequently resorted to. We charge the Communists with having made science a handmaiden of the all-powerful state, subservient to bureaucracy; they charge us with having made science a handmaiden of the exploiting class. There is plentiful evidence to support both charges, and each side has listed an extensive bill of particulars. Each side has also indulged in far-fetched extrapolations from this evidence and has offered counterexamples to refute the extrapolations made by the other side. These charges and countercharges need not concern us. We know that no science is free of social constraint, because science is part of a social fabric which is essentially a network of constraints. We also know that in order to function at all, all science must enjoy some measure of freedom. Little is gained by trying to establish relative degrees of freedom which science enjoys in this or that society, because the measures we propose will be surely influenced by our biases.

We can learn a great deal more about the freedom of science if we turn our attention to the other, deeper aspect of freedom. This is the freedom from inner rather than from externally imposed constraints. When internalized constraints are mentioned, we in the West immediately think of Freud and his influential theory of the unconscious. However, the idea of inner compulsions is as much a Marxist idea as a Freudian one.

Both Freudian psychology and Marxist sociology of knowledge find confirmation in the central idea of the modern theory of cognition, namely that to perceive means to select. Perception is organization of sensory inputs. These must fit into some "scheme" or gestalt, a picture that makes sense as a whole. This, in turn, means that some sensory inputs will be selected from the environment (if they fit) and others will be ignored (if they do not fit). If the latter stem from internal sources they will be suppressed, to use the Freudian term. In Marx's formulation, ethical systems are largely rationalizations of class interests. One need not accept this generalization as a dogma to recognize its validity in a large number of instances. When slavery was a controversial issue in the United States, most people in the North believed that slavery was morally wrong, and Northern preachers quoted the scriptures to prove it; while most white people in the South believed that slavery was morally right, and Southern preachers quoted the scriptures to prove it. It was hardly a coincidence that slave labor was profitable in plantation-type agriculture and unprofitable in industry. The so-called liberal-bourgeois notion of freedom, according to Marx, stems not from Natural Law, as our Founding Fathers thought, but from a rationalization of the freedom of contract, a social arrangement indispensable for the capitalist system of production.

When Soviet philosophers of science, therefore, declare that "bourgeois science is not free," they have in mind this sort of ideological constraint. Because ideological opposition is largely suppressed in the Soviet Union, the proponents of this view, not being subject to the discipline of facing serious criticism, go much further than the evidence warrants. They believe, or profess to believe, that scientific views contrary to the interests of the capitalist class are consciously, systematically, and overtly suppressed in the West. Again we need not accept this simplification in order to recognize the validity of the underlying idea. Even in the absence of systematic, overt ideological constraints, some constraints are nevertheless operating in Western science. They are operating, for example, in the channeling of research funds, in the recruitment of research personnel, in the standards of research competence, etc. Just as the invisible hand of the Market operates in private enterprise economics, so the invisible hand of ideology operates in guiding scientific research.

C. Wright Mills has had a great deal to say about pernicious influences on American sociology, and he supported his devastating critique by much factual material without having to depend on deductions from incontrovertible first principles, as doctrinaire Marxists tend to do. There is thus more than merely rhetorical support for the argument that "bourgeois science is not really free."

The constraints are not confined to the social sciences. The channeling of research funds in the physical sciences has influenced the selection of research areas not necessarily in accordance with the needs of physical science to develop along the lines of greatest promise. The recruitment of personnel into applied physical science (largely concerned with weaponry) is an even more serious problem. The competition for talent is keen and even allowing for interchangeability of problems, military research still drains off scientific manpower, which is lost to basic science or to applied research in nonmilitary areas.

In the behavioral sciences, the situation is even more serious. Here I can only restate the criticisms of Mills: the denigration of science by commercial agencies, who buy research on techniques of manipulating mass behavior solely in the interests of profit and frequently against the interests of the population manipulated; the trivialization of sociology (freewheeling nose counting), serving as an escape mechanism for avoiding important social issues, etc.

It seems, then, that American science can use more freedom, not of the sort associated with the absence of overt constraints, of which we have fortunately very few, but of the other sort, the freedom which is despoiled by social climate. In America, this climate is a result of primarily two factors: (1) the war-oriented economy and (2) the reluctance on the part of too many of our social scientists to subject the dynamics of our society to critical scrutiny, to question its unspoken assumptions.

On this score, Soviet science is even more vulnerable. However, it is by no means true that Soviet science is totally hamstrung by official ideology in all fields. Soviet physics has waged a heroic struggle on the philosophical front (to use an expression dear to Soviet philosophers), not, as these philosophers reiterate ad nauseam, in order to purge theoretical physics of idealistic tendencies but rather in order to harmonize the verbal framework of official ideology with the new physics. On the whole this struggle has been remarkably successful. The flourishing state of Soviet theoretical physics attests to this. To be sure their philosophical interpretations of quantum theories are different from those accepted by most Western physicists and philosophers but their dissent is intellectually defensible. In fact, on this matter it closely resembles the philosophical position of Einstein, who was virtually a minority of one in the West.

In Soviet biology, the situation has been at times much more precarious. For a while it looked as if the Lysenkoist obscurantism would wreck Soviet biology. However, this turned out to be a passing phase, an apparently reversible symptom of the Stalinist psychosis.

The really serious constraints operate in the Soviet Union on social science, as they do in the United States. Throughout the Stalinist era, there was no such thing as an empirical investigation conducted with a view of supporting or refuting a hypothesis concerning social structure, social behavior, or social evolution. This is still very largely true. What was called social science is still taught from textbooks like a catechism. The social structure of non-Socialist societies is described in terms of Marxist clichés. The class struggle as the prime mover of all social behavior is still a revealed truth, exactly as is the case with the Oedipal situation among the doctrinaire Freudians. Social evolution is declared to follow a universal law of development in line with the speculative anthropology of a century ago. To a large extent the intellectual framework which circumscribes social thought in the Soviet Union is conducive to a continuing sterility at least of social theory. Whatever progressive features of social thought one encounters, these stem rather from social engineering, for which centralized control provides extremely favorable conditions. One cannot help wondering what tremendous potentialities of progressive social thought would be released in the Soviet Union if the opportunities for social engineering were coupled with a genuine emancipation from the doctrinaire framework.

Needs of American and Soviet Science

To summarize, the lack of freedom in any scientific endeavor in our day (whether in the West or in the East) is traceable not so much to overt constraints, such as the delineation of taboo areas, suppression of publication, etc. (although this also happens), as to covert constraints, stemming from the intellectual climate itself. This idea was brought out forcibly by Marx, who pointed out the role of ideology in directing the very process of cognition. Ironically this factor is the most important in the Soviet Union, where the revolution is supposed to have emancipated the scientist from such constraints. I would venture to predict that a major breakthrough will occur in Soviet social science as soon as they begin to apply the Marxist ideas of the sociology of knowledge to their own society. And we, too, could benefit much from such an analysis.

RESPONSIBILITY

We turn to the other necessary ingredient of the soil on which science thrives, namely responsibility. With respect to this, the situation in the United States and in the Soviet Union is reversed. Whereas with us freedom of scientific inquiry is an accepted article of faith (whatever be the extent of its realization) and is a touchy subject in the Soviet Union, the role of science as a "servant of humanity" is axiomatic in the Soviet Union (whatever the extent of its realization) and a controversial subject with us. This is not to say that science does not serve evil purposes in the Soviet Union. The fraction of Soviet scientific effort which is channeled into military research is probably comparable with ours. But I am quite sure that the Soviet scientist feels compelled to rationalize as socially necessary his contributions to potential mass murder. With us, on the other hand, the social responsibility of the scientist is the touchy subject. A minority asserts this responsibility unequivocally. For the most part, however, the view prevails among American scientists that scientific objectivity necessitates the separation of facts and values and that the pursuit of all knowledge is a priori equally justifiable. It is this absolute relativism or moral nihilism which usually underlies the American scientist's participation in research on genocidal weapons and strategies or in research on manipulation of the mass psyche for commerical exploitation.

149

I believe that dualism in thinking about science and ethics is an unjustified extrapolation of the separation of fact and value, which *is* a prerequisite of fruitful scientific activity. One separates fact from value when one does not allow one's views about what ought to be to influence one's views about what is. This distinction was made at the very beginnings of scientific inquiry as a result of an insight that as far as the nonhuman environment is concerned, one's desires and the facts of life *are* separate. Science begins with the discovery that magic does not work. But is it indeed the case that "desire" and "fact" are separate in *all* instances? What about those phenomena which include events inside our skins? Is it not true that our desires often influence "facts" whether we like it or not, so that which "fact" presents itself for investigation depends vitally on the attitude with which one has approached the task of ferreting it out?

Every social scientist knows that attitudes elicited in opinion surveys depend on the way questions are put. Usually this is taken to be no more than an indication of the dependence of verbal responses upon verbal stimuli. But what if people are moved in one or another direction depending on what they are asked? Would not, in this case, the investigator's attitude determine a "social fact?" Social science methodology recognizes this complication and usually treats it as a difficulty peculiar to social science, a nuisance to be removed if at all possible. But it is not always possible to remove it; consequently the social scientist usually ignores such problems. There is, to be sure, an activity in which the interweaving of science and ethics is not shunned. This is so-called action research. Action research is not neutral with regard to results. Whereas in "objective" research every result is, in principle, an equally valuable contribution, in action research some results are successes and other results are failures. Therefore one tries to assure one set of results and to prevent another. It goes without saying that if one does this by simply ignoring or selecting facts, one is deceiving oneself and others. It is not true, however, that the separation of fact and value, which is a prerequisite to any social investigation, is the same as separating science and ethics. This is clear as soon as one sees science not as a "body of knowledge" or a "catalogue of techniques" but as a form of social activity or a subculture in human society. The body of knowledge or the catalogue of techniques are high-order abstractions. One often speaks of these as one speaks of the Latin language—as if its existence were independent of carriers and records. But the dependence of a language on carriers and records is vital. When we call Latin a dead language, we mean that its speakers have become extinct. We can also argue that Latin is a "live" language, meaning that its records have remained intelligible.

If science is a form of social activity, it too is viable only by virtue of the existence of carriers. Without scientists there would be no science, and the vast accumulation of records with which we sometimes identify science would become a dead language much more quickly than Etruscan ever did. For it is much farther from Vernacular to Scientific than from Etruscan to Latin.

Science needs, therefore, for its very survival an army of motivated practitioners. So much is obvious. The question is what sources of motivation can insure that science survives and flourishes. I believe it is safe to dismiss the venal sources. Money buys at best service, not devotion. There remain two other sources: the thirst for power and the love of harmony.

The first is the exploitative-sadistic component of our involvement with knowledge; the second the erotic-nurturing mode. The first is concerned with control of environment and of others; the second with understanding oneself and the world and the relation of self to the world and to other selves. The first seeks answers. The second seeks insights. I am not prepared to say which has been the predominant source of inspiration for science. Science has its roots both in alchemy and in philosophy. Faust craved both enlightenment and power. We do know, however, that both the thirst for power and the love of harmony are insatiable and that power and harmony are becoming ever more incompatible.

Not many American scientists are concerned with these questions. There are historical reasons for this; for example, the euphoria of the Age of Invention, and the resulting hypertrophy of the pragmatic image of science, the paucity of humanistically oriented education, ignorance of history, especially distrust of a philosophy of history, and finally the unprecedented breadth of the population base from which today's scientists are being recruited. But to explain a phenomenon does not mean to approve it. The lack of scientific *ideology*, of an understanding of science as a way of life rather than as a source of gadgetry, is the very serious and very obvious lack in American science. If it were not for this lack, the moral implications of science would not be so impatiently shrugged off when they are pointed out by the concerned minority.

I hope I have spelled out the meaning of the conclusion, namely that the need of Soviet science is for more freedom and the need of American science is for more responsibility. The needs are, in a way, complementary. The need of each sector is what the other has in greater abundance. There have been encouraging developments in both sectors. One of the first and most dramatic consequences of the thaw in the U.S.S.R. has been the increase of freedom in Soviet science. The burgeoning developments in cybernetics, structural linguistics, mathematical statistics, symbolic logic, and other previously banned fields attest to the results. Some respectable experimental psychology (unhooked from direct pedagogical application) has appeared. Empirical sociology (called "concrete sociology" probably to avoid the philosophically tainted word "empiricism") is no longer unknown. The Soviet Union needs more of the same, particularly in the social sciences. They need social science both to enhance their security and for immediate practical reasons. By security I mean not "national security," as it is conventionally understood in diplo-military circles but rather the sort of security which makes for social stability and progress — the security which stems from self-knowledge. For example, Soviet society is emerging from a quarter of a century of horrendous social disease — the Stalinist terror. Soviet people ought to understand the nature of this disease in order not to succumb to it again. For lack of a scientific orientation in such matters, and especially because the matter is severely threatening, they avoid analysis and instead pin a label on the disease, "cult of personality," just as prescientific physicians pinned labels on diseases they did not understand.

On the other hand, a society governed by central control, in which there is recognition that central control can be used constructively only with large popular support, needs social science as a basis for social engineering. It needs to answer questions like "What are effective incentives for increasing per capita productivity if it appears undesirable (for ideological reasons) to place too much emphasis on personal gain?" and "What are the advantages and disadvantages of centralization or decentralization?" and even "What is the optimal role differentiation between the sexes?" You don't get usable answers to these questions from textbooks on Marxism-Leninism.

I like to think that there are stirrings among American scientists symptomatic of an awakening responsibility. By and large our intellectuals, among whom are many scientists (as there are many intellectuals among scientists), are not happy about the general tone of American life, especially of our public life. Critics of the arms race and of the cold war policies are also found in intellectual and scientific circles. The reasons for our discontent are moral reasons. We find that public morality in the United States leaves much to be desired, not, perhaps, because we have more than our share of crime, delinquency, and chicanery, but because of the cynicism and apathy which have become the dominant social attitudes toward moral degradation. A moral view derived from the scientific-humanistic ethic would be a good antidote to cynicism and apathy. But if a scientific ethic is to be invoked, the practice of science must be made worthy of it. Science must be cleansed of venality, banality, and homicidal tendencies. This is the most important need of American science. The realization of this need marks the American scientist's sense of responsibility.

It is hardly necessary to add that the trend in the right direction in both Soviet and American science can continue only to the extent that the cold war becomes progressively less dominant in the life of both countries. It would appear, therefore, that the liquidation of the cold war, specifically an ideological disarmament, is the foremost need of both American and Soviet science.

A warless world is not simply a world in which wars do not occur. It is a world from which the threat of war has been removed. Only in such a world can the curse of destructive commitment be finally removed from science. Science so emancipated can then begin truly to embrace the emancipation of man.

IV

•

THE PURSUIT OF PEACE

Lincoln P. Bloomfield

•

ARMS CONTROL AND
WORLD GOVERNMENT

I. Introduction

The notion of a world government is today—and perhaps for all time—a fantastic one. That it is thought of as even a hypothetical framework for political and military planning grows, curiously enough, out of contemporary doctrines on arms control and disarmament. Political scientists have generally come to despair of quantum jumps to world order as utopian and unmindful of political realities. But fresh minds from military, scientific, and industrial life, as they focus on the increasingly dangerous arms race, have sometimes found the logic of world government irresistible.

What has served to bring the problem of world government out in the open in the 1960's is the United States government's public acceptance of the notion of general and complete disarmament. But though international political authority is an inescapable inference from the language of current American policies, its detailed implications have rarely been made explicit in Western pronouncements.

The problem is of course not an entirely new one. The 1946 United States plan for the international control of atomic energy assigned the proposed international agency managerial control or ownership of "all atomic energy activities potentially dangerous to world security," plus "power to control, inspect and license all other atomic activities." To carry this out would have required extraordinary powers at the center. But it was still some distance from that to the political control of the world as a whole

World Politics, vol. XIV, No. 4, July 1962, pp. 633-645.

implied in present American disarmament proposals. Through-out the postwar negotiating period, even when programs were advanced for drastic reduction and limitation of armaments, there is no record of any concrete suggestion or even discussion of a supranational political organization that would exercise effective control in the world.

Recent exchanges in the Great Power dialogue have now reopened the larger political question. On September 19, 1959, Premier Khrushchev announced to the UN General Assembly his plan for "general and complete disarmament" within four years. The American response was given by Secretary of State Herter on February 18, 1960, in a speech to the National Press Club. Mr. Herter said that the first goal of the United States in the forthcoming disarmament negotiations was the creation of a "stable military environment." To create such an environment, he urged certain arms control actions, such as measures to guard against surprise attack and to curtail the spread of nuclear weapons.

The second stage of Mr. Herter's counterproposal was general disarmament. Two American objectives existed in re-gard to the disarmament stage. The first was the creation of universally accepted rules of law, backed by a world court with effective means of enforcement—"that is, by international armed force." The second objective was disarmament itself—"to the point where no single nation or group of nations could effectively oppose this enforcement of international law by inter-national machinery."

The theme set forth by Mr. Herter was continued in the two proposals made by the United States in the spring of 1960, on March 15 and June 27. Under the latter proposal, an Interna-tional Disarmament Control Organization would be established within the framework of the United Nations in the first stage of disarmament. The second stage would include progressive establishment of an international peace force within the United Nations sufficient to preserve world peace under disarmament. And the Kennedy administration . . . carried over this theme, with its interior logic, into the disarmament plan enunciated on September 25, 1961, at the General Assembly of the United Nations.

Here, then, is the basis in recent American policy for the

notion of world government. It was not made explicit and, given the realities of domestic political life, may never be. But the United States position carried the unmistakable implication, by whatever name, of an international political authority sufficient in any event to keep the peace and with the power to enforce its judgments. By any reasonable semantic standards, this is a description of governmental power. Yet there is little evidence that we have thought through the political and military meaning of our position. In part this is because the question of feasibility is so overwhelming in today's world that the matter seems totally academic. The usual responses to the idea on the part of politically sophisticated people are so invariably negative that the only wonder is that the United States thought it would make good propaganda to enunciate it. And in part, alas, analysis too often follows policy.

But it is worth while for three reasons to try and see what we may have had in mind in our proposals. On policy grounds, it would be well to spell out with greater precision, if only for our own better understanding, that to which this country has committed itself. On grounds of sound scholarship, it may be worth while to apply analytical methods to a problem commonly approached on the basis of hunch alone. Finally, there is always the possibility that sophisticated people will turn out to have been wrong.

II. WHAT A WORLD GOVERNMENT WOULD LOOK LIKE

What, in the highly unlikely event that United States disarmament proposals and, consequently, an effective world authority were accepted, might that authority look like, within the bounds of reason and probability?

Limited in its scope, the authority has powers sufficient to monitor and enforce disarmament, settle disputes, and keep the peace. All other powers are reserved to the nations, as in the United States Constitution unspecified powers are reserved to the states. It possesses enforceable taxing powers to finance its political organs, its disarmament policing agency, and its international military force, which includes a nuclear component. The nations are disarmed to police levels. (The imperative reasons for an international nuclear capability will be discussed later in the article.)

Government powers are distributed to three branches. Without assuming that the Anglo-Saxon mold would necessarily be imposed on the new system, it can be assumed that primary functions would exist in some recognizable form, that they would be to some degree separated, and that each would be carried out through appropriate organs or agencies.

The legislative organ is enabled to make decisions, within the scope of the organization's powers for peacekeeping, on a weighted voting basis that combines population and capacity to contribute to the power of the system. A formula will have to be found that assures the United States (and presumably every other country) that vital decisions will not be made by any but the most substantial majorities, including the United States.

If the concept of realism can be applied to world government, this seems to represent minimum realism. For while there can be no individual veto, the Great Power veto will in this partial sense be extended into a limited world government. The precise formula for ensuring appropriate weight to the principal contributors while protecting the rights of the smaller nations has many possible variations. One way is through form. A bicameral legislature excels, through its upper house, at protecting the rights of the smaller units, while a unicameral body can do the same for the larger members by means of a dual vote.

Another way is through voting procedures. A qualified majority — two-thirds or three-fourths or even four-fifths — would be necessary to avoid control by a numerical majority that commanded only a minor fraction of the world's industrial power, financial ability, and so on. Further protection to the newly vulnerable great powers might take additional forms: for example, a legislative council in which the major nations would have a predominant vote (but no individual veto); a system of separation of powers among the branches of government as in the United States; or emphasis of the special position of the major nations in the executive branch.

The one design, however, that could not be applied successfully would be the Calhoun concept of the concurrent majority (in this case between the central authority and its constituencies) with its implied right of secession. "Effective control" has to mean the power to maintain the union.

The executive organ is operated by personnel elected by the

member governments, with administrative services carried out by international civil service personnel. An executive council, like the legislative branch, gives special weight—but without individual veto—to the most populous, industrially developed, and strategically significant states. Safeguards in the form of political supervision and rotation of personnel discourage usurpation of power by a "Praetorian Guard."

Without the optional clause, all states are bound to submit to the jurisdiction of the World Court for both legal disputes and legal aspects of political disputes. Justice is administered by an expanded network of international courts with regional panels. States and international agencies, but not individuals initially, are subjects of international law. An equity tribunal system is created for both legal disputes and legal aspects of political disputes, along with greatly expanded mediation, conciliation, and arbitration services, use of rapporteurs, and judgments by the courts *ex aequo et bono*. The constitution provides for the enforceability of decisions of the courts, for execution of the decisions of the executive, and for the carrying out of the laws passed by the legislature. The central authority itself can be sued, but, like the United States government today, cannot be forced to comply with court judgments. A human rights court modeled upon the comparable court under the European Community is empowered to hear individual complaints of violations of a covenant of civil rights that would accompany the constitution. Permissive and voluntary organs of cooperation exist in the economic, social, scientific, and technological and cultural fields as they do now, without powers of compulsion except under special provisions dealing with essential services—health, public safety, and the like.

A crucial feature of the system is its universality. Unlike the conventional American view of the United Nations, membership in the new regime, far from being a privilege, is mandatory. All the countries now divided would be included. None of the individual problems reflected in today's divided countries would by themselves have to be finally solved in order to set up such an organization. But they would no longer be solvable by force—or so the new ground rules stipulate.

National governments continue to make, execute, and enforce domestic laws with respect to all areas presently *in foro domestico* except for the raising and provisioning of armed forces, the declaration and waging of war, and the unhampered research, development, and production of military matériel. These hitherto untrammeled rights are limited by the terms of the new international constitution to the right to maintain sufficient police forces to ensure domestic security. The formula for such forces is derived from the present size of local, civil, and state police, plus such national law enforcement personnel as federal marshals, customs agents, border patrols, security police, law enforcement agents, and investigators. (There are obvious discrepancies between states, depending on their internal security problems and practices.)

The international force, compounded appropriately of ground, sea, air, and outer space elements, consists of 500,000 men, recruited individually and wearing the international uniform. It controls a nuclear force consisting of 50-100 mixed land-mobile and undersea missiles averaging 1 MT per weapon. The force is stationed and deployed in territorial enclaves equitably allocated among continents and areas for minimum temptation and likelihood of seizure by any single nation. Ten air-transportable divisions trained for vertical envelopment, armed with the latest field weapons (including a modest supply of tactical nuclear weapons), and provided with transport and communications facilities should be able to counter an aggressive thrust across one nation's borders of the dimension likely under the circumstances. Beyond that, the strategic nuclear deterrent in the hands of the central authority would presumably deter conventional attack on a massive scale in the same fashion as in American hands it presumably deterred Soviet conventional aggression in Europe in the late 1940's and early 1950's. (The latter analogy rests of course on an unproved hypothesis, as does the whole doctrine of massive retaliation associated with preponderance in nuclear weapons.) We must also assume the force's ability to deal with guerrilla activities, but without high confidence.

The international force would be decreasingly capable of coping with higher levels of aggression involving several countries up to a point describable as true international civil war. It should, however, be understood that the choice is not between an international system incapable of coping with important threats and one that can deal successfully with every contingency in the spectrum. At one end of the scale, the present international system has some capacity to cope even with Communist menaces. At the other end of the scale, we can guess that there would be finite limits to the capacity of a supranational system to handle such maximum challenges as international civil war. A civil war, domestic or international, can gather such force as to end the preponderance at the center. The hypothetical system adumbrated in this article, while its capacities go significantly beyond those presently in sight, remains subject to the basic laws of political life.

The individual states are open to international inspection against violation of the disarmament agreement, with permanent inspection of power and research nuclear reactors, accelerators and other high-energy equipment, electronic industries, steel mills, aircraft and space-vehicle production, major energy-producing facilities, ports, railheads, marshaling yards, major airports and rocket-launching facilities, central budgeting, bookkeeping, accounting, and auditing agencies, principal research and development operations and installations, and various other key and strategic points in the national economy.

The international inspectorate also monitors the atmosphere for clandestine explosions, for underground nuclear tests primarily through robot seismic stations combined with on-site inspection of suspicious events, and against tests in outer space through sensing devices in internationally operated solar satellites. In general, space technology remains in national and in some cases and places (communications, broadcasting, transportation, messenger service, etc.) private hands, but under international inspection. The international authority owns and operates only those space vehicles required both as a military deterrence system and to monitor enforcement of the disarmament agreement. Satellite observation vehicles are equipped to observe optically, electronically, and with infra-red and other sensing and detection devices, and are serviced by an internationally operated ground detection and tracking network.

Largely because of the requirements of the disarmament

program, a significant "UN presence" exists in all countries, consisting, *mutatis mutandis,* of technical assistance, political liaison, or even military personnel. The secondary functions of this presence include dissemination of impartial factual information as well as continuous liaison with local and national authorities.

III. The Role of Force in World Government

What is the basis for the apportionment of forces that I have suggested between center and parts? Here strategic analysis supplies tentative answers.

"Effective control" connotes a relative monopoly of political power, accompanied by preponderant military force, at the center of the system. The word "relative" indicates that the power relationship between the center and the parts is one of degree. Some examples illustrate the equation. In the United States the people have the constitutional right to "keep and bear arms"; the government monopoly is legally abridged to this extent. In the Congo Republic, during the most politically disturbed period, the central army was outnumbered by the provincial forces, putting into question the existence of effective central rule. In Kuomintang China the military power of the national government was often balanced by the military power of the warlords; the writ of the government hence could not extend uniformly through the country. Thus, under a supranational government, the degrees of relative power as between center and parts can occupy a wide range. The most logical combination of forces poses at once the question of nuclear weapons. One fundamental consideration supplies the answer here.

Modern science and technology are essentially irreversible. They can perhaps be slowed down or even stopped, either by some universal catastrophe or under a disarmament agreement that curtails the intensive allocation of economic and human resources to armaments. But the processes of fission and fusion and the design of engines of delivery cannot be unlearned. Moreover, assuming as we must that atomic power may become economical and fusion power — when harnessed — even more so, under total disarmament all of these technologies will be practiced in their peaceable aspects. Thus, however comprehensive the disarmament agreements, however much political power is transferred to a world government, and even if no significant amount of manpower is actually working on nuclear, chemical, and bacteriological weapons or on constructing military aircraft, ships, rockets, or space vehicles, there will always remain implicit in technically advanced societies the capacity to turn again to the production and fabrication of engines of war, probably with fair rapidity.

The very logic of "effective control" requires placing in the hands of the central authority military forces adequate to deal with breaches of the peace and acts of aggression through whatever means are necessary to preserve a preponderance of power at the center, even against the contingency of clandestine production of nuclear weapons. The conclusion is inescapable that the central authority, in addition to its conventional military capacity, will have to offset the inherent possibility of evasion by being equipped with nuclear weapons, along with delivery systems adequate to deter any reasonable expectation of clandestine violation and consequent attempt to destabilize or even destroy the new system.

It can be seen that even under a radically designed system of authority in a disarmed world the problem of deterrence will persist, including some of the features that characterize it today. The situation facing the central authority would not be very different from that confronting the United States in its need to be equipped with forces, both conventional and nuclear, adequate to deter any likely combination of hostile forces. Indeed, this is the problem inside any society. But the special feature in the new situation would be an element of profound uncertainty. Today national military forces are designed to deter known quantities or qualities of war-making capability in the arsenals of other nations. But our postulated regime, even with a good inspection system, will be to a degree uncertain whether nuclear weapons are hidden or being secretly made, or some highly potent psychochemical agent being developed in an isolated laboratory, or some potentially commanding weapon secreted illicitly in the payload of a communication, weather, navigation, or other type of satellite. These possibilities, however statistically improbable, would pose anew the problem of deterrence, in a different calculus, both for the general authority and for individual countries such as the United States in making their own calculations.

This fact reinforces the need for adequate inspection systems to prevent a marginal lead secretly gained in one nation from destabilizing the disarmed world. For while one mad tribal ruler in the hinterland might not be able to bring the rest of the world to its knees with his secretly prepared poisons, twenty-five secretly produced rockets with megaton warheads could supply one nation with an inordinate amount of political and strategic power. Adequate inspection would be designed to preclude such a development. But deterrence from the center would be the second line of defense, deterring in the first instance from political threat, and ultimately from actual military use.

IV. THE PROBLEMS TO BE SOLVED

It is sometimes assumed that if it were not for the Communists, the utopian design of a disarmed world at peace with justice would materialize. This assumption underestimates and possibly miscalculates the willingness of the other major countries to accept the revolutionary political changes implicit in current proposals for general and complete disarmament. The full meaning of that revolution is insufficiently understood.

For the United States, as well as for the other countries, a threshold will have been crossed from one historical condition to another profoundly different one. However many stages it passes through, however tacit or explicit the labels, however gradual or violent the process, there is a Rubicon that divides the Gaul of basically untrammeled national sovereignty from the Tuscany of meaningful supranational authority. Nothing could be more dangerous to sound thinking and planning than to elide this fundamental truth. By whatever process and under whatever name, the agency that is to control world affairs effectively requires in the most important ways the design customarily associated with government. A central authority with effective powers in the realms of disarmament and the settlement of international disputes, and with the capacity to deal with breaches of the peace and acts of aggression, and above all in possession of the most vital attribute of government—a preponderance of military power—is a government, however limited.

To grasp the profound difficulty in securing American acceptance, one only needs to recall that the United States Senate took the lead in demanding the veto power in the UN Charter. Other Western nations such as France are more nationalistic than we. And the nationalist revolution in its purest form is only now sweeping the world south of the equator.

Even if American acquiescence in the implications of its own proposals could be assumed, it is surely unsafe to make the further assumption that the ideological and power struggle between communism and the West will not continue indefinitely. This throws into question any program requiring that both sides subordinate themselves, their power, and their ambitions to a supranational authority. That is of course the central dilemma of world politics today, and it applies with ultimate force to the proposition of world government. The logical trap is completed with the familiar paradox: given an unabated continuation of Communist dynamism, the subordination of states to a true world government appears impossible; but if the Communist dynamic were greatly abated, the West might well lose whatever incentive it has for world government.

If, to test our hypothesis further, we assume that the West would favor a world under the effective control of the United Nations, the operative question is then how to transform and tame the forces of communism. Such a transformation is theoretically possible, but only under two conditions. The first is that through evolutionary processes Communist doctrine becomes drained of its messianic quality, forgoes its imperialistic ambitions, and comes to accept the notion of a higher authority—a notion totally antipathetic to its tenets. The other condition, which puts the possibility within a more foreseeable time span, is a crisis, a war, or a brink-of-war situation so grave or commonly menacing that deeply rooted attitudes and practices are sufficiently shaken to open up the possibility of a revolution in world political arrangements.

If we can for the sake of analysis make the further assumption that one or the other of these conditions has come about and that the Communists—both Occidental and Oriental—have consequently been brought to a significant mitigation of their doctrine, what kind of political environment could then be foreseen?

Remember, we are assuming a world in which relations between East and West are characterized by significantly higher degress of mutual trust, internationalist spirit, and unaggressiveness. But there is little in history to justify the belief that without the Communist threat in its present form the world political environment would be inherently stable. We have postulated by necessity a willing acceptance of limited world government by the Great Powers. We then have to postulate further either its acceptance by or imposition on all other nations.

This at once sets up future instabilities. Today the prime foci of instability are actually in third areas, centering on economic disparities and nationalistic strivings for independence, factors which Soviet and Chinese policies purposefully exploit. There is no reason to assume the disappearance under limited world government of the dynamic factors—the intergroup competitions, the racial and ethnic tensions, and the economic disparities that permeate human history and create the conditions for political upheaval. History, short of catastrophe, is not discontinuous. To paraphrase von Clausewitz, limited world government is a form of international conflict carried on under other institutional arrangements than unlimited state sovereignty. Thus, as international stability is restored under benign forms of world order, detailed disputes of a chronic or secondary nature can be confidently expected to re-emerge. The new regime will thus be faced with a continuous agenda of problems stemming from political ambition, inequalities, avarice, irrational behavior, the inhumanity of man to man, and the use or threat of violence to achieve political or social ends. This prospect can be ruled out only by the untenable assumption that history will have run its course and an end put to its dynamic, refractory, and otherwise troublesome qualities. Thus a world government, even if it could be created, would be subject to continuing pressures, the most exigent of which could lead to civil war on an international scale.

The crucial difficulty then is to ensure that no large-scale civil war can take place to test the "union," for war on a major scale would gravely threaten the system. It would revive the production and, given the instability of such a situation, the probable use of weapons of mass destruction. In any event such a war would be no more tolerable under a world government than it would be today, and for precisely the same humanitarian, social, and economic reasons.

But here the model runs into one of history's most vexing dilemmas. War is the traditional means for changing the international status quo, in the absence of effective provisions for peaceful change. When war is not possible—and when no such provisions exist—the traditional consequence is injustice, which in turn breeds even more ungovernable instabilities and ensuing violence. Perhaps the most sobering consideration about world government is the nightmare prospect of world order at the price of world tyranny—a kind of global Holy Alliance to preserve the status quo. Flexibility and capacity to adapt to change in time and with foresight become absolute imperatives in view of the proposed nuclear monopoly in the hands of the central authority.

To achieve the necessary viability and durability, then, the world authority must solve the problem that has pervaded all modern history and accommodate the dynamic forces making for change, without allowing them to lead to war. Specifically the system must, through its legislative action, its executive implementation, and its judicial interpretation, allow for changes in fact, in law, and in the system itself. Without a genuine breakthrough in this realm of peaceful change in which man has by and large so far failed, with persistently tragic results, nothing else about the world order has any meaning in terms of either the efficacy of the system or the values by which we would wish to continue to live.

V. The Prospects

Will any of this come about? Does it belong within any rational time span as we look ahead?

Under the first of our alternative conditions—the pacific evolution of the Communist world, including China—it is difficult to foresee a limited world government within twenty-five years at the earliest, fifty years more conservatively. If, however, one came about as a result of the second condition—a series of unnerving trips to or over the brink—it might happen at any time. It is this contingency that has the most relevance for the planner of both disarmament and world order, if he is not to substitute wishing for thinking.

If a world authority did become politically feasible, there is no dearth of applicable blueprints for its inner detail. There is no theoretical reason, for example, why the present United Nations could not be transformed by Charter amendment into an instrument of effective global power. Alternatively, the process could be a completely new start, in the way the Articles of Confederation were scrapped to write the Constitution. But it is not terribly important which method is used. The paramount issue is not, as some suppose, the difficulty of amending the Charter. It is to reach a political consensus about ground rules in the world. If this came to pass, it would surely be a secondary question whether to incorporate the changes in the present Charter or to write a new one. The overwhelming central fact would be the loss of control of their military power by individual nations. If this becomes achievable, the details will not be insurmountable.

Of the two paths, only the first—the longer-term evolutionary path—would be likely to follow the historical process of political community-building, involving a series of organic stages of consensus, value formation, and the experiences of common enterprise. Consideration of the other path, envisaging a grave crisis or war sufficient to bring about a sudden transformation in national attitudes through a series of traumatic shocks, raises large questions. Does it sufficiently lay the basis for genuine community, adequate to create a durable world order? Can it short-circuit the main course of history? We can only leave these questions unanswered. But their contingent nature reinforces the need for continuing policies aimed explicitly at achieving the foundation of consensus requisite for true community.

According to our reasoning, national disarmament is a condition *sine qua non* for effective supranational control. Yet the known difficulties of comprehensive disarmament are overwhelming. We can say that, perhaps as a consequence of a massive crisis, it may be neither inherently nor technically impossible to envisage a program whereby all nations scrap their armaments down to the police level, with a reasonable probability of detecting significant evasion or violation through inspection arrangements. But none of this implies that comprehensive disarmament is a political possibility in the foreseeable future even though it is technically feasible, and even though it is not unthinkable strategically, given adequate supranational surrogates for national arms. It *is* to say that effective international political control is not possible without it.

We can conclude that for both comprehensive disarmament and limited world government two problems are paramount. One is the historic quantum jump implied in centralization of military and political power in the world, a revolutionary concept that we ourselves may not have grasped or accepted any more than has our principal adversary. The other is the presently insurmountable difficulty of bringing into any unified, democratic, world-wide system the messianic forces of the Communist *imperium* so long as it is on the historic make. The very notion of a politico-military framework superior to both East and West today seems remote, for there has been doctrinal continuity between Litvinov's assertion that only angels can be impartial and Khrushchev's statement that there may be neutral nations but there are no neutral men.

The structure of a disarmed world can be perceived more easily than the fundamental building blocks of consensus and community that would have to underlie it. We can end only by speculating that if such a system ever came into being, even in grave crisis, it would thenceforth have its own inner dynamic. New forces could be set into motion that we cannot now comprehend, leading in the direction of constitutional and organic development that might bear as little resemblance to the planned first stage as the United States system in 1962 bears to the thirteen colonies under the Articles of Confederation.

Nikolai A. Pitersky

•

A SOVIET VIEW OF A DISARMED WORLD

Every day brings an increase in the numbers of those who want peace and disarmament and are prepared to appeal publicly for it. The idea of peaceful coexistence between the two social-political systems is winning acceptance in the minds of an ever growing number of people. Scientists, men holding public office, the intelligentsia, the workers, peasants, women, and youth of all countries have joined the fight for disarmament and peace. However, nearly all the speeches made, and articles published in the press, with very few exceptions deal exclusively with the first step towards the implementation of this idea—namely the need for disarmament, and its importance, together with ways of putting it into practice. There are probably many perfectly sincere supporters of disarmament who would skeptically dismiss any attempt to examine even a few of the problems which states and people will have to contend with after disarmament— in a world without arms.

We are told that it is rather early to talk of such problems, as the main task still remains to be done: an agreement must be reached on complete and general disarmament.

Our answer to this is that it is not good to undertake anything, it is not good to strive, without having an idea of the end for which you are striving. Moreover, a discussion of the problems we might encounter in a disarmed world will help us to avoid certain mistakes in the process of disarmament itself. But the most important reason for formulating the various problems of a disarmed world is that we are convinced that complete and general disarmament will be achieved, that *the world is ready for*

EDITOR'S NOTE: Rear Admiral Pitersky's article here is amplified in his "On the Establishment of International United Nations Forces," *Disarmament* (Paris), No. 5 (March 1965), pp. 5-8.

disarmament. Disarmament is not a utopia, it is feasible and practicable. Not only is disarmament feasible, *it has become an inevitable historical necessity.*

People everywhere are becoming more and more acutely aware of the urgent need to do something to bring about disarmament, because of the immense danger of the outbreak of a nuclear conflict.

The fight for disarmament and peace that the great masses of the people are waging is growing more intensive day by day, and assuming the most varied forms — demonstrations, marches, strikes. In all countries of the world, conferences are held on peace and disarmament, and the number of public organizations engaged in the fight for these aims is constantly increasing.

Impelled by the irreversible movement of the people of the whole world towards disarmament, the United Nations General Assembly has passed a resolution in favor of general and complete disarmament stating that the use of nuclear and thermonuclear weapons is contrary to the norms of international law, the laws of humanity, and the spirit, letter, and aims of the United Nations Charter, as a crime against humanity and civilization.

Other types of weapons of mass destruction — chemical and biological — are no less horrible and inhuman. The aggressor who uses any sort of weapon of mass destruction will not do so with impunity.

The overwhelming majority of military theorists in the Western countries, including the United States, also consider that *at the present time, a rocket-nuclear war is senseless.* Arthur I. Waskow, in his article "American Military Doctrine" published in the magazine *Survival* (May-June, 1962), states that *all strategists agree on one thing, that total thermonuclear war must be avoided.* However, there are certain differences of opinion among them with regard to the ways of preventing war.

A study of United States military theories and our own views on the possible nature of a future war enables one to draw the conclusion that, if both sides have thermonuclear weapons, no theory can avoid the dilemma: *either a mutually destructive war or peaceful coexistence. There is no other solution.* Common sense tells us that peaceful coexistence could be brought about more profitably without the useless expenditure of money on the arms race, which causes immense economic damage to both sides. Meanwhile the danger of war remains; it might break out in spite of the common sense and the good will of the Great Powers. War could break out as a result of many causes, such as an accident, recklessness, blackmail, and so on.

The development of science and military techniques has reached such a stage now that any war involving the use of rocket-nuclear weapons is suicidal.

As far back as 1918, the founder of the Soviet State, V. I. Lenin, said: "There will come a time when war will become so destructive, that it will just become impossible."[1] V. I. Lenin's most fervent wish was that war should become impossible.

In his speech to the World Congress for Disarmament and Peace, 10th June, 1962, N. S. Khrushchev said: "We have maintained, do and will maintain Lenin's principles of peaceful coexistence. They are the only doctrine for relations between states with different social systems which is in keeping with the historical conditions of this century, and on the basis of which peace can be preserved."

What do we understand by peaceful coexistence?

Above all, peaceful coexistence means a renunciation of war, of the use of force as a means of settling international disputes. It presupposes recognition of those governments, elected by the people, which are in power, and a renunciation of interference in the internal affairs of other countries carried out with a view to encroaching upon their territorial integrity or changing their political systems or way of life. Such interference is impermissible in any form and under any pretext. The policy of peaceful coexistence assumes a wide international cooperation between countries in the political, economic, social, and cultural fields, on a basis of full equality and mutual profit.

The Socialist countries do not need war. All Communists are opposed to wars of plunder. Marxist-Leninist theory, which Socialist states follow in their home and foreign policies, preaches the principles of peaceful coexistence between states with different social systems. The idea of coexistence between two opposing systems was defended by Lenin as far back as

[1] N. K. Krupskaia, *On Lenin,* Moscow: Gospolitizdat, 1960, pp. 40-41.

1920. Lenin's idea lay behind the Soviet disarmament proposals at the Genoa conference in 1922. The principles of peaceful coexistence to this day remain the general line of Soviet foreign policy.

In "The Programme of the Communist Party of the Soviet Union," passed by the 22nd Session of the C.P.S.U. in October 1961, we read: *"Peaceful coexistence of Socialist and capitalist states is an objective necessity for the development of human society. War can not and must not be used as a means of settling international disputes.* Either peaceful coexistence or catastrophic war — this alone is the way history is putting the question to us."

Complete and general disarmament naturally does not rule out the struggle between the ideologies of the two opposed social and political systems. But this struggle must be waged by peaceful means, without the use of armed forces.

A number of scientists and prominent figures in the Western countries (fortunately, they are few in number), when discussing the problem of security in a disarmed world, put forward the idea that some states might be dishonest in their manner of complying with obligations assumed, might keep weapons secretly and start an aggressive war, even using nuclear weapons hidden during the process of disarmament. So, they argue, the idea of establishing world-wide peace through complete and general disarmament is unrealistic. In particular, Professor Thomas Schelling, of Harvard, in an article published in April 1962, writes "Short of universal brain surgery, nothing can erase the memory of weapons and how to build them. If 'total disarmament' is to make war unlikely, it must reduce the incentives. It cannot eliminate the potential for destruction; the most primitive war can be modernized by rearmament as it goes along. . . . By the standards of 1944, the United States was fairly near to total disarmament when World War II broke out. . . . 'Disarmament' did not preclude U.S. participation; it just slowed it down."[2] Further on, he says that even if one of the sides did not have nuclear weapons at the beginning of the war, they would start to produce them. As a result of this, it might

[2]"The Role of Deterrence in Total Disarmament," *Foreign Affairs,* April 1962, pp. 392-393, 396, 402-403, 406.

come about that one of the sides will have nuclear weapons earlier than the other, and will force the other to capitulate. So, Schelling writes, the prohibition of weapons and the means of their production does not automatically create a stable military atmosphere. He agrees with the proposal for the creation of an international armed force, if it is superior militarily to any other combination of national forces, i.e., if it is large enough. The task of this force, he considers, would be to maintain order all over the world, not allowing war and new armaments. At the same time he writes that if the main powers keep or conceal any small stocks of nuclear weapons, the international police force would in that case simply be an additional deterrent. But Schelling does not say who is to command these forces and who to restrain them. He warns against the idea that under "complete" disarmament there is no military potential which must be controlled, kept in balance and stabilized. "There should be no divorce between deterrence and disarmament," Schelling concludes. "If disarmament is to work, it has got to improve deterrence. Until a much greater community of interest exists in the world than is likely in this generation, war will have to be made unprofitable. It cannot be made impossible."

This article, and various others like it, is an obvious attempt to lead the reader astray and to prove that until a "greater community of interests" has been achieved, disarmament is impossible. The principal leitmotiv is disbelief in the possibility of keeping peoples' lives free from war, the conviction that the parties to a disarmament treaty will not show integrity in complying with their obligations, and that control will be ineffective. According to Schelling the only way to avoid a terrible war is to maintain a balance of strength.

Schelling's argument does not take into account the qualitative changes which have occurred in the international scene and in military technology. In all previous wars, each belligerent party hoped to win the war, and thus gain economic and political advantages. Nowadays, with the present correlation of forces and with modern weapons, both sides can count only on mutual destruction. And the destruction will be such as can rightly be called a catastrophe for humanity. It is essential also to realize that dreams of seizing world dominion by force of arms are infeasible. This is a consideration that ought to be driven deep into the consciousness of all politicians and all the people of the world.

Besides this, it is difficult to suppose that a state, having concluded a disarmament agreement, would go to the trouble of disbanding the forces it already has, only to start acquiring arms again later, in the hope of outstripping its enemy. We do not exclude attempted aggression entirely. However, the possibilities for stopping any aggression will be quite sufficient.

In order to avoid deception in the disarmament process, we must demand very careful control over its implementation. After disarmament has been completed, this control must continue, not only in the form of superficial observation, from which war preparations could possibly be concealed, but also by verification of documents at the appropriate establishments — finance ministries, industrial enterprises, and so on. The wider public could also be brought into play to help in disarmament control. If the disarmament plan is widely published, together with the system of control and the addresses and telephone numbers of control agents, governmental bodies will find it difficult to conceal any violation of their disarmament obligations.

I have set out to examine some of the numerous problems which humanity will face after disarmament, namely: the role and tasks of the United Nations, international discord and the social struggle, the international police force and international law.

There is absolutely no doubt about the need for keeping the United Nations Organization in a disarmed world. This organization, created at the end of the Second World War, which brought humanity incalculable sufferings, has one main task — to spare the future generations from the scourge of war. This main aim — none other than guaranteeing the security of states — is one which the United Nations must serve in a disarmed world.

The vast majority of the aims and principles expounded in the United Nations Charter, which was passed more than seventeen years ago, remain valid today; the whole of humanity wants to see them implemented in an already disarmed world. But, in spite of the worthy provisions of the Charter, the credit side of the United Nations balance sheet looks as yet rather unimpressive. The explanation of this lies in the "cold war" and the fact that the Western countries, headed by the United States of America, have tried to use the United Nations for their own selfish aims. There are many other reasons for the limited effectiveness of the United Nations, one of the main ones being the existence of opposing military and economic blocs of states, which has made it impossible for some international questions to be properly approached and settled.

The very existence of the United Nations is based on the idea of peaceful coexistence between states with different social and political systems. Thus the principle of peaceful coexistence runs like a vital thread right through the whole of the Charter.

The clear and concise outline of the purposes and principles of the United Nations as stated in its Charter provides a perfectly suitable guide for states in their relations with one another after complete and general disarmament.

The United Nations is not a world government. Nevertheless, it makes it possible to harmonize the actions of all its members in order to promote cooperation between states with different economic and social systems and methods of government. Its appointed task is to bring about peaceful coexistence between states and the joint settlement of the main international issues and disputes by all countries, regardless of their political and social structure.

The primary task of the United Nations—to maintain international peace and security—is entrusted to one of the organization's principal bodies, the Security Council. The Charter as it now stands contains almost everything that is required as guidance for states in their international relations during the first years in a disarmed world.

Complete and general disarmament will create an atmosphere of trust and cooperation between states. This, however, does not mean that conflict and friction will disappear. Conflicts can be caused both by disagreements between states and as a result of internal struggles within this or that state. The United Nations will have a great part to play in settling by peaceful means whatever conflicts and disputes may arise.

After disarmament, the United Nations' role will become

more important. The United Nations in a disarmed world must become a truly universal body—and all countries of the world must become its members.

The United Nations' role and significance after disarmament will grow because it will be assigned new tasks in addition to the ones it already has. The most important of these new tasks will be that of supervising the manner in which states are complying with the Disarmament Treaty, and also that of organizing international cooperation in the economic, social, cultural, and scientific fields on a wider scale than at present.

For this purpose, it is essential that the United Nations be strengthened as much as possible, that its authority be enhanced, and that it be made an effective instrument for promoting peace and international cooperation.

The changed nature of international relations in a disarmed world will obviously require some changes in the structure and composition of the Secretariat and other principal United Nations bodies, together with the creation of entirely new ones. In particular, the membership of the Security Council must be expanded. After all the Trust Territories have become independent states, the Trusteeship Council may be disbanded. A body such as the Economic and Social Council will have to be expanded and its rights increased in view of the need for an improvement in the organization of international trade and cultural links. The International Disarmament Organization will remain and will continue its work after disarmament. The need will arise to establish a new body to coordinate scientific research work; its task will be to organize cooperation with regard to a number of technical projects on a world-wide scale, and to collect information on the scientific achievements of scientists of all countries in order to make rational use of the means available and the potential of scientists, and in order to produce the greatest scientific and technological effectiveness. This could be done by an exchange of literature, joint research projects, international conferences, and by sending individual scientists of one country to research institutions of another, and so on.

As disarmament goes into force, it is important that the question of where the International Disarmament Organization is to be located should be examined seriously and comprehensively. The Organization must be situated in such a place as will enable it to work unhindered and have liaison with the supervisory bodies. It must be borne in mind that the office of the supervisory organization in each country which is a signatory to the Disarmament Treaty must have an independent and direct link with the Headquarters of the Organization, and that this Organization will continue its activity in a disarmed world. Obviously a country must be chosen which will be most suitable for purposes of liaison, from the point of view of geographical situation.

Existing international discord will persist even after complete and general disarmament, as disarmament does not directly affect the political structure of the participant countries. However, the nature of the international relations will radically change — all international disagreements must be settled not by force but by peaceful means. This will be an immense gain for humanity. For the first time in history, military force will lose its significance and will cease to play a role in international relations. To a considerable extent, brute force will give place to reason, to an intelligent appreciation of everybody's interests. All the foundations of international relations will be altered, and, as a consequence, the life of each state will likewise change.

Of course, some differences will become more acute in nature, some will change, and some, with the passage of time, may entirely disappear.

The principal existing causes of discord of the imperialist period — the clash between labour and capital, between the imperialist powers and the peoples of colonial and dependent countries, between those same imperialist powers and the groups of countries struggling for a fair share in, and the redistribution of, the world capitalist market — these will all remain after complete and general disarmament has come into being. The ideological, economic, and political struggle between the two existing, opposed social and economic systems — capitalist and Socialist — will also continue.

Some of the conflicts listed above might be solved by means of social and political revolutions, others by means of talks and mutual concessions. We propose to conduct the struggle between the capitalist and Socialist systems through peaceful economic competition, based on the principle of peaceful coexistence. I feel it is essential to point out emphatically that social revolutions in the capitalist countries arise not as a result of the "export of revolution" as is claimed by certain bourgeois ideologists, but solely because of the action of the internal laws of economic development and the class struggle in those countries. Since sane people everywhere have come to the conclusion that it is now futile to hope to settle the historical conflict between capitalism and communism by war, there is only one course left, the course of peaceful competition between the two systems.

"Our argument is that there are in the world two systems; one system of states has capitalism as its basis, whereas the other is based on the doctrine of Marxism-Leninism, on socialism. An ideological and political struggle is going on between these two systems. We do not want this struggle to be turned into a war between the states with different social systems, but we rather want these questions settled by peaceful competition. Let each country in the socialist and capitalist worlds prove the superiority of its own system in a peaceful way."[3]

We thus propose to transfer the clash between the two systems, after disarmament, into the field of economic competition. Immense opportunities open up for increased prosperity for all the states of the world as a result of complete and general disarmament. It is important that all capitalists, whatever country they come from, should at long last realize that the old methods of trying to achieve economic and political superiority by armed force have become irrevocably a thing of the past. New methods, new relations between states, based on peaceful measures, on respect for the sovereignty and the mutual interests of states — this is what is required in the conduct of economic policy.

In conformity with the Disarmament Treaty, military blocs and alliances must be dissolved, troops withdrawn from foreign territories, and military bases dismantled. This will greatly lessen the divergences and tensions which have hitherto marred relations between states.

Moreover the elimination of military bases on foreign soil

[3]Speech by N. S. Khrushchev at the World Congress for General Disarmament and Peace in Moscow, 10 July, 1962.

will enable small and dependent countries to free themselves from military pressure exerted on them by the great capitalist powers, and to prevent them from being used for aggression. Small countries, including those which are neutral, can be certain to see their economies prosper, and their standard of living rise, once they have done away with the crippling burden of military expenditure.

The existing political and economic alliances and groups of states in both the capitalist and Socialist worlds may remain in being, though some of them will have to be changed.

I consider it quite possible that a union of the economically underdeveloped countries might be formed, with a view to combating exploitation by the large capitalist monopolies, and achieving greater economic effectiveness by a united effort in the use of natural wealth.

In spite of the strengthening of cooperation between states and groups of states in various fields—in science, technology, and economics—conflict between some of them is inevitable.

In a disarmed world, owing to the conflicts mentioned above, various forms of international conflict not involving the use of armed force are possible, in addition to the class struggle within capitalist countries. The main ones are:

1. Competition between two systems of states, the purpose of which is to show which system guarantees the popular masses the greatest material and cultural benefits, gives most true individual freedom and guarantees the best development of productive forces, culture, and science in the interests of the people. This struggle started with the October Revolution in Russia. It has already shown the considerable advantages of the Socialist system.

After complete and general disarmament there will be an enormous increase in the opportunities for competition in giving technical and economic aid to the underdeveloped countries, as also for establishing cooperation between these latter and both Socialist and, we hope, capitalist countries.

2. The struggle between the underdeveloped and the imperialist countries. After the Second World War, as a result of the tempestuous and irresistible growth of the national liberation movement of the colonial peoples towards national and

economic independence, half the population of the world freed itself from the colonial yoke. The day is not far off when those who are still under colonial rule against their will will acquire freedom, and there will remain no more colonial countries and trust territories.

Because of the greed of the colonialists, the economy of the colonies has lagged behind in its development, and the working population is indigent. In those states which were formerly colonies, almost the entire economy is still in the hands of the imperialist monopolies which continue to exploit the primary resources and the labour of the people of these countries. The struggle of the former colonial peoples for complete economic independence has yet to run its course. For this reason, we do not exclude the possibility of the outbreak of a liberation fight (popular uprisings) against the colonialists with a view to changing a system which the people do not accept.

3. The struggle for possession of the sources of primary commodities and for markets for manufactured products between monopolists of individual states and groups of states. This struggle might be exceptionally severe, and whole groups of both economically advanced and underdeveloped countries might be drawn into it.

To counteract this trend for the worse, the Socialist states are already advancing an extensive program of international economic and cultural cooperation.

In particular the leaders of the Socialist countries taking part in the Council for Economic Mutual Aid, at its June session in 1962, expressed a desire for an expansion of trade with the capitalist countries. They proposed to convene an international conference on the problems of trade, which would discuss the question of creating an international trade organization, which would embrace all areas and countries of the world, without any discrimination. The question of convening an international conference on the questions of trade was included on the agenda of the 17th Session of the United Nations General Assembly, on the initiative of the Soviet Union, and an affirmative decision was passed on it.

The Socialist countries propose to organize cooperation with the Western European states in the elaboration of primary commodities in short supply, in increasing the sources of energy, the joint exploitation of waterways, and in other fields.[4]

The draft Declaration on the transfer to peaceful needs of the means and resources, released as a result of disarmament, which was submitted to the 17th Session of the General Assembly by the Soviet Foreign Minister, A. A. Gromyko, 21st September, 1962, dwells in detail on the prospects for economic development of all countries, for bringing all countries and continents to the same level of economic development, and of raising the economically backward countries up to the level of the highly developed countries.

The draft Declaration shows that the transfer of colossal resources from military to peaceful purposes, and the expansion of international economic exchange and mutual aid will be of profit to all countries, large and small, highly developed and underdeveloped, will create conditions favourable to a growth in production, and will guarantee work for new millions of people. Demand will increase because living conditions will have improved; this in turn will lead to a growth in the capacity of markets, and new markets for manufactured products will appear. The rise in general well-being will thus help even to render the conflicts I enumerated above less acute. There are immense opportunities for cooperation and for lessening international tensions in a disarmed world. It is simply a question of understanding what these opportunities are, and of making good use of them.

At the same time, we must foresee the possibility that the Disarmament Treaty might be violated, and provide for ways of preventing this.

The Western powers, using as their pretext the idea that they do not want to allow aggression in a disarmed world, propose to set up a powerful international armed force, armed with nuclear weapons. After the discussion of the United States and U.S.S.R. draft disarmament treaties at a meeting of the Committee of Eighteen, the Western powers proposed that this force should be under the command of a specially created

[4]N. S. Khrushchev, "Essential Questions in the Development of a World Socialist System," in *Problems of Peace and Socialism*, No. 9, September 1962.

permanent United Nations military body. In other words, the idea of the Western powers was that this force should be supranational.

Attempts have been made to implement the idea of an International Armed Force before: at the Versailles Peace Conference at the end of the First World War and after the Second World War in 1946-1947 and in 1958 at the United Nations, the question of setting up an international armed force was discussed. However, owing to irreconcilable differences of opinion between states over the nature and composition of the force and its numerical strength, the discussion was fruitless.

In raising the issue once again, the Western powers argue that one of the sides, having secretly violated its obligations under the Disarmament Treaty, might commit an act of aggression. They state that the country which commits the aggression might be able to use the national forces which it had left after disarmament and thus start an aggressive war. And as, according to their claims, the national forces belonging to a nation with a large population must be very considerable, and their weapons, whether hidden or newly produced, powerful, it follows that the international force must be far superior to them in numerical strength or armaments, in other words, "so that not one state should be able to challenge it." In order to make absolutely sure that the force will be more powerful than any potential aggressor-state, it is proposed that it should be armed with nuclear weapons.

I am firmly convinced that the proposal to establish such a supranational armed force is dictated by the Western powers' desire to keep powerful weapons in their grasp, and certainly not to maintain security, but rather to preserve military and strategic advantages for themselves, and put other countries in a position of inequality. Formally this armed force would be deemed to be an instrument of the United Nations, but in actual fact it would be within the control of the Western powers, because with the present United Nations structure, power in the United Nations executive bodies is largely in their hands.

"In these conditions," said N. S. Khrushchev, "to agree with the American proposal would be tantamount to agreeing to suicide, we would disarm ourselves, and then give NATO a chance to use the international armed force to dictate its terms to us."[5]

Such an international armed force, in all probability, could be used against the countries of the Socialist camp, and also to put pressure on small, weak countries under the specious pretext "of maintaining international peace and security." Moreover, without reference to the Security Council, they can be used against the national liberation movement of colonial peoples and dependent countries and, ultimately, exploited for purposes of interference in the internal affairs of other states.

Accordingly, the idea of supranational, international, armed forces is in no way in the interests of peace and security.

Before giving our views on the composition, command, strength, and location of international forces which I suggest to name international security forces, let us consider the possibility of aggression and possible ways of stopping it.

I imagine that responsible political and military leaders are aware what fate is in store for them if they deceive mankind and violate a disarmament treaty. Their own people will never forgive them. These persons will always be forced to remember their responsibilities, for it is the whole of mankind which will be judging them.

American monopolist circles, which are the virtual political rulers of the United States, will be forced to reckon with the opinions of the whole of mankind, with the opinion of the American people, which is just as concerned as any other people to see the establishment of lasting peace and friendly cooperation among all countries.

The attitude of mankind to war and peace was well expressed by a delegate at the World Congress for General Disarmament and Peace, held in Moscow in July 1962: "Today mankind is being forced under pain of death to prefer the risk of peace, which, however dangerous it may be, is nevertheless insignificant in comparison to the deadly risk of war." In other

[5]Speech made by N. S. Khrushchev at the World Congress for General Disarmament and Peace, 10 July, 1962.

words, even if disarmament does constitute a certain risk, it would be a much greater risk not to disarm. This is so obvious that it needs no proof.

Apart from the moral responsibility which would be borne by the leaders of any aggressor state, sanctions could also be brought to bear. The United Nations disposes of a whole armory of political, economic, and military measures for halting the military action of any state after general disarmament.

Articles 41 and 42 of the United Nations Charter empower the Security Council to take, against any state violating international peace and security, such measures as would be sufficient for the restoration of international law and order. Under the United Nations Charter and Articles 36 to 38 of the draft "Treaty on General and Complete Disarmament under Strict International Control," proposed by the Soviet Government on the 15th of March 1962, for consideration by the Eighteen Nation Committee in Geneva, the states party to the treaty would, if necessary, be able to make available to the Security Council a part of their remaining police or militia contingents designed for joint, international, coercive action. These security forces, however, could be used only with the necessary agreement among the permanent members of the Security Council.

These forces would be under the command of representatives of the three principal groups of states in the world, on the basis of equal representation. All questions of command would be decided by agreement among its members, who would represent all three groups of powers. The observance of this binding condition would exclude all possibility of the use of international armed forces in the interests of one state or group of states.

Among the organs of the United Nations there is a Military Staff Committee set up to advise the Security Council on questions connected with the use of armed forces for the maintenance or restoration of international peace and security.

This Military Staff Committee could be used as the high command for planning military operations and the command of forces made available by the members of the organization for implementing Security Council decisions designed to normalize the situation in regions where aggression has occurred.

In order to enable the Military Staff Committee to discharge these functions, it would be necessary to make certain changes in the situation with regard to the Military Staff Committee and the Security Council.

My own views on the creation of an international police or security force, as we shall call them, are as follows:

International security forces should consist of contingents from national security forces. These forces should be stationed and trained in their own countries. The location, size, and strength of the contingents which states party to the Treaty would bind themselves to make available to the Security Council under Article 43 of the United Nations Charter would be determined by special agreements between these states and the Security Council.

The contingents designated for joint international, coercive action under their own officers would come from national security forces retained by states after disarmament. Apart from military contingents, states would be obliged to make available to the Security Council the necessary assistance and services and, if necessary, accord the right of passage through their territory to the international security forces.

The decision to use the international security forces would be taken by the Security Council under Article 42 of the United Nations Charter. The command of these forces would be based on the principle of equal representation of the three principal groups of states, as mentioned above. The same principle of command would be observed if it were decided to transfer operational command to the Military Staff Committee.

The tasks of these forces would be the maintenance or restoration of international peace and security and the prevention and halting of military aggression by one state against another. In no circumstances and under no pretext would these forces be used for intervention in the internal affairs of states, including cases of revolutionary uprising.

In deciding on measures to halt aggression the Security Council would be guided by a clear definition of all the forms of aggression, a definition which would permit of no ambiguity.

One of the criteria in determining an aggressor state would be the fact that that state had been the first to invade another state, regardless of the excuse.

N. Pitersky

The strength of the international security forces would gradually be raised to a level where they could prevent aggression on the part of a powerful state.

It would therefore have to be determined by the size of national armed forces, as determined by international agreement, which would depend largely on the size of the population. However, in determining the size of national armed forces, account would have to be taken also of the extent of their territory, the length of their frontiers, and their economic resources.

The *composition* of international security forces should be based on the following principle: all member states of the United Nations should make forces available to the Security Council in accordance with the size of their own national forces.

The strength of national armed forces could be calculated for the transition period on the basis of not more than 0.1% of the population plus one man for each kilometer of frontier or coastline, provided that the total does not exceed 300,000 men for each country. Each state, in our view, would have to make available to the Security Council, at its request, up to a quarter of its national security forces. There will, obviously, be deviations from this general principle, since some states, because of their economic situation and geographical position, will find it appropriate to maintain smaller national security forces. If it is borne in mind that in 1961 there were about 20 million men serving in armed forces throughout the world, the reduction of this total to 2.5 to 3 million and then to 1 million members of security forces after disarmament will bring tremendous economic relief to all peoples.

In view of the fact that arms expenditure will be substantially reduced through the use of simpler and cheaper weapons, the maintenance of each serviceman as well as his weapons, uniform, and food will cost considerably less than at present.

Under the agreement with the Security Council and Article 43 of the United Nations Charter, member states of the United Nations will have to maintain a certain proportion of their forces, designated for joint, international action, at such a continuous level of readiness and battle training as to permit of an early halting of any attempts to violate the peace, from whatever quarter they may come.

Armaments should consist of small arms — rifles, submachine guns, pistols — and artillery. To enable these units to be moved quickly, they should be motorized and equipped with serial troop carriers, and parachute troops should be equipped with air transport. The contingents designated for action in the international security forces as well as the rest of the national forces should be armed by and in each country independently. However, the caliber and type of weapon should be determined by special international agreement.

Various objections may be made to the principle I have proposed. In particular, it is often said that if atomic and other powerful weapons were destroyed and the national forces retained by states were equipped only with light arms, mere strength of numbers would be enough to guarantee victory, and that consequently there would be a danger that states with large populations might commit aggression against neighboring states which, although highly developed, had small populations, and subject these states to their rule.

It should be taken into account that under the proposed General and Complete Disarmament Treaty, the International Disarmament Organization would remain in being even after disarmament.

Inspectors, on detecting troop movements and concentrations, which are indispensable preliminaries to invasion, would immediately inform the headquarters of the international disarmament organization, without the knowledge of the state in question, so that the various sanctions, including, if necessary, the use of international security forces, could be brought to bear.

International law, governing relations between states on the basis of universally acknowledged norms, is at present often violated.

The United Nations Charter and state sovereignty have been repeatedly violated.

In conditions of general and complete disarmament the sphere of application and effectiveness of international law would be substantially increased. This would also create favorable conditions for the codification of international law. International law could become a permanently operative code of peaceful coexistence, embracing the multifarious questions of relations between states with different social systems.

Disarmament would create favourable conditions for fulfilling the purposes and principles of the United Nations Charter which state that relations between states should be based on the principles of equality, economic cooperation, and respect for the national rights of states, regardless of their political and social systems and their size. All controversies between states could be settled by peaceful diplomatic and constitutional means. The United Nations Charter and the generally acknowledged norms of international law would have to be strictly observed.

Many questions of international law will probably, therefore, be reviewed. It may be necessary, for instance, to amend various treaties, conventions, and agreements to take account of the interests of small and economically underdeveloped countries.

In the light of general and complete disarmament, amendments may be also made in the Charter of the United Nations, designed to strengthen amd improve fundamental principles of the United Nations as an international organization supporting the strict observance of the General and Complete Disarmament Treaty, broad international cooperation, and the maintenance of international peace and security.

WALTER C. CLEMENS, JR.

•

IMPLICATIONS FOR UNITED STATES POLICY

The United States and most Western countries have more grounds than Moscow and certainly more than Peking to be interested in stabilization of the existing political order and the establishment of arms controls that would tend to preserve the military balance, but at a lower level. The have nations of the West have strong material if not moral incentives to reduce the danger of central war, cool the revolutionary ardor of China and other dissatisfied nations, and bring order out of chaos in the developing countries. Precisely because of the opportunities inherent in its great wealth, the United States has reason to reduce the imbalances in its scientific resources and cultural values that result from the present allocation of human and material riches to the defense effort, imbalances that prevent America from becoming more like Athens and less like Sparta.

CONTAINMENT AND COOPERATION

What should be the United States approach to the now bipolar Communist world? If we wish to move from a condition of cold war to cease-fire and peaceful change, should Washington seek to encourage both Moscow and Peking simultaneously to move toward accommodation with the West? The answer to this question warrants much deeper consideration than can be provided in this brief essay, but the overlap of United States and Soviet interests on many subjects of common concern and the vast disparity between these interests and those of China suggest that the more realistic approach would follow two main stages: first, to convince the Soviet government that its interests

191

would be best served by comprehensive arms control and peacekeeping arrangements; second, assuming this giant step proved successful, to bring China into this world of arms control. In any case we face a situation in which time is not on our side. The longer we delay, the more numerous and devastating weapons each party produces, complicating the problem of inspection; the more countries join the nuclear club; and the greater danger that existing weapons will be used, whether by accident or calculation.

It is possible, of course, that China's views toward disarmament may evolve as Soviet theory has, quoting Lenin from 1922 instead of 1916 and even going beyond the limits he saw to collaboration with the adversary.[1] The Soviet state, like China, was once isolated and insecure. It had few allies and many foes who worked within and outside the country. Russia stood brooding, excluded by her own choice and by the League of Nations and Washington, from the community of nations. As the Soviet government developed a greater stake in the existing order, its concern became more with security than with revolution. Will the same transformation overtake China? History does not repeat itself mechanically and the number of variables is legion. In the first place China's economic-demographic problems may not be solved in this century, thus creating a constant source of frustration, aggressive feeling, and expansionist tendencies. Further, even if China masters her material problems, she could follow the jingoist route followed by many nations, including the United States in 1898. On the other hand, most revolutionary movements do seem to lose their momentum in time, and the reduction of internal problems and external threats removes at least some causes of a bellicose foreign policy. The economic cost of attempting to overtake the other nuclear powers militarily would provide a sharp incentive for China to limit her military investment and concentrate on developing the nonmilitary factors of power in which she, as the world's most populous nation, is potentially quite strong. Finally, China need not use the

[1]See above, pp. 131-134. For a study of similarities and differences between the Soviet and Chinese revolutions, see Robert Vincent Daniels, "The Chinese Revolution in Russian Perspective," *World Politics,* vol. XII, No. 2, January 1961, pp. 210-230.

"peace" issue to wrestle with Russia for leadership in the Communist world. Assuming such competition continues, Peking could just as well utilize other bases to challenge Moscow, such as the model of China's economic development as a paradigm for underdeveloped, agrarian economies.

For the foreseeable future, however, political and other factors seem likely to ensure that Peking's views on peace and disarmament will resemble those of the pre-1917 Lenin. The fact that no prospect is in sight for reconciling China's ambitions with stabilization of the military-political environment only heightens the urgency of taking steps toward collective security where such progress is possible because of overlapping interests, namely, between the West and the Soviet Union. The danger is that Washington and Moscow may determine how to establish a less tenuous modus vivendi only to find out that the arms controls they might undertake cannot be taken because of threats from China and other militarily growing powers. The rapid proliferation of nuclear weapons therefore dictates that the states most interested and able to maintain international order move quickly toward the building of a warless world—*with or without* complete and general disarmament.

Since Soviet attitudes toward arms control seem to derive primarily from strategic calculations, the first step would be to convince the Kremlin that its security could be better provided in a system of balanced arms controls than in an unbridled arms race. To make this point may require that the West parley from strength, but also with a willingness to compromise and without any threatening demeanor or desire to seek one-sided advantages, for such behavior has usually tended only to stiffen Soviet intransigence.

Second, Western interests could benefit from a long-range strategy utilizing public and private resources to reduce the gap between the perceived "is" and perceived "ought to be" in the emerging nations. Such a program is not only morally incumbent upon the have nations of the affluent West, but politically expedient to thwart Communist—especially Chinese—subversion in the third world and to prod the Communist states into an interest in reducing military expenditures. As many economists have pointed out, the West has the resources to intensify the arms race even while radically increasing its investment — human and material — in the developing countries. Such a program, while providing a stimulus to some sectors of the United States economy, could also tend to compel the Soviet Union to choose — because of its more limited resources — between continuation of the arms race and increased development programs to maintain Soviet influence in the third world. The Western objective would not necessarily be to drive out all Soviet technicians from the developing nations, but rather to create new conditions in which specialists from East and West might eventually work together in assisting less fortunate peoples.[2]

Third, the West should stress the material inducements for Communist participation in building a warless world — the improvement in living standards, the prospect of long-term credits and trade, and joint cooperation in space and technology. The Communist states of Asia, even more than those of Europe, have an objective interest in such programs.[3]

Fourth, the United States must decide what compromises, if any, it is willing to make to buy Soviet participation in the institutions required to sustain order in a warless world. Two questions of principle are central: first, the level of armaments to be retained; and second, the nature of international peacekeeping machinery. Moscow's stands on both issues raise profound problems for Western security.

The Soviet GCD proposal modified to allow the superpowers to retain a nuclear umbrella until the end of the disarmament process is certainly more in accord with United States interests than earlier Soviet proposals to eliminate all strategic delivery vehicles at the outset. Because the United States leads Russia in ICBMs, however, Washington has generally favored a freeze of such weapons or a *proportional* reduction, instead of reductions to a common size. Whether we seek to preserve United States superiority or settle for parity at a lower level depends in part on our assessment of many complex factors — the inexorability of Communist expansionism; the sufficiency of

<hr/>

[2]See Seymour Melman, *The Peace Race,* New York: George Braziller, Inc., 1962; see also below pp. 240-252.

[3]For a systematic approach to developing cross-national bonds, see Vincent P. Rock, *A Strategy of Interdependence,* New York: Charles Scribner's Sons, 1964.

a minimum nuclear deterrent instead of a graduated response capability to defend Western interests; the prospects for a shift in the balance of power due to a technological breakthrough or the spread of nuclear weapons.

Without attempting here to provide an answer to these profound questions, a principle can nevertheless be suggested for proceeding toward a minimum nuclear deterrent—assuming commitment to this goal—in a manner that respects many of the vital interests of both Washington and Moscow. In the first stage of disarmament both sides would reduce their ICBM forces proportionately, thus maintaining absolute United States superiority, but with little on-site inspection—thus protecting Soviet secrecy. In the second stage, however, Washington would surrender its superiority and reduce to the same absolute number of missiles as Moscow, while the Soviet Union would renounce its advantages of secrecy and permit on-site inspection to ensure against violations of the agreement or surprise attack. Such a program would have the advantages of stabilizing the arms race and reducing the total megatonnage that might explode if war did erupt. Before either superpower drastically reduced its missile forces, however, it is obvious that some limitation would also have to be accepted or imposed on the nuclear weapons of other countries.

The Soviet position on international peacekeeping machinery troubles the United States because Moscow insists that international forces be limited to national contingents placed at the disposal of the Security Council by United Nations members in accord with Chapter VII of the Charter.[4] Great power conflicts prevented implementation of Chapter VII at the outset of the cold war, but even now the fact remains that any forces so established could not be used in the face of a negative vote by a permanent member of the Security Council. If this hurdle were passed, the *troika* command structure proposed by Moscow

---

[4]The following analysis is based on the Draft Treaty on General and Complete Disarmament under Strict International Control, submitted by the Soviet Union to the Eighteen Nation Disarmament Conference on March 15, 1962, with the qualifications noted above in notes 14 and 15, p. 137. Text of the March 1962 draft is in *Documents on Disarmament, 1962* (2 vols.), Washington, D.C.: United States Arms Control and Disarmament Agency, 1963, vol. I, pp. 103-126.

would still present serious difficulties for international forces, because a combined neutralist and Communist vote in the command organization could cripple all operations. Finally, according to the Soviet proposal such forces could be armed only with the light weapons permitted each nation in a disarmed world. Hence their quantity might be insufficient to deter or repulse the quality of forces of a state that clandestinely retained or produced weapons prohibited by the disarmament treaty.

The United States, in contrast to the Soviet government, has favored an international peacekeeping force not subject to Security Council veto and one with sufficient armaments to assure that "no state could challenge it." As one United States delegate to the Eighteen Nation Disarmament Conference pointed out: the goals of the United States proposal "imply nothing less than a world in which the fundamental rights and duties of states would in fact be subject to enforcement by collective sanctions and where change in such rights and duties not only should not, but actually could not, be altered by unilateral force."[5]

While the Soviet proposal for an international peacekeeping force seems far less comprehensive than the American, it may be worthy of study if for no other reason than that its more limited ambitions make it more feasible in a world of nation-states. As Dr. J. I. Coffey of the Bendix Systems Division has pointed out:

> It would be far easier to establish, maintain, and deploy a United Nations Peace Force based on national contributions than one recruited internationally, and far more feasible to develop a consensus with the U.S.S.R. concerning the use of this force, however difficult that might be, than to create the supranational government needed to control and give direction to a standing force so large and so well-equipped "that no state could challenge it."[6]

United States security vis-à-vis the Soviet Union would in any case depend—at least until the very end of the long road to GCD—upon maintenance of some national deterrent force,

---

[5]Alan F. Neidde. "Peacekeeping and Disarmament," *American Journal of International Law,* vol. LVII, No. 1, January 1963, p. 69.
[6]J. I. Coffey, "The Soviet View of a Disarmed World," *Journal of Conflict Resolution,* vol VIII, No. 1, March 1964, pp. 5-6.

perhaps on a kind of nuclear umbrella. Even if this force were finally eliminated in a system of total disarmament, the main deterrent to Soviet aggression would be a threat that the United States would abrogate the disarmament treaty.

If the security of the great powers against other great powers did not depend upon the international peace force, the narrowly conceived and limited force proposed by the Soviet Union might be quite adequate for preventing interstate violence between lesser powers—though perhaps not China.

The success of great power efforts to bring greater order into international politics and to halt the spread of nuclear arms would depend in part upon the creation of a role and a reward for all countries in the construction of a peaceful world. The great powers would be expected to set an exemplary example by significantly reducing their own armaments, even if a nuclear umbrella were to be retained by the superpowers until the end of the GCD process. Many nonaligned nations might welcome the prestige that came from providing the main contingents composing the United Nations peacekeeping force, whether on a permanent or ad hoc basis. China's participation in these arrangements would begin by seating the Peking delegation in the United Nations, probably on an expanded Security Council. For China as for all the developing nations the most powerful inducement to cooperate in a world without war would consist in expanded development programs made possible by reductions in the defense budgets of all countries, large and small.

WHO WOULD WIN?

The notion that adversaries may have common interests in limiting their competition and in collaborating to mutual advantage is strange to the black-and-white mentality of the cold war. But this principle is increasingly accepted not only by game theorists and strategists in the West but by Soviet ideology which has defined "peaceful competition" to include elements of "cooperation" as well as "struggle" between the Socialist and capitalist camps.[7] That Moscow as well as the West understood

[7]See "The Dialectics of Coexistence," in Robert C. Tucker, *The Soviet Political Mind,* New York: Praeger, 1963, pp. 201-222.

the importance of joint efforts to preserve the peace was strikingly demonstrated in the aftermath of the 1962 Cuban missile crisis, for example, in the positive Soviet response to President Kennedy's "Strategy of Peace" address (which reaped only scorn in Peking[8]).

Although a high degree of cooperation and perceived interdependence would be prerequisites for the establishment of a disarmed world, it is to be assumed that conflict and rivalry between states will continue. What kind of competition will this be? The Russian terms for the English word "competition" suggest two kinds of conflict: the Russian *konkurentsiia* connotes competition in the sense of the business world or of a zero-sum game, i.e., what one party gains, the other loses; a second Russian word, *sorevnovanie,* connotes the friendly rivalry, say, of athletes. And when Soviet spokesmen speak of "peaceful competition," they use the second term.

The logical dimensions of conflict extend even further than these two senses of competition. At one extreme one can imagine an intense drive by one government or alliance to overpower another by any means short of war. This, it would seem, would be the strategy to be worked out by Waskow's future Rand Corporations.[9] At another extreme, one can conceive of a situation in which cooperation among nations would become so intensive that all elements of competition would cease.

It is possible that East-West relations in a warless world could touch on all these points on the spectrum ranging from zero-sum conflict to helpful cooperation. But it seems unlikely that a warless world could be maintained or even achieved if international tensions continued at a high level. If conflict were

[8]"Kennedy's Big Conspiracy," *Peking Review,* vol. VI, No. 26, June 28, 1963, pp. 12-14. The Kennedy speech was reprinted in full in *Pravda* and *Izvestiia,* June 13, 1963. Khrushchev's comments on the address were made in reply to questions by editors of the two newspapers and printed in *Pravda,* June 15 and *Izvestiia,* June 16, 1964. The First Secretary accepted "with pleasure the appeal for an improvement" in United States-Soviet relations, but criticized Kennedy's address for not coming to grips with the basic problems of the cold war—such as the West's refusal to sign a German peace treaty, United States "occupation" of Taiwan, and other manifestations of United States aggession. Khrushchev's comments are translated in *Current Digest of the Soviet Press,* vol. XV, No. 24, July 10, 1963, pp. 21-23.

[9]See above, p. 112.

intense, nations would hardly develop the trust necessary to disarm in the first place; but if disarmament did take place, despite continued tension, nations would be tempted to rearm (a) because of suspicions that the other side was rearming or (b) in order to prevent what was perceived as a "loss" in international stature. The most useful and healthy attitude might well be a sense that both sides can grow stronger from competition.

The plain fact is that if country "A" sees the warless world as a way to "defeat" country "B," the chances of obtaining and preserving such a world are slim indeed. Even if A plans his victory by means short of war, his hostile attitude will deter B from disarming. This is true whether A is Moscow or Washington or Peking. Soviet assurance that revolution will spread, but mainly by indigenous forces, implies a basic hostility that would deter many United States Senators from consenting to a major treaty requiring some faith in Moscow's assurances of peaceful intent, even if the agreement seemed to be self-enforcing. Similarly, the historical underdogs, Moscow and Peking, are highly sensitive to foreign attempts to undermine their territorial, political, and economic accomplishments, for past Western domination and intervention have left a bitter aftertaste in both Russia and China.

How would Communist interests fare in a world in which peace was ensured by an international military force? What would be the worst and the best possible results—from the Communist standpoint? The worst that could happen would be a disintegration of Communist power in Russia, Eastern Europe, in China, and around the world. If the Communist parties were no longer backed by unquestioned military superiority in the countries where they now rule, if the non-Communist nations could no longer be portrayed as threatening the Communist homeland, if the tempo of Communist expansion grew still slower, dire consequences could follow within the Communist movement. The raison d'être and authority of Communist elites might be eroded; demands for freedom of choice and better living standards might increase; nominally Communist nations might seek allies and trading partners wherever they desired. These tendencies would be exacerbated by the appeal of "bourgeois" freedoms and comforts, and by the ability of the Western nations to use their present economic superiority to influence the underdeveloped nations and even some Communist states. "Coexistence in the realm of ideology," which Soviet propagandists declare taboo, would become a fact.

The best possible results, from the Communist perspective, would be that the economic laws of history could operate without intervention by military factors. The achievements of the Communist states would not be threatened by war. The revolutionary classes throughout the world would not be disadvantaged by the military superiority of the ruling classes. The Communist countries, relieved of armaments expenditures, might plan and develop their resources so that the Communist model became the ideal of all peoples. The Western governments, no longer able to point to the possibility of "Red aggression," might lose their ability to cooperate with one another or to subjugate the workers within their countries.

Given a warless world, would either of these two extreme patterns of development actually take place? It must be remembered, first, that a minimum of one or more decades will probably be required to achieve such a world. The very coming into being of such a world will probably depend on a diminishing of tension and an increase of confidence between East and West. Once in being, such a world could generate forces which reduced still more the enmity between peoples. Once the military element were gone from international relations, Russia could afford to look at Eastern Europe in other than strategic terms, as a buffer zone which must be held secure against possible Western attack. As Western economies become more socialized and Communist economies less centralized, there will be less ground for concern over ideological purity. Once the material needs of all nations begin to be met and free trade begins to flourish, there will be less cause to expand territorially and more perceived interest in maintaining the peace.

Of course neither Communist nor Western leaders can foresee the future with any certainty, and they may well prefer whatever security they sense from unlimited armaments to the hypothetical advantages of a disarmed world. If leaders of both camps really believe in their own political and economic systems, however, they should not fear a warless world. Marxists, particularly, should welcome an environment in which economic factors were allowed to operate without the inhibition of military elements of power. Westerners, on the other hand, should welcome a world without war because in most areas where Communist governments (not to be identified with national independence movements) have come to power, they have done so as a result of international and related civil wars.

International cooperation, if it is to make peace secure, must go beyond agreement not to fight; it must include shared efforts in the productive enterprises of a scientific and humanistic civilization. One reason for the relative peace of the nineteenth century was that the dynamic, industrializing nations of Europe could direct their energies to imperialist ventures in Africa and Asia. For a time, at least, they could move away from Europe, without confronting one another. Toward the end of the nineteenth century, however, the frontier became closed and what Lenin called the "redivision" of the world began, a process that brought the European powers into direct conflict. Twentieth-century man is confronted with frontiers much vaster and more challenging than those that absorbed the energies of nineteenth-century imperialists. As President Kennedy said after astronaut Gordon Cooper's flight, "Peace too, has its victories." Outer space, population control, conflict resolution, mass education, longevity—these are but a few of the gigantic problems challenging the pioneer spirit. These problems are urgent, costly, and exciting to solve. They offer ample opportunity for the sublimation of men's competitive drives. And their solution requires the kind of international cooperation which contributes to the greater mutual confidence on which a warless world must rest.

The magnitude, the expense, and the complexity of the problems facing the world may provide the greater challenges which will force East and West to see that their best interests require more cooperation and less conflict. The concept that Protestant and Catholic could live peaceably together must have seemed just as strange to the seventeenth-century Christian engaged in the Thirty Years' War as does the notion of a warless world to twentieth-century man. But on this point Soviet ideology rings true: "life itself" impels nations to wider and ever closer cooperation.

FIRST DOCUMENTS OF A

WARLESS WORLD

•

JOINT STATEMENT OF AGREED PRINCIPLES FOR DISARMAMENT
NEGOTIATIONS[1]

Having conducted an extensive exchange of views on disarmament pursuant to their agreement announced in the General Assembly on 30 March 1961,

Noting with concern that the continuing arms race is a heavy burden for humanity and is fraught with dangers for the cause of world peace,

Reaffirming their adherence to all the provisions of the General Assembly resolution 1378 (XIV) of 20 November 1959,

Affirming that to facilitate the attainment of general and complete disarmament in a peaceful world it is important that all States abide by existing international agreements, refrain from any actions which might aggravate international tensions, and that they seek settlement of all disputes by peaceful means,

The United States and the U.S.S.R. have agreed to recommend the following principles as the basis for future multilateral negotiations on disarmament and to call upon other States to cooperate in reaching early agreement on general and complete disarmament in a peaceful world in accordance with these principles.

1. The goal of negotiations is to achieve agreement on a program which will ensure that (a) disarmament is general and complete and war is no longer an instrument for settling international problems, and (b) such disarmament is accompanied by the establishment of reliable procedures for the peaceful settlement of disputes and effective arrangements for the maintenance of peace in accordance with the principles of the United Nations Charter.

[1]United Nations Document A/4879, September 20, 1961.

2. The program for general and complete disarmament shall ensure that States will have at their disposal only those non-nuclear armaments, forces, facilities, and establishments as are agreed to be necessary to maintain internal order and protect the personal security of citizens; and that States shall support and provide agreed manpower for a United Nations peace force.

3. To this end, the program for general and complete disarmament shall contain the necessary provisions, with respect to the military establishment of every nation, for:

    a. Disbanding of armed forces, dismantling of military establishments, including bases, cessation of the production of armaments as well as their liquidation or conversion to peaceful uses;

    b. Elimination of all stockpiles of nuclear, chemical, bacteriological, and other weapons of mass destruction and cessation of the production of such weapons;

    c. Elimination of all means of delivery of weapons of mass destruction;

    d. Abolishment of the organization and institutions designed to organize the military effort of States, cessation of military training, and closing of all military training institutions;

    e. Discontinuance of military expenditures.

4. The disarmament program should be implemented in an agreed sequence, by stages until it is completed, with each measure and state carried out within specified time-limits. Transition to a subsequent stage in the process of disarmament should take place upon a review of the implementation of measures included in the preceding stage and upon a decision that all such measures have been implemented and verified and that any additional verification arrangements required for measures in the next stage are, when appropriate, ready to operate.

5. All measures of general and complete disarmament should be balanced so that at no stage of the implementation of the treaty could any State or group of States gain military advantage and that security is ensured equally for all.

6. All disarmament measures should be implemented from

beginning to end under such strict and effective international control as would provide firm assurance that all parties are honoring their obligations. During and after the implementation of general and complete disarmament, the most thorough control should be exercised, the nature and extent of such control depending on the requirements for verification of the disarmament measures being carried out in each stage. To implement control over and inspection of disarmament, an International Disarmament Organization including all parties to the agreement should be created within the framework of the United Nations. This International Disarmament Organization and its inspectors should be assured unrestricted access without veto to all places as necessary for the purpose of effective verification.

7. Progress in disarmament should be accompanied by measures to strengthen institutions for maintaining peace and the settlement of international disputes by peaceful means. During and after the implementation of the program of general and complete disarmament, there should be taken, in accordance with the principles of the United Nations Charter, the necessary measures to maintain international peace and security, including the obligation of States to place at the disposal of the United Nations agreed manpower necessary for an international peace force to be equipped with agreed types of armaments. Arrangements for the use of this force should ensure that the United Nations can effectively deter or suppress any threat or use of arms in violation of the purposes and principles of the United Nations.

8. States participating in the negotiations should seek to achieve and implement the widest possible agreement at the earliest possible date. Efforts should continue without interruption until agreement upon the total program has been achieved, and efforts to ensure early agreement on and implementation of measures of disarmament should be undertaken without prejudicing progress on agreement on the total program and in such a way that these measures would facilitate and form part of that program.

September 20, 1961

First Documents of a Warless World

ANNEX I[2]
LETTER FROM JOHN J. MC CLOY, UNITED STATES REPRESENTA-
TIVE AT THE UNITED STATES-U.S.S.R. EXCHANGE OF VIEWS ON
DISARMAMENT, TO V. A. ZORIN, DEPUTY MINISTER OF FOREIGN
AFFAIRS OF THE U.S.S.R.

20 September 1961

Dear Mr. Zorin:

At the 18 September 1961 session of our bilateral discussions on disarmament you indicated that the draft of a joint
statement of agreed principles which I submitted to you on
behalf of the United States Government on 14 September 1961
would be acceptable to the Government of the Soviet Union
provided the following clause were omitted from paragraph 6:

> Such verification should ensure that not only agreed
> limitations or reductions take place but also that re-
> tained armed forces and armaments do not exceed
> agreed levels at any stage.

This sentence expresses a key element in the United States
position which we believe is implicit in the entire joint statement
of agreed principles that whenever an agreement stipulates that
at a certain point certain levels of forces and armaments may be
retained, the verification machinery must have all the rights and
powers necessary to ensure that those levels are not exceeded.

It appears from your statements that the Soviet Union will
be unwilling to agree to a joint statement of agreed principles
unless the above-mentioned clause is omitted therefrom. My
Government has authorized me to inform you that, in the
interests of progress toward resuming disarmament negotiations, it is willing to remove the above-mentioned sentence from
paragraph 6 of the joint statement of agreed principles since it is
an item to which the Soviet Union has not agreed.

This is done upon the express understanding that the
substantive position of the United States Government as out-
lined in the above-quoted sentence and in our memorandum of
14 September 1961 remains unchanged, and is in no sense

[2]United Nations Document A/4880, September 20, 1961.

prejudiced by the exclusion of this sentence from the joint statement of agreed principles.

The United States continues to adhere to and will continue to advance the principle contained in the omitted sentence as a necessary element in any comprehensive disarmament negotiations or argeement.

Very truly yours,

(*Signed*) John J. McCloy

ANNEX II[3]

LETTER DATED 20 SEPTEMBER 1961 ADDRESSED BY THE REPRESENTATIVE OF THE U.S.S.R. IN THE U.S.S.R.-UNITED STATES BILATERAL NEGOTIATIONS ON DISARMAMENT TO THE REPRESENTATIVE OF THE UNITED STATES IN THE NEGOTIATIONS

Dear Mr. McCloy,

I have received your letter of 20 September 1961, in which you express a reservation with regard to the position which the United States of America intends to adopt in subsequent negotiations on disarmament.

According to the agreement which we reached in the course of a bilateral exchange of views, the United States agreed not to include, in the joint statement by the Governments of the U.S.S.R. and the United States on the principles for disarmament negotiations, the proposal with which you are conversant and the adoption of which would imply acceptance of the concept of the establishment of control over armaments instead of control over disarmament. In your letter you say that this proposal "expresses a key element in the United States position."

In this connection I must state that, as you know, the position of the U.S.S.R. on the question of control over general and complete disarmament has been thoroughly and clearly explained in the statements of the Soviet Government and its leader N. S. Khrushchev. The Soviet Union favors the most thorough and strict international control over the measures of general and complete disarmament. While strongly advocating effective control over disarmament and wishing to facilitate as

[3]United Nations Document A/4887, September 25, 1961.

much as possible the achievement of agreement on this control, the Soviet Union is at the same time resolutely opposed to the establishment of control over armaments.

It appears from your letter that the United States is trying to establish control over the armed forces and armaments retained by States at any given stage of disarmament. However, such control, which in fact means control over armaments, would turn into an international system of legalized espionage, which would naturally be unacceptable to any State concerned for its security and the interests of preserving peace throughout the world. The position of the United States on this question, if it insists on the proposal described above, will inevitably complicate agreement on a program of general and complete disarmament, on the general principles of which we have agreed.

The Soviet Union will continue to make every effort towards the earliest preparation of a treaty on general and complete disarmament under effective international control.

I have the honor to be, etc.

V. Zorin
Permanent Representative of
the U.S.S.R. to the United Nations

MEMORANDUM OF UNDERSTANDING BETWEEN THE UNITED STATES OF AMERICA AND THE UNION OF SOVIET SOCIALIST REPUBLICS REGARDING THE ESTABLISHMENT OF A DIRECT COMMUNICATIONS LINK[1]

For use in time of emergency the Government of the United States of America and the Government of the Union of Soviet Socialist Republics have agreed to establish as soon as technically feasible a direct communications link between the two Governments.

Each Government shall be responsible for the arrangements for the link on its own territory. Each Government shall take the necessary steps to ensure continuous functioning of the link and prompt delivery to its head of government of any communica-

---

[1]United States Department of State, Treaties and Other International Acts Series 5362. Signed and entered into force on June 20, 1963.

tions received by means of the link from the head of government of the other party.

Arrangements for establishing and operating the link are set forth in the Annex which is attached hereto and forms an integral part hereof.

Done in duplicate in the English and Russian languages at Geneva, Switzerland, this 20th day of June, 1963.

FOR THE GOVERNMENT
OF THE UNITED STATES
OF AMERICA:

CHARLES C. STELLE
Acting Representative of the
United States of America to
the Eighteen-Nation Com-
mittee on Disarmament

FOR THE GOVERNMENT
OF THE UNION OF SOVIET
SOCIALIST REPUBLICS:

S. K. TSARAPKIN
Acting Representative of the
Union of Soviet Socialist
Republics to the Eighteen-
Nation Committee on
Disarmament

ANNEX

The direct communications link between Washington and Moscow established in accordance with the Memorandum, and the operation of such link, shall be governed by the following provisions:

1. The direct communications link shall consist of:
   a. Two terminal points with telegraph-teleprinter equipment between which communications shall be directly exchanged;
   b. One full-time duplex wire telegraph circuit, routed Washington-London-Copenhagen-Stockholm-Helsinki-Moscow, which shall be used for the transmission of messages;
   c. One full-time duplex radio telegraph circuit, routed Washington-Tangier-Moscow, which shall be used for service communications and for coordination of operations between the two terminal points.

If experience in operating the direct communications link

should demonstrate that the establishment of an additional wire telegraph circuit is advisable, such circuit may be established by mutual agreement between authorized representatives of both Governments.

2. In case of interruption of the wire circuit, transmission of messages shall be effected via the radio circuit, and for this purpose provision shall be made at the terminal points for the capability of prompt switching of all necessary equipment from one circuit to another.

3. The terminal points of the link shall be so equipped as to provide for the transmission and reception of messages from Moscow to Washington in the Russian language and from Washington to Moscow in the English language. In this connection, the U.S.S.R. shall furnish the United States four sets of telegraph terminal equipment, including page printers, transmitters, and reperforators, with one year's supply of spare parts and all necessary special tools, test equipment, operating instructions and other technical literature, to provide for transmission and reception of messages in the Russian language.

The United States shall furnish the Soviet Union four sets of telegraph terminal equipment, including page printers, transmitters, and reperforators, with one year's supply of spare parts and all necessary special tools, test equipment, operating instructions and other technical literature, to provide for transmission and reception of messages in the English language.

The equipment described in this paragraph shall be exchanged directly between the parties without any payment being required therefor.

4. The terminal points of the direct communications link shall be provided with encoding equipment. For the terminal point in the U.S.S.R., four sets of such equipment (each capable of simplex operation), with one year's supply of spare parts, with all necessary special tools, test equipment, operating instructions and other technical literature, and with all necessary blank tape, shall be furnished by the United States to the U.S.S.R. against payment of the cost thereof by the U.S.S.R.

The U.S.S.R. shall provide for preparation and delivery of keying tapes to the terminal point of the link in the United States for reception of messages from the U.S.S.R. The United States shall provide for the preparation and delivery of keying tapes to the terminal point of the link in the U.S.S.R. for reception of messages from the United States. Delivery of prepared keying tapes to the terminal points of the link shall be effected through the Embassy of the U.S.S.R. in Washington (for the terminal of the link in the U.S.S.R.) and through the Embassy of the United States in Moscow (for the terminal of the link in the United States).

5. The United States and the U.S.S.R. shall designate the agencies responsible for the arrangements regarding the direct communications link, for its technical maintenance, continuity and reliability, and for the timely transmission of messages.

Such agencies may, by mutual agreement, decide matters and develop instructions relating to the technical maintenance and operation of the direct communications link and effect arrangements to improve the operation of the link.

6. The technical parameters of the telegraph circuits of the link and of the terminal equipment, as well as the maintenance of such circuits and equipment, shall be in accordance with CCITT and CCIR recommendations.

Transmission and reception of messages over the direct communications link shall be effected in accordance with applicable recommendations of international telegraph and radio communications regulations, as well as with mutually agreed instructions.

7. The costs of the direct communications link shall be borne as follows:

    a. The U.S.S.R. shall pay the full cost of leasing the portion of the telegraph circuit from Moscow to Helsinki and 50% of the cost of leasing the portion of the telegraph circuit from Helsinki to London. The United States shall pay the full cost of leasing the portion of the telegraph circuit from Washington to London and 50% of the cost of leasing the portion of the telegraph circuit from London to Helsinki.

    b. Payment of the cost of leasing the radio telegraph circuit between Washington and Moscow shall be effected without any transfer of payments between the parties.

First Documents of a Warless World

The U.S.S.R. shall bear the expenses relating to the transmission of messages from Moscow to Washington. The United States shall bear the expenses relating to the transmission of messages from Washington to Moscow.

Treaty Banning Nuclear Weapon Tests in the Atmosphere, in Outer Space, and Under Water, August 5, 1963[1]

The Governments of the United States of America, the United Kingdom of Great Britain and Northern Ireland, and the Union of Soviet Socialist Republics, hereinafter referred to as the "Original Parties,"

Proclaiming as their principal aim the speediest possible achievement of an agreement on general and complete disarmament under strict international control in accordance with the objectives of the United Nations, which would put an end to the armaments race and eliminate the incentive to the production and testing of all kinds of weapons, including nuclear weapons,

Seeking to achieve the discontinuance of all test explosions of nuclear weapons for all time, determined to continue negotiations to this end, and desiring to put an end to the contamination of man's environment by radioactive substances,

Have agreed as follows:

ARTICLE I

1. Each of the Parties to this Treaty undertakes to prohibit, to prevent, and not to carry out any nuclear weapon test explosion, or any other nuclear explosion, at any place under its jurisdiction or control:

a. in the atmosphere; beyond its limits, including outer space; or under water, including territorial waters or high seas; or

[1]United States Department of State, Treaties and Other International Acts Series 5433. Initialled July 25, 1963; signed August 5, 1963; entered into force on October 10, 1963, after ratifications by the United Kingdom, United States, and U.S.S.R.

b. in any other environment if such explosion causes radio-active debris to be present outside the territorial limits of the State under whose jurisdiction or control such explosion is conducted. It is understood in this con-nection that the provisions of this subparagraph are without prejudice to the conclusion of a treaty resulting in the permanent banning of all nuclear test explosions, including all such explosions underground, the conclu-sions of which, as the Parties have stated in the Pream-ble to this Treaty, they seek to achieve.

2. Each of the Parties to this Treaty undertakes further-more to refrain from causing, encouraging, or in any way participating in, the carrying out of any nuclear weapon test explosion, or any other nuclear explosion, anywhere which would take place in any of the environments described, or have the effect referred to, in paragraph 1 of this Article.

ARTICLE II

1. Any Party may propose amendments to this Treaty. The text of any proposed amendment shall be submitted to the Depos-itary Governments which shall circulate it to all Parties to this Treaty. Thereafter, if requested to do so by one-third or more of the Parties, the Depositary Governments shall convene a confer-ence, to which they shall invite all the Parties, to consider such amendment.

2. Any amendment to this Treaty must be approved by a majority of the votes of all the Parties to this Treaty, including the votes of all of the Original Parties. The amendment shall enter into force for all Parties upon the deposit of instruments of ratification by a majority of all the Parties, including the instru-ments of ratification of all of the Original Parties.

ARTICLE III

1. This Treaty shall be open to all States for signature. Any State which does not sign this Treaty before its entry into force in accordance with paragraph 3 of this Article may accede to it at any time.

2. This Treaty shall be subject to ratification by signatory

States. Instruments of ratification and instruments of accession shall be deposited with the Governments of the Original Parties —the United States of America, the United Kingdom of Great Britain and Northern Ireland, and the Union of Soviet Socialist Republics—which are hereby designated the Depositary Governments.

3. This Treaty shall enter into force after its ratification by all the Original Parties and the deposit of their instruments of ratification.

4. For States whose instruments of ratification or accession are deposited subsequent to the entry into force of this Treaty, it shall enter into force on the date of the deposit of their instruments of ratification or accession.

5. The Depositary Governments shall promptly inform all signatory and acceding States of the date of each signature, the date of deposit of each instrument of ratification of and accession to this Treaty, the date of its entry into force, and the date of receipt of any requests for conferences or other notices.

6. This Treaty shall be registered by the Depositary Governments pursuant to Article 102 of the Charter of the United Nations.

ARTICLE IV

This Treaty shall be of unlimited duration.

Each Party shall in exercising its national sovereignty have the right to withdraw from the Treaty if it decides that extraordinary events, related to the subject matter of this Treaty, have jeopardized the supreme interests of its country. It shall give notice of such withdrawal to all other Parties to the Treaty three months in advance.

ARTICLE V

This Treaty, of which the English and Russian texts are equally authentic, shall be deposited in the archives of the Depositary Governments. Duly certified copies of this Treaty shall be transmitted by the Depositary Governments to the Governments of the signatory and acceding States.

First Documents of a Warless World

AGAINST THE PLACING OF NUCLEAR WEAPONS IN SPACE:
GENERAL ASSEMBLY RESOLUTION (XVIII), UNITED
NATIONS RESOLUTION AGAINST ORBITING OF
NUCLEAR WEAPONS ADOPTED OCTOBER 17, 1963[1]

1884 (XVIII). QUESTION OF GENERAL AND COMPLETE
DISARMAMENT

The General Assembly,

Recalling General Assembly resolution 1721 (XVI) which expressed the belief that the exploration and use of outer space should be only for the betterment of mankind,

Determined to take steps to prevent the spread of the arms race to outer space.

1. *Welcomes* the expressions by the United States of America and the Union of Soviet Socialist Republics of their intention not to station any objects carrying nuclear weapons or other kinds of weapons of mass destruction in outer space;

2. *Solemnly called upon* all States:

A. *To refrain* from placing in orbit around the earth any objects carrying nuclear weapons or any other kinds of weapons of mass destruction, installing such weapons on celestial bodies, or stationing such weapons in outer space in any other manner;

B. *To refrain* from causing, encouraging, or in any way participating in the conduct of the foregoing activities.

First Committee Action: Adopted on October 16, 1963, by acclamation.

Plenary Action: Adopted on October 17, 1963, by acclamation.

THE REDUCTION OF FISSIONABLE MATERIALS PRODUCTION

STATEMENT BY PRESIDENT LYNDON B. JOHNSON, APRIL 20,
1964[2]

We must remember that peace will not come suddenly. It will not emerge dramatically from a single agreement or a single meeting. It will be advanced by concrete and limited accommo-

---

[1]United Nations Press Release GA/2910, December 17, part II, p. 1.
[2]*The New York Times,* April 21, 1964, p. 14.

214

dations, by the gradual growth of common interests, by the increased awareness of shifting dangers and alignments, and by the development of trust in a good faith based on a reasoned view of the world.

Our own position is clear. We will discuss any problem, we will listen to any proposal, we will pursue any agreement, we will take any action which might lessen the chance of war without sacrificing the interests of our allies or our own ability to defend the alliance against attack.

In other words, our guard is up but our hand is out.

I am taking two actions today which reflect both our desire to reduce tension and our unwillingness to risk weakness.

I have ordered a further substantial reduction in our production of enriched uranium to be carried out over a four-year period. When added to previous reductions, this will mean an over-all decrease in the production of plutonium by 20 per cent, and of enriched uranium by 40 per cent.

And by bringing production in line with need, and the chart shows now that our production is here, and our need is here, and our reduction today will bring it here, we think we will reduce tension while we maintain all the necessary power. We must not operate a W.P.A. nuclear project just to provide employment when our needs have been met. And in reaching these decisions I have been in close consultation with Prime Minister Douglas-Home.

And simultaneously with my announcement now, Chairman Khrushchev is releasing a statement in Moscow at 2 o'clock our time in which he makes definite commitments to steps toward a more peaceful world. He agrees to discontinue the construction of two big new atomic reactors for the production of plutonium over the next several years, to reduce substantially the production of U-235 for nuclear weapons, and to allocate more fissionable material for peaceful uses.

This is not disarmament. This is not a declaration of peace. But it is a hopeful sign and it is a step forward which we welcome and which we can take in the hope that the world may yet one day live without the fear of war.

At the same time I have reaffirmed all the safeguards against weakening our nuclear strength which we adopted at the time of the test ban treaty.

First Documents of a Warless World

N. S. KHRUSHCHEV'S STATEMENT ON REDUCING PRODUCTION OF
FISSIONABLE MATERIALS[3]

A certain relaxation of international tension has been achieved of late as a result of active, persistent efforts by all peace-loving states and peoples. It can be said with full confidence that a big contribution to this has been made by the conclusion of the treaty banning nuclear weapon tests in the atmosphere, in outer space and under water—the first agreement in history designed to put a brake on a further intensification of the nuclear arms race.

It was with great satisfaction that the peoples also met the understanding between the U.S.S.R. and the United States, sealed in a resolution of the United Nations General Assembly, to refrain from orbiting vehicles carrying nuclear weapons. The Soviet Union, the United States and a number of other states took steps toward some reduction in their military budgets for 1964.

All this facilitated a definite strengthening of confidence in the relations between states and the creation of a more favorable situation for the adoption of further measures that would lead to the discontinuance of the arms race, to the solution of the main problem, the problem of disarmament.

Advocating an early solution of the problem of disarmament, the taking of effective steps toward the discontinuance of the arms race, especially the nuclear race, the Soviet Government seeks to take advantage of any opportunity to achieve in international affairs mutual understanding with other states with regard to the necessity of avoiding a nuclear war.

On behalf of the Soviet Government I should like to declare that the opportunity for improving such mutual understanding has now arisen in connection with the question of the manufacture of fissionable materials for nuclear weapons.

It is common knowledge that plutonium and uranium-235 are the starting materials for the manufacture of nuclear weapons. It is inside their atoms that chain reactions originate that engender devastating nuclear explosions.

For many years already the nuclear powers have been

[3]TASS News Agency, April 20, 1964.

steadily stockpiling plutonium and uranium-235, vying with each other who has more of these materials for nuclear weapons, and in doing so assuming very considerable expenditures, since plutonium and uranium-235 are produced on the basis of intricate technological processes, demanding expensive equipment and large expenditures of power.

The nuclear arms race, the competition of nuclear powers in stockpiling fissionable materials, have not been initiated by the Soviet Union. We were not the first to include this monstrous weapon of mass annihilation into military arsenals. But we must show concern for safeguarding the security of our country and all Socialist states and do this on a scale that is in line with the situation.

A moment has now come when the possibility emerged of taking steps toward a reduction of the manufacture of fissionable materials for military purposes. The Soviet Government has examined the question to what limit our country can go in this direction, given the present balance of nuclear power in the world arena, without in any way weakening the defenses of the Soviet Union and the firmness of the nuclear rocket shield, reliably safeguarding the security of all countries of the Socialist community.

Carefully weighing all data that have a bearing on the nuclear potential of the Soviet Union, on the one hand, and of the nuclear powers, parties to NATO (North Atlantic Treaty Organization) on the other, analyzing all circumstances, the Soviet Government took the following decision:

1. To discontinue now the construction of two new big atomic reactors for the production of plutonium.
2. In the next several years to reduce substantially the production of uranium-235 for nuclear weapons.
3. Accordingly, to allocate more fissionable materials for peaceful uses—in atomic power stations, in industry, agriculture, in medicine, in the implementation of major scientific, technical projects, including the distillation of sea water.

President Lyndon Johnson of the United States and Prime Minister Sir Alec Douglas-Home of the United Kingdom have notified me that they would issue statements on the practical measures in the field of reducing the manufacture of fissionable materials for military purposes, which will be undertaken by the United States and the United Kingdom respectively.

We are convinced that this latest step, though it does not yet constitute factual disarmament, will be assessed by the peoples as continuation of the course set at the conclusion of the treaty banning nuclear weapon tests and will promote a further improvement in the international atmosphere.

But one must go further. It is the profound belief of the Soviet Government that the efforts must be redoubled in searching for a solution of the main problems of disarmament, in adopting more and more effective measures of strengthening universal peace. This is demanded by the vital interests of all states, all peoples.

The Soviet Government is ready to take such further steps in agreement with other powers.

V

•

PEACE AND HUMAN RIGHTS

Samuel B. Gould

●

LEARNING FOR PEACE
INSTEAD OF SURVIVAL

I

Our discussions today are taking place against a backdrop of world events that with terrifying swiftness have turned vague theories into harsh realities. We now know from experience what it feels like to come to the brink of nuclear war. We know what the presence of horrible weapons of destruction all in readiness for use can mean to us personally and as a nation. We know the pride that comes of having faced up to an aggressor, but we also know the sober fact that the whole world is in jeopardy whenever such a facing up becomes a necessity. In the instance of the Cuban missile crisis we were fortunate, but shall we always be so fortunate?

Armament versus disarmament is no longer just a subject for debate and conference. It now presents on the one hand the very real possibilities for instantaneous mass annihilation once the single die has been cast; on the other hand it presents the hope of a time lag created by the lack of weapons. Joined to this is the equally real possibility of a breathing space for discussion and negotiation. Disarmament is not a guarantee of peace, however, since it does not remove the causes of war. It merely sets the instruments for destruction a few steps out of reach. Disarmament, when and if it comes, will be a tremendously important achievement, and it should be striven for unceasingly.

Address to the Institute on World Affairs, Santa Barbara, California, December 1, 1962.

But it does not mean peace by itself; it means no more than the temporary postponement of hostilities.

Furthermore, effective disarmament is possible only in a world of rationality and a reasonable degree of trust. Today's world in its totality offers no such rational or trustful promise. Still, the possibilities of universal disarmament should be pursued, whether the pursuit takes months or years or decades, since nations unprepared for war are more likely to look for peaceful solutions to their problems.

Similarly, international control of nuclear weapons vs. lack of such control is no longer a question for the long future. The point we have reached in the development of such weapons puts us into what Max Lerner and others have called "the age of overkill." In other words, we are now producing death-dealing weapons in quantities far beyond what is necessary to destroy our whole planet. Each day's new tests and discoveries make world destruction that much more simple and total. Nor do we find ourselves able to judge accurately what our present actions are doing to future generations. And let us remember that just as with other armaments, the creation of nuclear testing or even the destruction of all nuclear weapons is not in itself a guarantee of peace.

This brings me to the crux of what I have to say about a warless world as it relates to education, for in this aspect of life as well as every other we seem to be laboring under a delusion. We talk about peace and the need to prepare for peace in every way possible, but in truth what we are mainly talking and thinking about is not peace but survival. Similarly the nature of our education today is much less oriented to a preparation for peace than to a philosophy of survival. This is why I have characterized education as being on a tightrope, for it finds itself constrained to balance itself precariously between an honest desire to teach according to humanistic principles and an ever present necessity to train for survival in an age of horrendous dangers.

Real peace is more than the mere absence of war. It is based upon a positive and constructive philosophy and is rooted in the deepest conviction that man is indeed his brother's keeper. It starts with the stirrings of the individual conscience. We have done little in our schools, in our churches, and even in our families to create such a conscience. Every effort to awaken the conscience of America to a dedication to peace is met with violent accusations of muddle-headedness and even treason. For many of us the Sermon on the Mount is a beautiful bit of poetry to read, provided one does not take it too seriously, especially the passage that starts, "Blessed are the peacemakers. . . ." For many of us the Christmas wish of "Peace on earth, good will toward men" is fine for greeting cards and other displays, but it has very little to do with our actual motivations. We preach one rule and live according to another; and if we dare to do otherwise, we are suspect among our neighbors.

The phenomenon of world peace is also something quite apart from the practice of pacifism. Refusal to fight or defend ourself under any provocation is no guarantee of peace in the world as we know it. It may, in fact, be an open invitation to conquest and tragedy. When madmen like Hitler rise to dictatorial power, they must be stopped. The traditional policy of nonviolence in India is commendable, but what application does it have to the attack by Red China? Should India lie down supinely and allow itself to be overrun? Will this bring about world peace? Or will it, in fact, encourage world slavery?

Education in modern American society, then, finds itself on a tightrope with the increasingly present danger of falling in the wrong direction. To put the matter another way, it stands balancing itself in the center of a dilemma that brings the pressure of criticism upon it regardless of which horn it grasps to keep from falling. Shall it prepare the new generations for the world as it is, or shall it prepare them for the world as it should be? If it does the former, it continues to solidify and harden the crust of cynicism, deviousness, and sophisticated self-interest that seem to be the accepted and necessary adjunct to international relationships as we see them developed by astute national leaders, particularly those of ambitious nations. If it does the latter, it opens the way to what seems to be weakness and idealistic folly and it runs counter to the desires of the people, at least those desires being expressed most vocally. What are its motivations under such circumstances, and can they be other than what they are?

Learning for Peace

II

The three most prevalent and powerful motivations of American education today do not offer too much hope, if a lasting peace is our goal. Yet they have become almost inevitably characteristic in the past few decades as the tide of human circumstances has continued to rise around us.

The first of these motivations is that of *materialism*. A great part of education is devoted to assuring to students the means for making a living, for acquiring social status, and for making the comforts of life more obtainable. Wherever we turn we see examples of this, reflecting the preoccupation of our adult population with these same elements. In and of itself, this motivation would not be so bad if it did not so completely dominate the educational scene through high school and the undergraduate college years. By so doing, it overshadows those aspects of education that are more selfless in purpose and that probe more deeply into the proper shaping of human character. With such an emphasis, the process of preparing coming generations so that they will think and move constructively toward a warless world becomes difficult if not impossible to create. Concentration upon self and personal well-being shunts off to one side the broader and far-reaching aspects of life. It places limitations upon thought and action that tend to overshadow the deeper and more meaningful motivations we hope for in each individual.

The motivation of materialism also has an escapist influence not to be underestimated. When one is concerned with his own personal progress to the exclusion of so much that is beyond individual well-being, the result is a tendency toward actual unwillingness to think or talk or act about the great problems of the world as a whole. The latter become a threat to our pursuit of happiness, since this pursuit is so self-centered. We thus can forget easily that there are times when we should put aside our personal concerns in favor of those that affect the progress of mankind. Let me give a specific and perhaps oversimplified example of how this works by using a recent broadcasting experience of Channel 13 in New York. It may or may not be significant, but it sets a tone deserving of notice.

In late October of 1962, when the Cuban crisis was suddenly

thrust upon America, a policy decision was made at Channel 13 to set aside the regular programming schedule whenever necessary in order to bring to its viewers the most complete reporting and analysis of the world situation. The first major debate in the Security Council of the United Nations occurred on Tuesday, October 23rd, the day following President Kennedy's address to the nation. Representatives of Cuba, Russia, and the United States were the main figures in this debate. The feeling of tension was high, and the debate was acrimonious, to say the least. Together with the commercial stations, Channel 13 carried the debate until eight o'clock that evening, at which time the former went back to their regular commercial programming, interrupting with occasional bulletins. Channel 13, however, felt a responsibility to carry the debate to its conclusion and to follow it with an analysis by experts, giving them whatever time they needed to explore the situation fully. This was done and, from all reports, was followed by a very large and interested audience.

The original program scheduled for part of this time was called "The Art of Film," and was a two-hour presentation of four Charlie Chaplin films with suitable critical commentary. During the evening Channel 13 received more than five hundred phone calls from viewers who protested vehemently at the substitution. World affairs notwithstanding, to them the important thing was to see the Chaplin films. (May I say parenthetically that five hundred phone calls represent the attitudes of far more than five hundred persons and that the Channel 13 audience is presumably and I think actually composed of thinking people.)

The example may be insignificant, but I think it represents a point of view frequently uncovered today, a desire to escape from the broader realities and responsibilities of life when they are disturbing or interruptive of one's personal eagerness to find recreational or entertaining or cultural diversion. It is a selfishness born of materialism and insufficiently combated by our educational approaches.

The second major motivation in modern education is that of *scientific exploration*. Here again, we should not hold such a motivation in question except if it be dominated by those aspects of science which concentrate upon preparation of personnel and invention of instruments related to the national defense. Nor can we honestly hold even this in question when we consider the demands of the present-day world. The fact is that a very large portion of our scientific effort is directed toward defense either directly or indirectly, and there seems to be no way to change the pattern. The only hopeful attribute of this category of scientific work is that it stimulates more basic research which can and does have much deeper influence upon scientific progress as a whole.

But it cannot be denied that many of our ablest minds are being diverted to experimentation which is expected to have practical and immediate application whether for weapons or for a higher standard of living. Even at the far-flung frontiers of space exploration there are military overtones. Furthermore, in spite of an increasing awareness of scientists that there are moral implications in their work in which they must share responsibility, such awareness is by no means developed to a point of really effective influence.

Once more our educational systems are forced to straddle the issue. They cannot ignore the pressures of what appears to be inevitable necessity even though they may yearn wistfully for the opportunity to open new vistas of philosophical understanding for our scientists. Every major scientific invention has tremendous sociological results, but these are never dealt with as problems concomitant to the invention. The lag in human adjustment grows greater day by day, and our educational systems are almost timid about pointing this out, to say nothing of taking action. The basic process of bringing some sort of order and selectivity out of our modern "explosion of knowledge," as it has been so aptly termed, is staggering enough without attempting in any systematic fashion to glean even a meager harvest of wisdom from such knowledge. We are becoming more and more willing to accept the type of answers only the electronic computers can offer us. There is serious doubt as to whether these answers will provide a warless world for ourselves or our descendants.

The third great motivation in education is one of *activism*. We live in a world of movement, of action, of change, and education is profoundly affected by this. Few men allow themselves the luxury of meditation or of quiet self-communion; the thoughtful life is disappearing steadily from our daily orbit; we have no time anymore, as the poet said, "to stand and stare." Education has thus become equated with immediate action and relentless dynamism. Contemplative man is an anachronism of the times and is recalled only as a figure in history, benevolent, harmless, and unheroic. We are worse than our nineteenth-century utilitarian brethren in espousing their "up and doing" philosophy, and we truly believe we must "improve each shining hour" with frenetic bursts of endeavor lest we be considered traitors to the creed of growth and progress.

Our modern unwillingness to think of progress except in tangible terms and our tendency to place a lesser value upon the progress of the mind in exploring deeper and more enduring attributes surrounds education with a temporal quality that has great effect upon its emphases and directions. The important aspects of life in our view are those that are present and contemporary and immediate. The pace at which we live and the diffuse nature of our lives contribute to this, and education reflects much of this same pace and a corresponding proliferation of activities with which it increasingly surrounds itself. The atmosphere of most of our campuses and schools is one of constant bustle and rigid rationing of time and energy; the leisurely, unhurried necessities of individual scholarly pursuits are too often pre-empted by superficial activities of the group. Faculties rarely if ever meet to discuss intellectual matters except as these may obliquely relate to the mechanics of a curriculum; at all educational levels they gather merely to debate professional items that are unintellectual in the main. Students are bemused with a vast choice of peripheral opportunities, many of which are only tangential to education but which they dare not ignore for fear of being considered nonconformist.

Good educational institutions have great guilt feelings about all this. They see these motivations toward materialism, toward science, and toward activism dominating their intellectual enterprises and sapping the strength of their deeper academic resolve. Yet they feel they cannot brush aside the world as it is and, indeed, must concentrate their educative powers upon preparing the student for the immediate realities, shallow as some of

these may be. There is very little time for education that pre-
pares one mentally and spiritually for peace, and so the major
effort continues to be made upon the more acceptable and
timely process of preparing for survival and physical well-being.

III

From what I have been saying, you must have gathered by now
that I believe education today has great empty spaces in its
conceptual structures, spaces that must be filled if we are to get
on seriously with the task of making a world in which war is
obsolete. The motivations that rule the present must be put into
balance with other and deeper motivations, more difficult to
achieve, and more lasting in their significance. But there is real
question as to whether educational systems would be supported
by their constituencies in any efforts to strike such a balance.
Tradition points in the other direction, as many of us realize, for
education has long since adopted the pattern of following the
desires and demands of the people rather than that of leading
with boldness and courage and persuasiveness. Certainly, however, the possibilities of better balance should be examined
even if one may be pessimistic about whether they will be
accepted.

Education for peace requires a far more all-encompassing
historical approach than we have been willing to create hitherto.
Today, when a university or college announces a thorough-
going program in the non-Western cultures, it is still considered
news. Yet, our daily papers are filled with items from other
countries that are unintelligible or misleading except to those
with the background to interpret them. The citizen of today and
tomorrow needs to know the significant facts about and the
implications of the great movements of history, not just in the
West but world-wide. Nor is this historical approach complete
except as it touches upon economics, anthropology, political
science, art, literature, philosophy, and other disciplines. Obviously some new sort of distillation and coordination of knowledge and concepts is necessary if one is to cover all this, for
these disciplines cannot be taken up piecemeal. They must
rather reflect major threads that run through the fabric of
existence, threads that identify clearly man's major struggles

through history and that show the bright and dark spots, the hopeful and the dangerous elements. From this can come some sort of rational basis for an interest in and an understanding of international affairs in all their ramifications, a basis for man to use in meditating upon man's motives and yearnings and pressures toward recognition. How far beyond the purely superficial have we gone in American education toward developing any such basis? To do it we might have to recast entire departmental relationships and methods, reorganize our knowledge, and overcome the prejudices that have solidified over many years. Few of us are in a mood even to dare the attempt.

The study of man himself as an individual with mysterious inner drives and fears and exhilarations is also necessary to education for peace. In contrast to the natural sciences, those relating to the behavior of man are still inexact, fumbling, and frequently vulnerable to criticism. But they must be refined by the same sort of intellectual perceptiveness and encouraged by the same sort of enthusiasm and support hitherto reserved to the physical sciences, if we ever expect to understand ourselves and one another. Sociological progress in research of basic consequence is lagging far behind today, and much of its effort and resources are being expended on consumer characteristics or customer motivation in traditionally materialistic fashion. It needs a great dignity of purpose, and could well concentrate upon discovering and exposing those aspects of man that help him to be free rather than those that make of him a manipulated creature.

Peace cannot be achieved without ethical man, but education in America approaches the problem of ethics only tangentially. One can get a college or university degree with only the most distant and clouded view of the verities of life, with no sense of the classical tradition from which many of these verities flow, and with a taste for skepticism unrelieved by hope. To counteract the values made paramount today by our adult population, education would have to oppose much of what it sees, and this would only compound the confusion that exists in our minds and makes us strangely unhappy at the same time that it keeps us reasonably adjusted to modern demands. It may well be that the greatest conflicts we face are within ourselves and that our inability to conquer these contributes consistently to the general instability of mankind. Until we meet these conflicts squarely, until we put people first and things second, until we fashion an educational process that goes beyond the temporal and sets itself firmly upon a foundation reflecting man's understanding of and compassion for man—until we do these things and more, we can be accused in truth of merely holding the present popular line and ignoring the necessity for preparing youth to live in a new kind of world. Yet in the face of all this, education seeks its most constant and reassuring refuge in scholarship, set apart from values, and the expansion of knowledge has no purposeful relationship to the expansion and deepening of man's spirit.

IV

How to substitute a broad and sturdy platform for education instead of its present tightrope is the question I raise with you. What the platform should be is not too hard to determine; on the other hand, how to move people, people in large numbers and people in authority, to a willingness and even a passion to build such a platform poses staggering difficulties. The most important component required is that of courage. It will take courage to counteract the numbness that nuclear weapons development has created in the American people. It will take courage to be flexible in our educational approaches. It will take courage to go beyond what is presently acceptable in the public view, to discard the peripheral, to surround the educational task with ethical and philosophical and humane resolve, to think in broader and more conceptual terms, to challenge the vested interests whether lay or professional.

The vision of a world without war or, more specifically, a world of peace has been with us for centuries. In spite of our countless failures to make a reality of that vision, it is still attainable. But it can only be reached by going beyond the point of survival to the more lasting and firmer ground on which all men can stand because of their interdependence, their humanity, their understanding, their compassion. Education rightly conceived and developed, rightly understood for its true purposes, can take this nation a long way toward such a place. This is the greatest single contribution we can make to all the generations of Americans to come.

PAUL G. HOFFMAN

•

A WORLD WITHOUT WANT

World development is a primary factor in bringing about a world without war, but over 100 nations on this globe are, by any standards, dreadfully poor. The peoples of these countries are in active, sometimes explosive, rebellion against the conditions under which they have been living. They are determined not to accept poverty, illiteracy, chronic ill health, and despair as their way of life. They number more than 1.3 billion human souls. Add to this figure 700 million people in Red China and we find that more than two-thirds of the world's population are stirred by what has been so aptly called "the revolution of rising expectations."

This revolution can produce other Congos, other Cubas — indeed it could plunge the whole world into chaos. It could make difficult, if not impossible, even imagining a world without war. This need not be. The overwhelming share of responsibility for the economic and social progress of any country rests with the people of that country but they must have our help. The pressure for progress is so great today that we cannot wait for the slow development which was characteristic of most of the industrially advanced nations. Processes which took centuries for us must be compressed into decades for the underdeveloped countries. Fortunately, there are tremendous new allies in this struggle. Science and technology have given us exciting new tools with which to improve their lives, just as they have opened up new pathways to the stars. Our knowledge and our aspira-

Address given at The Institute of World Affairs, Santa Barbara, California, Friday, November 30, 1962.

tions have brought within reach the capacity to create, in freedom, a world without want before this century ends.

President Kennedy in an address before the General Assembly of the United Nations in September 1961 proclaimed this decade the United Nations Development Decade. The immediate task is to get off to a good start in that decade in our campaign to abolish poverty, illiteracy, and chronic ill health from the face of the earth. This task cannot await a warless world but, as I have already suggested, may contribute to the achievement of such a world.

Improving the lot of poorer peoples must be achieved principally by speeding the economic development of the poorer countries. This task, in addition to being one of staggering dimensions, is also of bewildering complexity. In order to bring about the economic development of a country, many factors have to be taken into account—its social structure, its political framework, the psychology of the people, to say nothing of its mores and traditions and the conditions to be found in each territory, which differ greatly. A development program, to be successful, has to be hand-tailored to the conditions of the country.

There is a further condition which must be met before a world-wide attack on poverty can be fully effective. Certain myths have to be disposed of.

We are told by its proponents that the peasant cultivator lives an idyllic life close to the bosom of Mother Earth. His wants and needs are simple. He is happy. Indeed, we are told, it is we who are unhappy; our goal should be to emulate the simple dignity of the man in the fields.

Of course the advocates of this romantic view know the peasant cultivator only from the pages of a colorfully illustrated travel magazine or from a brief glimpse through the windows of an air-conditioned railroad car. Their noses have not been rubbed in the grime and misery of the peasant's daily life. They have never had to work to exhaustion day after day for the equivalent of half a loaf of bread.

No, the happy native exists almost solely in conversations at cocktail parties in well-appointed living rooms. A recent investigation disclosed that there are as many stomach ulcers (which are reputed to be induced partly by tension) per thousand persons in Indonesia as in New York.

There is a pernicious myth that lighter-skinned peoples who predominate in industrialized countries are superior to people with colored skin. Many still believe, despite evidence to the contrary, that the darker-skinned peoples are incapable of absorbing the education, of acquiring the skills, and of exercising the judgment needed for economic development.

With some who believe in this myth, there is no use presenting evidence or discussing the question. But with others, whose only guilt is an unthinking acceptance of inherited misconceptions, a simple look at the leaders of much of Asia, Africa, and Latin America and at what the peoples of such areas as India, Mexico, and Puerto Rico have already accomplished in an amazingly short time is enough to destroy these attitudes.

Any close look at the peoples of underdeveloped nations will reveal that the human race is made up of about the same cross section of types in every country. Intelligence, capacity, ability, and even poverty know no color line.

Another myth—or rather system of myths—concerns colonialism. On the one hand, many of the citizens of former colony-owning countries feel that they made a substantial contribution to the welfare and development of their former colonies. On the other hand, deep-seated resentments in the former colonies blind the citizens to everything but the memory of exploitation. Both points of view are emotionally charged, and the peoples of both groups are extremely sensitive on the subject.

An objective look at colonialism shows that the truth is somewhere in between. Colonialism, in many ways, was exploitative and often ugly. But the colonial powers frequently made substantial contributions to health and education and in many instances injected the first industrial capital into the underdeveloped lands—the roads, docks, mining equipment, railroads, and other appurtenances of industrialization. In some instances, they brought another prerequisite of development: stable government. And they certainly brought to the peoples of the colonial areas an awareness of the possibilities of material improvement.

To assign colonialism the full blame for underdevelopment is unfair. In some cases it held development back, but in others it should be credited with the first few steps forward.

Parallel with the myth about colonialism is another myth: that independence, in and of itself, guarantees development. History contradicts this belief. Some long-independent countries are among the least developed, and independence can, at the beginning, add to the problems of development. On the other hand, when the initial handicaps are overcome, independence does provide an incentive for sharply accelerated development.

One of the most prevalent myths about development concerns its cost for the industrialized nations. Because budget makers and legislators find it convenient to describe these costs in terms solely of dollars or other currencies, we have come to think that these costs simply represent outpourings of cash—dollar bills—which in turn are extracted from the taxpayer's wallet.

This is not true. What the underdeveloped nations want and need—and what we have given them and will give them in large part in the future—is goods and technical services. True, these things must be paid for with money, but far less money comes from the taxpayer's pocket than the figures would indicate. Some "foreign aid" is, in effect, a subsidy for a country's exports. Goods sent to the underdeveloped countries mean jobs for workers in the industrialized nations. They mean greater profits through increased trade. They mean absorption of surplus commodities with a consequent firming of prices. They mean that, because of economic expansion, more taxes can be collected without a corresponding rise in tax rates.

In short, the betterment of business that results from aid to the underdeveloped countries serves to make the actual out-of-pocket cost of such a program substantially less than its book cost.

Fortunately, in speeding development, the United Nations and the specialized agencies have accumulated over the past years a vast amount of experience. The mere listing of specialized agencies engaged in developmental activities gives some idea of the scope of its work. There is the World Bank, the International Development Association, and the International

Finance Corporation which are the principal sources of invest-ment capital. There is the International Monetary Fund, which is helping to preserve monetary stability; UNESCO, which is helping to wipe out illiteracy; the International Labor Organiza-tion which has had more than 40 years' experience in training technicians; UNICEF, engaged in a most laudable activity of protecting children; the International Telecommunications Union, which is helping develop communications systems; the International Civil Aviation Organization, which is doing a tre-mendous job in expanding aviation facilities throughout the world; the World Meteorological Organization, which is doing great work in providing better information about weather and rainfall. There is the United Nations Bureau of Technical Assistance Operations which is helping countries in various fields — and the United Nations OPEX which supplies interna-tional civil servants to new countries. Perhaps one statistic will reveal the extensive nature of economical and social activities of the United Nations — out of a total of some 19,000 people employed by the United Nations and its specialized agencies, 16,700 are engaged in the economic and social field, leaving 2,300 to carry on administrative and political activities. Those of us who are among the 16,700 sometimes wonder why it is that 95 per cent of the publicity about the United Nations is concerned with its political activities.

One encouraging aspect of this staggering and bewildering task is that in at least 90 of the 100 countries, there is convincing evidence that sufficient physical resources are available to make possible decent living standards for their people. The problem is first discovering what the resources are by investigations in depth and then taking the steps necessary to make effective use of those resources. Inherent in their human resources are ample potentialities for bringing this about — but I must underscore the word "potentialities."

Fortunately, as I have stated, modern technology and science can greatly speed the process of bringing to light the physical resources of the poorer countries. One example of this is the aerial surveys where contemporary methods — steadily being improved — can already compress into a decade investiga-tions that not long ago would have taken a century. Thus aerial photography and its skilled interpretation — one of the marvels of our age — reveals resources hitherto concealed by precipitous mountain ranges, dense forests, desert sand, and inaccessible mudflats. This can show, and is showing, where certain crops might be grown, the economic potentialities of forest areas, promising regions for settlement, how best to lay out irrigation and drainage networks, where the most powerful head of water for hydroelectric power can be obtained, where highways might most usefully and economically be built.

Aerial cameras, supplemented by magnetometers, scintillation counters, and other electronic devices, have dispatched the old-time prospector, with his pick and mule, into the Hollywood film library and into history. This equipment can not only analyze the earth's surface but pierce that surface with an incredibly penetrating eye and reveal the probable presence of minerals and petroleum. It was by such means that areas which camel-borne explorers had rejected as hopeless attracted ground crews to tap some of the richest oil deposits in the world.

Another exciting new instrument for discovery — the peaceful atom — has relegated the willow wand to old wives' tales. Nuclear tracers are bringing new accuracy to ground-water investigations, while radioactive isotopes are giving unthought-of answers to the imponderables of plant breeding and fertilization, of animal husbandry and of insect control.

Nor is this the end. Electronic computers are being used for building mathematical models of river beds showing where dams should be built, flood control barriers introduced, irrigation works installed — all this at less cost, with greater speed and higher efficiency than older methods.

These incredible new tools are adding to the proof coming to the United Nations each day that the low-income countries are richly endowed with the physical resources required for their prosperity and sustained economic growth.

In the case of the human resources, the problem is different, and more difficult. The human resources of the less-developed countries have been shamefully neglected.

Every low-income country is extremely short of trained government administrators, technicians and professional men, teachers, business leaders and skilled workers, people who can make effective use of physical resources. Yet all experience shows that the people of these countries can become skilled farmers, good administrators, technicians, and skilled workers. And they are avid to do so.

The educational and training task that lies ahead is appalling in its magnitude. Of the 1.3 billion people in the 100 underdeveloped countries and territories associated with the United Nations, around 750 million of those at or over school age still cannot read or write. The achievement of literacy alone, however, will not help enough. Scores of millions must be given secondary education as well. There are immense needs for vocational training. Finally, as an overriding factor in economic development, vast numbers of people must be trained for highly skilled occupations. At a conservative estimate for the immediate future, the 100 underdeveloped countries and territories need to train one million people as top-level administrators, professional personnel, management and business executives, and middle-level technicians for building and industrial programs, health services, education, and supervisory positions in government and industry.

What *this* means in terms of closing the educational gap between the advanced countries and the less-developed countries is given to us in a nutshell by Professor R. H. Harbison of Princeton University. In a recent study of human resource problems in economic development, he defines high-level manpower as persons who have twelve or more years of formal education. He then goes on to point out that in the less-developed countries of Africa fewer than one person in every thousand of population would have this level of education. In the United States 280 persons in a thousand have had at least twelve years of schooling.

The United Nations and many national governments have stepped up their assistance to raise the capacities of people in the underdeveloped world. But a much greater effort is required than is presently contemplated. And there is no time to lose in getting on with this all-important task, for much more education and technical training are indispensable to achieve really significant economic advance.

We have lost altogether too much time already. Why it took

those of us engaged in trying to assist these countries so long to learn that there is an intimate relationship between the economic development of a country and the development of its people, I don't know, but it is only recently that education and training are receiving appropriate attention.

I said earlier that a development program must take into account not only the social, political, and economic factors, but also psychological factors. The first psychological factor that must be faced in any country is whether the leaders and the people of that country are willing to work hard and make the genuine sacrifices in order to improve. Unless they are, external aid will not be effective. It can only assist people who are determined to help themselves.

Quite often in talking to a representative of the less-developed countries the statement is made to me, "We need a Marshall Plan for Africa, Asia, the Middle East," as the case may be. When this is said, my reply is that the Marshall Plan is being given altogether too much credit for the spectacular recovery of Western Europe. In the year of the most massive American aid, five billion dollars' worth of goods were poured into the European countries. These goods were vital and there could not have been recovery without them. But the gross national product of the Marshall Plan countries in that year was $125 billion — so our contribution in physical resources was 4 per cent. As far as human effort is concerned, 99 per cent was provided by the Europeans.

I go on to say, unless they are prepared to make similar contributions, our assistance would be of no avail.

There is another block to development which must be eliminated and that is the paternalistic approach. We must stop talking about the rich helping the poor and instead make it clear that all countries are involved as partners in the great adventure of trying to bring about an expanding world economy. May I add that no country is so rich that it cannot profit tremendously by such an expansion and no country is so poor that it cannot help another country.

In the operation of the United Nations Special Fund we have, I believe, been successful in taking into account these psychological factors. We are purely a financing agency, subcontracting the actual operation of our projects to the specialized agencies of the United Nations. We assist countries in investigations of their natural resources. We assist them in setting up applied research laboratories—most importantly we assist them in establishing training institutions ranging from vocational instructor's schools to technical universities. The Special Fund is supported by voluntary contributions from governments. Eighty-seven of the 110 member nations of the United Nations [in 1962] contribute toward our fund. Our Governing Council has approved, to date, 246 projects calling for a total expenditure of approximately $500 million. We are supplying $210 million, the countries themselves $290 million, which explains why I repeated and repeated the word "assist." We help only those projects for which the countries themselves accept responsibility and to which they contribute as substantially as they can of their own resources.

Preinvestment work, the kind I have been describing, is, I believe, essential not only to prevent loss of investment capital due to inadequate preparation and study but also, and far more important, for uncovering resources of which the country did not have knowledge. Of the external assistance going to less-developed countries in 1962, it is my estimate that approximately $600 million is being devoted to activities of this kind. We like to think of these dollars as seed money, or as multipliers.

In addition to the $600 million of capital that will flow from the more advanced countries to the less-developed countries for preinvestment activities, I would guess that approximately $5.4 million of capital will flow in the form of loans and investments —public and private. Of this amount, perhaps $1.5 million will be loans which in banking parlance are called "soft." They are for non-revenue-producing facilities such as schools, hospitals, health services, communication systems, etc. These loans will prove sound only if there is sufficient improvement in the general economy or, in other words, if the developmental programs succeed. However, although these loans may be "soft," the financial support they provide is vital to a country. They build what we bureaucrats call the infrastructure which is the foundation that must be laid before many revenue-producing projects can get under way.

A World without Want

There is just one more figure I would like to give you—the amount of additional capital beyond that presently flowing to the less-developed countries which will be needed in the Development Decade. I would put it at $30 billion, of which $10 billion could be in the form of bankable loans and private investment with $3 billion additional needed for preinvestment activities, and the remaining $17 billion in "soft" loans. Twenty billion dollars is, of course, a huge sum of money to put out in risky investments and in grants. Of this $20 billion, approximately $8 billion would have to come from the United States. Let us not forget, however, that in this decade, if defense expenditures continue at the present rate, the United States alone will be investing some $500 billion in order to maintain what Winston Churchill has called "the balance of terror." Let us not forget also that one value coming out of this vast expenditure is the time it buys for constructive work, work that will make possible sharp reductions in defense expenditures as our world becomes better stabilized.

What can we expect in results in the next ten years? Assuming that we do move toward peace and a warless world and not away from it, there are twenty of those 100 countries I have been talking about whose people could move from poverty to decent living conditions. May I add that if those countries do move in that direction—and under free institutions—it will be proved to the other eighty countries that they can achiêve a similar result. And in the remaining twenty years of this century we can come close to reaching that goal President Kennedy proposed of wiping poverty, illiteracy, and preventable ill health off the face of the earth. We can have or come close to having a world without want. If that is accomplished, we who have lived in this century can hold our heads high.

SEYMOUR MELMAN

•

CONVERTING AMERICA'S ECONOMY
TO A WARLESS WORLD

The American economy now uses up two-thirds and more of its prime productive resources, its engineers and scientists, for military purposes. The conversion from such an economy to that of a warless world is not likely to be a quick transformation. Instead a process of conversion can be set in motion which will move the economy in the direction of a warless world. Even under optimistic estimates of possible disarmament conditions I do not envision this process as requiring less than five years. Accordingly, the concern of this essay is to estimate the nature of the conversion process toward a warless world.

Conversion toward warlessness must begin from the present condition which is the result of a substantial conversion from a peaceful to a military-oriented economy. In 1963, 6.7 million Americans earned their livelihood directly from military or civilian defense-related employment; 3.7 million of these were employed by the military establishment itself; and almost 3 million Americans in 1963 were engaged in defense-related private industry. These were primarily the industries producing aircraft, missiles, ships, electronics, and miscellaneous ordnance items.

Defense was one of the main growth industries of the last twenty years. By 1962, more than half of the federal budget and 10 per cent of the value of all goods and services (gross national product) consisted of national defense activity. About two-thirds of all the research men, engineers and scientists of the United States are now employed in this defense activity, for the federal government has become the principal sponsor of technical research and development. The virtual nationalization of this industry corresponds to the concentration of technical talent on military work. More than 89 per cent of the research and development expenditures by the federal government in 1963 are for defense purposes.

The military industrial economy has tended to be concentrated in a few states and localities. This concentrates the conversion problem. The following are the states which, in 1962, had over 10 per cent of personal income deriving from defense industry or federal defense payroll: Maryland, 11.3%; District of Columbia, 10.5%; Virginia, 15.1%; New Mexico, 10.9%; Utah, 12.8%; Washington, 13.8%; California, 11.6%; Alaska, 26.1%; Hawaii, 19.8%.[1]

In the following states, during 1962, employment in five principal defense-related manufacturing industries and defense agencies amounted to 10 per cent or more of total nonagricultural employment: Connecticut, 10.6%; Virginia, 10.1%; Utah, 12.7%; Washington, 12.2%; California, 11.2%; Alaska, 10.2%.

A recent study has disclosed that the most significant correlation of economic activity and defense economy is found in the county rather than the state units. Thus New York state does not appear in the above listing of states but the counties of Long Island include high concentrations of defense dependency.

The concentration of engineering, technical and scientific manpower in the defense sector of the economy limits the capability for large new capital investments without converting a significant proportion of the engineers and scientists to the field of expansion.

The growth of government is a further dominating feature of military economy. Military spending for 1964 exceeds the sum of all budgets of the federal government from the period 1933 to 1939. In 1939, total federal expenditures for education, labor, welfare, housing, and the like amounted to 42.5% of the federal budget. By 1965, all the outlays for these purposes will amount to 7.4% of the federal budget. Far from tending toward a welfare state, the federal government has devoted a diminish-

[1]*The Economic and Social Consequences of Disarmament,* Washington, D.C.: United States Arms Control and Disarmament Agency, June 1964, pp. 40-41.

ing proportion of its resources to the human care of human beings.

The growth of the federal government has been concentrated in the cold war institutional machine. In the federal government this includes primarily the Department of Defense, the Atomic Energy Commission, the Central Intelligence Agency, the National Security Agency. All told these organizations employed over a million people by 1960. Surrounding these agencies are a group of nominally private organizations such as the Institute for Defense Analysis, the RAND Corporation, the Special Operations Research Organization, and the Hudson Institute. Finally, about 50 per cent of the research and development funds of American universities derive from the Department of Defense and the Atomic Energy Commission. At the same time, a number of universities have become beholden to the budget of the federal government for a major portion of their total income. By 1959-1960 federally sponsored research dominated the total income of the following institutions: California Institute of Technology, 83.5%; Massachusetts Institute of Technology, 81.8%; University of Chicago, 63.9%; Princeton University, 75.4%. Owing to the substantial expansion of defense expenditure from 1960 onward it is likely that these proportions have remained the same or have been somewhat enlarged.

The movement of American economy toward a warless world means the conversion of federal employment, industrial employment, and private institutional employment from defense to civilian activity.

INSTEAD OF WAR ECONOMY: NEW MARKETS AND NEW JOBS FOR AMERICANS

In order to finance new markets and new jobs for Americans, $20 billion could be transferred from the defense budget while maintaining present United States forces. The 1963-1964 $2.5 billion savings announced by Secretary McNamara is hardly a beginning in the direction of a sensible defense budget—before international, controlled disarmament is acted upon.[2]

[2]*A Strategy for American Security—An Alternative to the 1964 Military Budget: A Report Submitted by a Group of Independent Specialists,* Seymour Melman (ed.), April 1963. 27 pp.

America's Economy in a Warless World

There is no justification for costly defense spending that piles up overkill. The strategic missiles and aircraft of American armed forces can already deliver the equivalent of more than six tons of TNT for every human being on earth. Even if 90 per cent of United States strategic aircraft were lost and 75 per cent of the strategic missiles were destroyed, the remaining weapons would be able to overkill the population-industrial centers of the Soviet Union at least 270 times over.[3] Enough is enough.

Large savings in the defense budget make possible the repair of areas of our national life that have been badly depleted during the last twenty years. But large investment for generating new markets and new jobs is not possible so long as two-thirds and more of our engineers and scientists are used up in defense work and 89 per cent of the government research and development is for military purposes.

Entire industries have become technologically and economically depleted because of the sustained withdrawal of technical talent and capital into the defense field. By 1963 the United States attained the unenviable position of having the oldest stock of metal-working machinery of any major industrial country in the world. Sixty-four per cent of our machine tools were ten years old or older. For West Germany the figure was 55 per cent, in the Soviet Union it was 50 per cent and declining, while the American stock continues to age. Productivity in every class of metal-working production is thereby limited and our whole industrial system is affected. Stagnation has become a characteristic of many industries (shipbuilding, machinery production), resulting in declining employment.

Parallel with industrial depletion there has been a deterioration in the condition of water supply, care of natural resources, and increased contamination of the very air we breathe. Productive investments in all these areas have been held up by the concentration of technical brains and money in the defense sphere.

The first stage of the American war on poverty is to be operated via the Economic Opportunity Act with a budget of $947.5 million. For 35 million Americans in poverty, this aver-

---

[3]*Ibid.*; see also Statement to the United States Senate Committee on Appropriations Defense Subcommittee by Seymour Melman, June 14, 1963.

ages $27 per person. This compares favorably with spending for this purpose by the Government of India, but compares unfavorably with the activity of the Government of Ghana which marshals about $37 per capita for economic development. By contrast the United States investment in manufacturing averages over $16,000 per job.

In 1964 the Senate Subcommittee on Employment and Manpower calculated the cost of meeting the backlog of national needs in housing, urban renewal, mass transit, highways, pollution control, soil and forest conservation, and community planning. These new markets require financing of $43-53 billion per year for ten years, then $31-41 billion per year for another decade. New markets that are financed at a level of $50 billion per year would generate *directly* 6,250,000 jobs (assuming $8,000 as the cost of an average year of work to be done). The productive nature of this work would multiply indirect employment. Adding private investing, the prospect of 10 million new jobs in new markets is what America needs as a foundation for competent solution of many present and foreseeable problems: conversion from military economy; erasing unemployment; solving the job needs of Negroes; job needs for our youth. Useful work for all as a national condition is within our reach. The following is the additional cost per year of a national program for upgrading the main education areas: $10 billion federal, $4 billion state.

These estimates are based upon an end of school segregation and job discrimination. For only then can the damage to the children involved begin to be repaired. Should segregated schools remain, the cause of educational deprivation would remain operative, and attempts at educational upgrading would be rendered futile.

	Five-year Program	Per Year
I. Remedial Education		
A. The Goal: To repair the human damage caused by segregated or inadequate facilities, understaffing, or other deprivation.	$10-20 billion	$2-4 billion
II. Improving Our Educational System		
A. The Goal: To provide for all the youth of this nation, education of high quality.		
B. The Cost: Increase salaries of instructional staff 50%.	$17.85	

244

Construction of new classrooms.	20.36	
Provide for improvement in teaching methods (Research and Training).	3.49	
Federal share of above at 50 per cent.	20.90	
Increased federal funds for colleges.	14.00	
Total federal share	34.90	$6.98 billion

III. Job Training and Retraining
  A. The Aim: To provide for, a nation's working population those skills necessary for their continued employment and/or the continued growth and prosperity of the nation.
  B. The Cost:

Provide high-school diploma for 2½ million unemployed.	1.25	
Provide job training for 4 million unemployed.	4.00	
Total	5.25	$1.05 billion
GRAND TOTAL	$50.15-60.15 billion	$10.03-12.03 billion
(Federal share)		

NOTE: All figures in this Table are in billions.

If, say, $14 billion a year were spent at an average outlay of $8,000 per job year, then the additional spending for education would generate directly 1,750,000 new jobs.

During the last 25 years, human welfare has been allotted a declining portion of our tax dollars. In the year 1939, total federal expenditures for education, health, labor, welfare, housing, and community development were $3.7 billion. This was 42.5 per cent of the 1939 federal budget. In the 1965 budget the spending for these same purposes is now estimated to be $7.2 billion, and this will be 7.4 per cent of the 1965 budget.

America's racial explosion has its roots in unrepaired economic deprivation. The remedy lies in education, jobs, and decent homes, and in the human hope that is generated by a serious start of a war on poverty.

New markets and new jobs for Americans are the indispensable requirements for peace at home.

Even though part of the unmet needs of our people will be met through private capital investment, public financing will be required. Implementation of many constructive projects by private firms can be combined with public financing. Decentralized administration can be used to avoid the growth of unwieldly central bureaucracies. The United States highway program suggests a model for financing large new capital investments in our country through public funds. In this case the federal government provided 90 per cent of the funds and the states 10 per cent. This proportion can be varied for the whole range of new market areas according to average income per person. Thus, the states, counties, or cities with lowest average income per person could receive 95 per cent of the capital needed from federal funds. The areas with highest income per person could receive only 50 per cent. This will concentrate job-creating new capital projects at the points of greatest need.

A first-year effort could start with a modest $5 billion for these purposes. Immediate blueprinting on new investments should be started so that the rate of new financing could be raised swiftly to $10 billion the second year and $25 billion the third year.

Well-planned conversion programs in every factory, town, region, and state are essential for efficient changeover of industrial and manpower resources from military to civilian work. The bills for establishing an Economic Conversion Commission in the federal government and in governments of states suggest the essential framework for an efficient conversion process and for economic growth.

Industrial conversion under disarmament would be greatly eased by the negotiation of contracts with military producers that go into force on the day following the termination of military contracts. Such contracts for civilian work require both a budget of national requirements and good planning at the firm and plant level. In detail, each firm and plant should plan for products and markets that are alternatives to its present military business. For each of these possibilities, production systems should be designed and engineering estimates prepared for cost and volume. The same planning should include preparation for retraining of employees and estimates of the lead-time required to put production plans into motion. Such local plans can be matched against estimated private markets and the budget of national civilian investments.

Within a framework of a vigorous program for new markets and new jobs there need be no fear for jobs when defense plants and military bases have been closed. There need be no fears of competition for existing jobs from Negroes or our youth as they enter into gainful employment.

Three principles may be suggested to guide programs aimed at reducing poverty in the United States while at the same time making the transition to conversion of military to civilian industry.

First: *Constructive private and government planning, in concert, is needed to generate useful work for all.* Private planning is traditionally acceptable in America as an economic technique. During the last thirty years the American consensus has developed toward acceptance of use of the government as well as an instrument for planning. With respect to government there are new issues: planning for what? Government planning for military purposes is widely valued. The principle of using government as an instrument for planning useful work for all is partly accepted. Government can be used as an instrument for economic development without fear of a dictatorial result if two conditions are satisfied: our society must retain multiple sources of decision-making—no monopoly of decision power must be permitted; second, the right of independent organization must be retained. Under these conditions government can be used together with private plans to generate useful work for all.

Second: *Private and public bodies, including local, state, and federal governments, should be encouraged to formulate concrete plans for investing in new productive activity.* These plans should include detailed estimates of cost, employment effects and income to be generated, and the lead time required to set new work in motion. Specifying lead time is critical, for that enables one to know how long it takes to set new investments, private and public, in motion once a decision to do so has been taken.

Third: *Conversion from military to civilian economy can be made a major opportunity to find people and develop skills needed for new productive undertakings.* For example, large numbers of engineers, technicians and scientists are being and will continue to be released from military work because of the attainment of over-abundance in some military spheres, or owing to possible disarmament agreements. Part of present shortages of qualified science teachers in public schools, high schools, and junior

Seymour Melman

colleges could be filled by making available a one-year teacher-training program to engineers and scientists released from military work. Salaries in upper-quartile school systems compare favorably with those received by many engineers and scientists. Recent sampling of graduate engineering groups suggests that as many as 10 to 20 per cent would give serious attention to such professional opportunities. It is also reasonable to expect that engineers and technicians released from military work, for whatever reason, would become available to blueprint and to direct major new productive undertakings in our own country and abroad.

FROM COLD WAR TO WORLD-WIDE WAR ON POVERTY

Competition among social systems will continue as less reliance is placed on military modes of competition. Therefore, the economic-industrial capability of the United States will become increasingly prominent as an explicit political factor in the world relations of American society.

The major contest for political allegiance between East and West centers on the underdeveloped countries of the world. For the 1.7 billion inhabitants of Asia, Africa, and Latin America, the central question is: how is it possible to industrialize rapidly? The classic Soviet formula is this: industrialization at speed can only be achieved with a thoroughly managerial society, centrally organized in a dictatorial hierarchy that wields a monopoly of decision-power. The absence of personal and political freedom is regarded as a necessary price of rapid growth. In the West there is the implicit counterclaim that industrialization can be achieved with personal and political freedom. The implication has been that this, in turn, is possible only under an economy of private firms. This appears to be a prescription for a slow process, especially where a large middle class is not present, and thus denies the impatient demand that industrialization be carried out at a speed that makes a major difference within a single lifetime.

I believe that we can formulate the broad outlines of a method that combines rapid industrialization with freedom.

The achievement of rapid industrialization with freedom is frustrated by the need to accumulate industrial resources out of

248

the meager means of impoverished peasants. For extracting industrial investment funds out of peasants who earn $60-100 per year, Stalin and Mao Tse-tung utilized ruthless police measures. But the United States can transform the political conditions of the industrialization process in the developing countries: first, by supplying the machines and money for industrialization; and second, by promoting methods for ensuring personal and political freedom while making use of the efficiencies of large, planned organizations.

The magnitude of the task is suggested by India's third five-year plan which envisions an investment of ten dollars per person per year. A more intensive level of investment is to be reached under the second development plan in Ghana where investment for industrialization will amount altogether to about $37 per year per capita. If we apply these annual per capita investment rates to the total population of Asia, Africa, and Latin America, this suggests an annual range of capital investment for industrialization from about $17 billion to about $65 billion per year for the entire area.

The upper end of this range of investment intensity amounts to about 10 per cent of the gross national product of the United States. In a world-wide industrialization program this probably represents an outside figure. The rate at which people can learn the ways of industrial life is surely a major restriction on the pace of economic development. Also, this estimated amount includes the population of countries like China which, for political reasons, would be outside such an effort—at least in a foreseeable future.

An increase in American production of this size is feasible as part of a conversion process from military to civilian industry. America's industrial goods-producing industries have been concentration points of unused capacity but are the crucial sources for supplying the capital goods necessary for industrialization. Indeed, it is more than likely that the capability of the United States for supplying the necessary products for industrialization is well in excess of the ability of the developing countries to absorb such goods.

In the presence of efficient conversion from military to civilian economy, the United States will possess unmatched industrial and agricultural reserves with which to sponsor productive capital investment on a large scale throughout the world. This can be carried out by imaginative methods including large banking operations for productive capital loans, proposed by Morris Forgash, President of the U.S. Freight Corporation, in his plan for a bank for accelerating economic development.[4] Large investments for these purposes would change the complexion of political opportunities for the developing countries and would transform the political and social crisis conditions which deteriorate eventually into military confrontations of the sort we have experienced in Cuba and Vietnam.

A second requirement for success in combining freedom with rapid economic development is the use of methods of organization — economic and political — that will give strong support to personal and political freedom in society. This result is supported by two conditions in economic and social life: the right of independent organization, widely applied; and second, the existence of multiple sources of decision-making in society.

The right of independent organization means not only the right of free association of individuals but also the right to form economic and other organizations in society. The essential point here is that no existing organization prevents new organizations from being formed. In the industrial system of the United States this condition is substantially satisfied by the existence of a variety of autonomous organizations. Even the largest managements must heed the opinions of trade unions, government bodies, and all manner of political pressure groups. The wide exercise of this right creates multiple sources of decision-making in society. The right of independent organization, extending from industrial enterprises to poetry circles, is one of the elements that critically differentiates the Soviet system from Western democracy.

The Soviet model offers the counterpoint to these conditions. That form of society prohibits independent organization, and only one source of decision-power is permitted — the party-state machine. In economic life the contrast is sharp indeed.

---

[4]Morris Forgash, *A Plan for a World Bank for Economic Acceleration of Backward Countries,* in Seymour Melman, *Our Depleted Society,* New York: Holt, Rinehart and Winston, 1965.

America's Economy in a Warless World

Independent managements, independent unions, or even truly independent literary circles are prohibited in the Soviet scheme. By contrast, the presence of these rights in the industrialized countries of the West contributes strongly to diversity in sources of decision-making. This, in turn, is a major support for individual freedom.

These are conditions that restrain political monopoly and support freedom in American society, even while large firms play a major part in the American economy, and the role of government in economic life becomes more extensive. Planning can be combined with personal and political freedoms.

The practice of independent organization in industrial life and the existence of multiple sources of decision-making are powerful incentives to rapid growth of industrial productivity. The interplay in decision-making by management and workers in the United States has pressed management to apply methods of mechanization and organization that enhance the productivity of both labor and capital. The result of this process is plain for all to see: the productivity of the United States is the highest in the world.

ECONOMIC EFFECTS IN THE UNITED STATES

A world-wide development effort will have an exhilarating effect on the American economy. Production capacity will be used to the maximum, especially in the industrial goods-producing industries. Therefore, the production cost of many products should be reduced. This will open up opportunities for price reduction, with widespread effect on the modernization and re-equipment of American domestic industry, even while industrial goods are being exported in large quantities.

The labor force will have full employment conditions under the peace race. Many problems of labor training and utilization that stem from the increased automation of production will become less awkward problems under full employment. An expanding economy provides the best background for occupational retraining, and even for the transfer of entire industrial plants.

An international industrialization program will have far-reaching effects on the future demand for American-made industrial goods. Furthermore, as the industrializing countries grow in their own economic capability, they become users of the more intricate types of fabricated goods. This development will proceed in accord with the general pattern whereby American foreign trade is most developed with industrialized countries.

The world-wide war on poverty will give the American economy competence to adapt to reductions in military programs. The problems of economic conversion under partial or total disarmament are most easily dealt with within the framework of an expanding, full-employment economy.

From a political standpoint it is significant that the United States could start a world-wide war on poverty, while also inviting Soviet participation in a Bank for Economic Acceleration of Backward Countries, aimed at raising agricultural efficiency by financing land reform. Bold initiative for this peace policy coming from the United States will have an electrifying effect throughout the world. It would transform the conditions under which the American people must consider solutions for both international and domestic problems.

While greater success in a world war on poverty gives political advantage, lesser success does not impose damaging loss. Indeed, the very act of participating in this contest has a life-serving and freedom-serving effect for all the societies involved.

Pope John XXIII

•

PACEM IN TERRIS

ENCYCLICAL LETTER ON ESTABLISHING UNIVERSAL PEACE IN TRUTH, JUSTICE, CHARITY AND LIBERTY, APRIL 11, 1963

INTRODUCTION

ORDER IN THE UNIVERSE

Peace on earth, which all men of every era have most eagerly yearned for, can be firmly established only if the order laid down by God be dutifully observed.

2. The progress of learning and the inventions of technology clearly show that, both in living things and in the forces of nature, an astonishing order reigns, and they also bear witness to the greatness of man, who can understand that order and create suitable instruments to harness those forces of nature and use them to his benefit.

3. But the progress of science and the inventions of technology show above all the infinite greatness of God, Who created the universe....

PART III
RELATIONS BETWEEN STATES

SUBJECTS OF RIGHTS AND DUTIES

Our Predecessors have constantly maintained, and We join them in reasserting, that nations are reciprocally subjects of rights and

Published by the National Catholic Welfare Conference, Washington, D.C., with some changes from the translation originally issued by the Vatican Polyglot Press.

253

duties. This means that their relationships also must be harmonized in truth, in justice, in a working solidarity, in liberty. The same natural law, which governs relations between individual human beings, serves also to regulate the relations of nations with one another. . . .

IN TRUTH

86. First among the rules governing the relations between states is that of truth. This calls, above all, for the elimination of every trace of racism, and the consequent recognition of the principle that all states are by nature equal in dignity. Each of them accordingly is vested with the right to existence, to self-development, to the means fitting to its attainment, and to be the one primarily responsible for this self-development. Add to that the right of each to its good name, and to the respect which is its due. . . .

. . . it can happen that one country surpasses another in scientific progress, culture and economic development. But this superiority, far from permitting it to rule others unjustly, imposes the obligation to make a greater contribution to the general development of the people.

89. In fact, men cannot by nature be superior to others since all enjoy an equal natural dignity. From this it follows that countries too do not differ at all from one another in the dignity which they derive from nature. Individual states are like a body whose members are human beings. Furthermore, we know from experience that nations are wont to be very sensitive in all matters which in any way concern their dignity and honor, and rightly so. . . .

IN JUSTICE

91. Relations between nations are to be further regulated by justice. This implies, over and above recognition of their mutual rights, the fulfillment of their respective duties.

92. Since nations have a right to exist, to develop themselves, to acquire a supply of the resources necessary for their development, to defend their good name and the honor due to them, it follows that they are likewise bound by the obligation of

effectively guarding each of these rights and of avoiding those actions by which these rights can be jeopardized. As men in their private enterprises cannot pursue their own interests to the detriment of others, so too states cannot lawfully seek that development of their own resources which brings harm to other states and unjustly oppresses them. This statement of St. Augustine seems to be very apt in this regard: *What are kingdoms without justice but large bands of robbers.*[56]

93. Not only can it happen, but it actually does happen that the advantages and conveniences which nations strive to acquire for themselves become objects of contention; nevertheless, the resulting disagreements must be settled, not by force, nor by deceit or trickery, but rather in the only manner which is worthy of the dignity of man, i.e., by a mutual assessment of the reasons on both sides of the dispute, by a mature and objective investigation of the situation, and by an equitable reconciliation of differences of opinion. . . .

ACTIVE SOLIDARITY

98. Since the mutual relations among nations must be regulated by the norm of truth and justice, they must also derive great advantage from an energetic union of mind, heart and resources. This can be effected at various levels by mutual cooperation in many ways, as is happening in our own time with beneficial results in the economic, social, political, educational, public health and sports spheres. We must remember that, of its very nature, civil authority exists, not to confine its people within the boundaries of their nation, but rather to protect, above all else, the common good of that particular civil society, which certainly cannot be divorced from the common good of the entire human family.

99. So it happens that civil societies in pursuing their interests not only must not harm others, but must join their plans and forces whenever the efforts of an individual government cannot achieve its desired goals; but in the execution of such common efforts, great care must be taken lest what helps some nations should injure others.

[56]*De civitate Dei,* Book IV, ch. 4; Patrologia Latina, 41, 115; cf. Radio Message of Pius XII, Christmas Eve, 1939, *A.A.S.* XXXII, 1940, pp. 5-13.

100. Furthermore, the universal common good requires that in every nation friendly relations be fostered in all fields between the citizens and their intermediate societies. Since in many parts of the world there are groups of people of varying ethnic backgrounds, we must be on our guard against isolating one ethnic group from its fellow men. This is clearly inconsistent with modern conditions since distances which separate people from each other have been almost wiped out. Neither are we to overlook the fact that men of every ethnic group, in addition to their own characteristic endowments by which they are distinguished from the rest of men, have other important gifts of nature in common with their fellow men by which they can make more and more progress and perfect themselves, particularly in matters that pertain to the spirit. They have the right and duty therefore to live in communion with one another.

THE PROPER BALANCE BETWEEN POPULATION, LAND AND CAPITAL

101. Everyone certainly knows that in some parts of the world there is an imbalance between the amount of arable land and the size of the population, and in other parts between the fertility of the soil and available farm implements. Consequently, necessity demands a cooperative effort on the part of the people to bring about a quicker exchange of goods, or of capital, or the migration of people themselves. . . .

DISARMAMENT

109. On the other hand, it is with deep sorrow that We note the enormous stocks of armaments that have been and still are being made in more economically developed countries, with a vast outlay of intellectual and economic resources. And so it happens that, while the people of these countries are loaded with heavy burdens, other countries as a result are deprived of the collaboration they need in order to make economic and social progress.

110. The production of arms is allegedly justified on the grounds that in present-day conditions peace cannot be preserved without an equal balance of armaments. And so, if one country increases its armaments, others feel the need to do the same; and if one country is equipped with nuclear weapons, other countries must produce their own, equally destructive.

111. Consequently, people live in constant fear lest the storm that every moment threatens should break upon them with dreadful violence. And with good reason, for the arms of war are ready at hand. Even though it is difficult to believe that anyone would dare bring upon himself the appalling destruction and sorrow that war would bring in its train, it cannot be denied that the conflagration can be set off by some unexpected and unpremeditated act. And one must bear in mind that, even though the monstrous power of modern weapons acts as a deterrent, there is nevertheless reason to fear that the mere continuance of nuclear tests, undertaken with war in mind, can seriously jeopardize various kinds of life on earth.

112. Justice, then, right reason and consideration for human dignity and life urgently demand that the arms race should cease; that the stockpiles which exist in various countries should be reduced equally and simultaneously by the parties concerned; that nuclear weapons should be banned; and finally that all come to an agreement on a fitting program of disarmament, employing mutual and effective controls. . . .

113. All must realize that there is no hope of putting an end to the building up of armaments, nor of reducing the present stocks, nor, still less—and this is the main point—of abolishing them altogether, unless the process is complete and thorough and unless it proceeds from inner conviction: unless, that is, everyone sincerely cooperates to banish the fear and anxious expectation of war with which men are oppressed. If this is to come about, the fundamental principle on which our present peace depends must be replaced by another, which declares that the true and solid peace of nations consists not in equality of arms but in mutual trust alone. We believe that this can be brought to pass, and we consider that, since it concerns a matter not only demanded by right reason but also eminently desirable in itself, it will prove to be the source of many benefits.

114. In the first place, it is an objective demanded by reason. There can be, or at least there should be, no doubt that relations between states, as between individuals, should be regulated not by the force of arms but by the light of reason, by the rule, that is, of truth, of justice and of active and sincere cooperation.

115. Secondly, We say that it is an objective earnestly to be

desired in itself. Is there anyone who does not ardently yearn to
see dangers of war banished, to see peace preserved and daily
more firmly established?

116. And finally, it is an objective which will be a fruitful
source of many benefits, for its advantages will be felt everywhere, by individuals, by families, by nations, by the whole
human family. The warning of Pius XII still rings in our ears:
Nothing is lost by peace; everything may be lost by war.[60]...

118. In the highest and most authoritative assemblies, let
men give serious thought to the problem of a peaceful adjustment of relations between political communities on a world
level: an adjustment founded on mutual trust, on sincerity in
negotiations, on faithful fulfillment of obligations assumed. Let
them study the problem until they find that point of agreement
from which it will be possible to commence to go forward
towards accords that will be sincere, lasting and fruitful....

IN LIBERTY

120. It has also to be borne in mind that relations between states
should be based on freedom, that is to say, that no country may
unjustly oppress others or unduly meddle in their affairs. On the
contrary, all should help to develop in others a sense of responsibility, a spirit of enterprise, and an earnest desire to be the first
to promote their own advancement in every field.

THE EVOLUTION OF ECONOMICALLY
UNDERDEVELOPED COUNTRIES

... 124. Our Predecessor Pius XII already proclaimed that *in the
field of a new order founded on moral principles, there is no room for
violation of freedom, integrity and security of other nations, no matter
what may be their territorial extension or their capacity for defense. It is
inevitable that the powerful states, by reason of their greater potential
and their power, should pave the way in the establishment of economic
groups comprising not only themselves but also smaller and weaker states
as well. It is nevertheless indispensable that in the interests of the common
good they, as all others, should respect the rights of those smaller states to
political freedom, to economic development and to the adequate protec-*

[60]Cf. Radio Message, Aug. 24, 1939, *A.A.S.* XXXI, 1939, p. 334.

tion, in the case of conflicts between nations, of that neutrality which is theirs according to the natural, as well as international, law. In this way, and in this way only, will they be able to obtain a fitting share of the common good, and assure the material and spiritual welfare of their people.[62]

125. It is vitally important, therefore, that the wealthier states, in providing varied forms of assistance to the poorer, should respect the moral values and ethnic characteristics peculiar to each, and also that they should avoid any intention of political domination. If this is done, *a precious contribution will be made towards the formation of a world community, a community in which each member, whilst conscious of its own individual rights and duties, will work in a relationship of equality towards the attainment of the universal common good.*[63]

SIGNS OF THE TIMES

126. Men are becoming more and more convinced that disputes which arise between states should not be resolved by recourse to arms, but rather by negotiation.

127. We grant indeed that this conviction is chiefly based on the terrible destructive force of modern weapons and a fear of the calamities and frightful destruction which such weapons would cause. Therefore, in an age such as ours which prides itself on its atomic energy it is contrary to reason to hold that war is now a suitable way to restore rights which have been violated.

128. Nevertheless, unfortunately, the law of fear still reigns among peoples, and it forces them to spend fabulous sums for armaments, not for aggression they affirm—and there is no reason for not believing them—but to dissuade others from aggression.

129. There is reason to hope, however, that by meeting and negotiating, men may come to discover better the bonds that unite them together, deriving from the human nature which they have in common; and that they may also come to discover that one of the most profound requirements of their common nature is this: that between them and their respective peoples it is not fear which should reign but love, a love which tends to

[62]Cf. Radio Message, Christmas Eve, 1941, *A.A.S.* XXXIV, 1942, pp. 16-17.
[63]Encycl. *Mater et Magistra* of John XXIII, *A.A.S.* LIII, 1961, p. 443.

express itself in a collaboration that is loyal, manifold in form and productive of many benefits.

PART IV
RELATIONSHIP OF MEN AND OF POLITICAL COMMUNITIES WITH THE WORLD COMMUNITY

INTERDEPENDENCE BETWEEN POLITICAL COMMUNITIES

The recent progress of science and technology, since it has profoundly influenced human conduct, is rousing men everywhere in the world to more and more cooperation and association with one another. Today the exchange of goods and ideas, travel from one country to another have greatly increased. Consequently, the close relations of individuals, families, intermediate associations belonging to different countries have become vastly more frequent and conferences between heads of states are held at shorter intervals. At the same time the interdependence of national economies has grown deeper, one becoming progressively more closely related to the other, so that they become, as it were, integral parts of the one world economy. Finally, the social progress, order, security and peace of each country are necessarily connected with the social progress, order, security and peace of all other countries.

131. Given these conditions, it is obvious that individual countries cannot rightly seek their own interests and develop themselves in isolation from the rest, for the prosperity and development of one country follows partly in the train of the prosperity and progress of all the rest and partly produces that prosperity and progress.

INSUFFICIENCY OF MODERN STATES TO ENSURE THE UNIVERSAL COMMON GOOD

132. No era will destroy the unity of the human family since it is made up of human beings sharing with equal right their natural dignity. For this reason, necessity, rooted in man's very nature, will always demand that the common good be sought in sufficient measure because it concerns the entire human family.

133. In times past, it seemed that the leaders of nations might be in a position to provide for the universal common

good, either through normal diplomatic channels, or through top-level meetings, or through conventions or treaties, by making use of methods and instruments suggested by natural law, the law of nations, or international law.

134. In our time, however, relationships between states have changed greatly. On the one hand, the universal common good poses very serious questions which are difficult and which demand immediate solution especially because they are concerned with safeguarding the security and peace of the whole world. On the other hand the heads of individual states, inasmuch as they are juridically equal, are not entirely successful no matter how often they meet or how hard they try to find more fitting juridical instruments. This is due not to lack of goodwill and initiative but to lack of adequate power to back up their authority.

135. Therefore, under the present circumstances of human society both the structure and form of governments as well as the power which public authority wields in all the nations of the world, must be considered inadequate to promote the universal common good.

CONNECTION BETWEEN THE COMMON GOOD AND POLITICAL AUTHORITY

136. Moreover, if we carefully consider the essential nature of the common good on the one hand, and the nature and function of public authority on the other, everyone sees that there is an intrinsic connection between the two. And, indeed, just as the moral order needs public authority to promote the common good in civil society, it likewise demands that public authority actually be able to attain it. From this it follows that the governmental institutions, on which public authority depends and through which it functions and pursues its end, should be provided with such structure and efficacy that they can lead to the common good by ways and methods which are suitably adapted to various contingencies.

137. Today the universal common good poses problems of world-wide dimensions, which cannot be adequately tackled or solved except by the efforts of public authority endowed with a wideness of powers, structure and means of the same propor-

tions: that is, of public authority which is in a position to operate in an effective manner on a world-wide basis. The moral order itself, therefore, demands that such a form of public authority be established.

PUBLIC AUTHORITY INSTITUTED BY COMMON CONSENT AND NOT IMPOSED BY FORCE

138. This public authority, having world-wide power and endowed with the proper means for the efficacious pursuit of its objective, which is the universal common good in concrete form, must be set up by common accord and not imposed by force. The reason is that such an authority must be in a position to operate effectively; yet, at the same time, its action must be inspired by sincere and real impartiality: it must be an action aimed at satisfying the universal common good. The difficulty is that there would be reason to fear that a supranational or world-wide public authority, imposed by force by the more powerful nations might be an instrument of one-sided interests; and even should this not happen, it would be difficult for it to avoid all suspicion of partiality in its actions, and this would take from the force and effectiveness of its activity. Even though there may be pronounced differences between nations as regards the degree of their economic development and their military power, they are all very sensitive as regards their juridical equality and the excellence of their way of life. For that reason, they are right in not easily yielding obedience to an authority imposed by force, or to an authority in whose creation they had no part, or to which they themselves did not decide to submit by their own free choice.

THE UNIVERSAL COMMON GOOD AND PERSONAL RIGHTS

139. Like the common good of individual states, so too the universal common good cannot be determined except by having regard for the human person. Therefore, the public and universal authority, too, must have as its fundamental objective the recognition, respect, safeguarding and promotion of the rights of the human person; this can be done by direct action when required, or by creating on a world scale an environment in which leaders of the individual countries can suitably maintain their own functions.

Pacem in Terris

140. Moreover, just as it is necessary in each state that relations which the public authority has with its citizens, families and intermediate associations be controlled and regulated by the principle of subsidiarity, it is equally necessary that the relationships which exist between the world-wide public authority and the public authorities of individual nations be governed by the same principle. This means that the world-wide public authority must tackle and solve problems of an economic, social, political or cultural character which are posed by the universal common good. For, because of the vastness, complexity and urgency of those problems, the public authorities of the individual states are not in a position to tackle them with any hope of a postive solution.

141. The world-wide public authority is not intended to limit the sphere of action of the public authority of the individual state, much less to take its place. On the contrary, its purpose is to create, on a world basis, an environment in which the public authorities of each state, its citizens and intermediate associations, can carry out their tasks, fulfill their duties and exercise their rights with greater security.[64]

MODERN DEVELOPMENTS

142. As is known, the United Nations Organization (U.N.O.) was established on June 26, 1945, and to it there were subsequently added specialized agencies consisting of members designated by the public authority of the various countries with important international tasks in the economic, social, cultural, educational and health fields. The United Nations Organization had as its essential purpose the maintenance and consolidation of peace between peoples, fostering between them friendly relations, based on the principles of equality, mutual respect, and varied forms of cooperation in every sector of human endeavor.

143. An act of the highest importance performed by the United Nations Organization was the Universal Declaration of Human Rights, approved in the General Assembly of December 10, 1948. In the preamble of that Declaration, the recognition

[64]Cf. Address of Pius XII to youths of Catholic Action from the dioceses of Italy gathered in Rome, Sept. 12, 1948, *A.A.S.* XL, p. 412.

and respect of those rights and respective liberties is proclaimed as a goal to be achieved by all peoples and all countries.

144. We are fully aware that some objections and reservations were raised regarding certain points in the Declaration, and rightly so. There is no doubt, however, that the document represents an important step on the path towards the juridical-political organization of all the peoples of the world. For in it, in most solemn form, the dignity of a human person is acknowledged to all human beings; and as a consequence there is proclaimed, as a fundamental right, the right of every man freely to investigate the truth and to follow the norms of moral good and justice, and also the right to a life worthy of man's dignity, while other rights connected with those mentioned are likewise proclaimed.

145. It is therefore our ardent desire that the United Nations Organization—in its structure and in its means—may become ever more equal to the magnitude and nobility of its tasks, and may the time come as quickly as possible when every human being will find therein an effective safeguard for the rights which derive directly from his dignity as a person, and which are therefore universal, inviolable and inalienable rights. This is all the more to be hoped for since all human beings, as they take an ever more active part in the public life of their own country, are showing an increasing interest in the affairs of all peoples, and are becoming more consciously aware that they are living members of the whole human family.